IMAGES
of America

LANCASTER

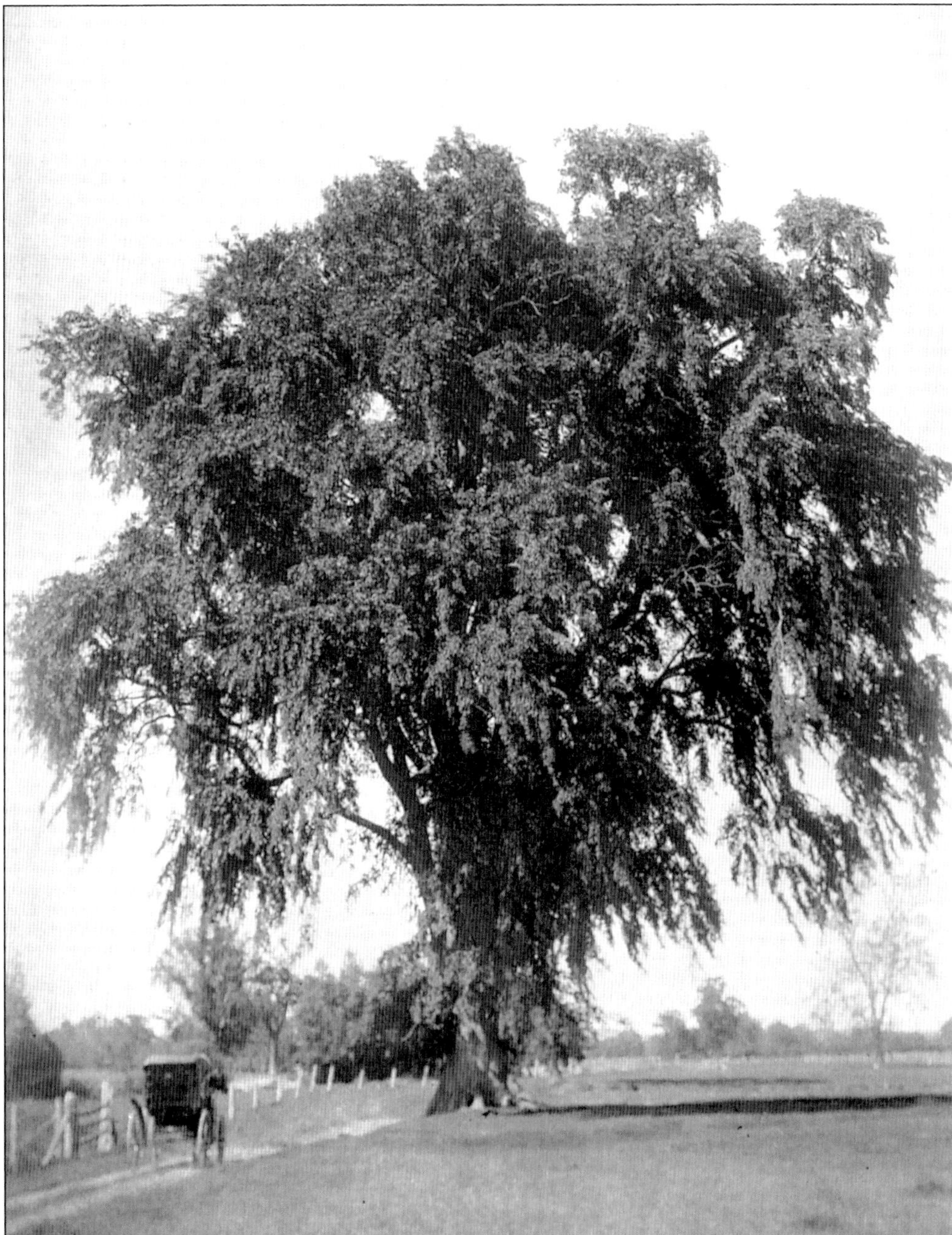

The Great Elm. During the 18th and 19th centuries, Lancaster was famous for its huge elm trees. Considered the largest in New England, the Great Elm, in 1888, had a circumference of of 23 feet at 5 feet above the ground. The height was 95 feet and the branch spread was 114 feet. Eight people with arms outstretched could reach around it. The tree was located on Lover's Lane near the Nashua River in the Five Corners area of town. Unfortunately, during a "cyclonic outburst of the elements," the tree was blown down on July 20, 1907. The Massachusetts Forestry Association, founded in 1898, chose this tree for their seal. It is also used in the logo of the Lancaster Historical Society.

IMAGES
of America

LANCASTER

Heather Maurer Lennon

ARCADIA
PUBLISHING

ISBN 978-0-7385-0904-4

Published by Arcadia Publishing
Charleston, South Carolina

Printed in the United States of America

Library of Congress Catalog Card Number: 2001090243

For all general information contact Arcadia Publishing at:
Telephone 843-853-2070
Fax 843-853-0044
E-mail sales@arcadiapublishing.com
For customer service and orders:
Toll-Free 1-888-313-2665

Visit us on the Internet at www.arcadiapublishing.com

God gives all men all earth to love,
But since man's heart is small
Ordains for each one spot shall prove
Beloved over all.

—From Rudyard Kipling's *Sussex*, as inscribed on the tombstone of Col. John E. Thayer in the Old Settler's Burial Field.

This book is dedicated to those who also find in Lancaster a very special sense of place.

On the cover: Through the years, Lancaster has been the home to many musical organizations. Pictured in a rustic setting is the 19th-century Lancaster Cornet Band.

Contents

Acknowledgments

Many of the images and pieces of information in this book come from the archives of the Lancaster Historical Commission. Especially featured are the photographs of James MacDonald and Alice Greene Chandler. A very special thank-you goes to Michael Sczerzen, Joan Richards, and Elizabeth Colley, who have been a tremendous help throughout this project, and to Phyllis Farnsworth for her review. I also thank the following individuals and institutions for their input in the form of images and information. Credit for the images will be indicated as follows:

Atlantic Union College (AUC)
Charles E. Tuttle Company (Tuttle)
Eugene and Beryl Christoph (Christoph)
Elizabeth Winslow Colley (Colley)
Clinton Daily Item (Item)
Devens Historical Museum (DHM)
Paul L'Ecuyer (L'Ecuyer)
First Church of Christ, Unitarian (FC)
Charlotte Follansbee (Follansbee)
Kathleen Griffin (Griffin)
Dr. Geraldine I. Grout (Grout)
William A. Kilbourn (Kilbourn)
Leila Lawler (Lawler)
Little, Brown and Company (LB)
Luther Burbank Home & Gardens (LBHG)
Gloria Willruth Maurer
Frank and Lois Ponte (Ponte)
John Charles Schumacher-Hardy (Schumacher-Hardy)
Michael Sczerzen (Sczerzen)
South Lancaster Village SDA Church Heritage Center (VC)
Estelle Taylor (Taylor)
Constance Tefft (Tefft)
Thayer Memorial Library (TML)
Jean Watson (Watson)

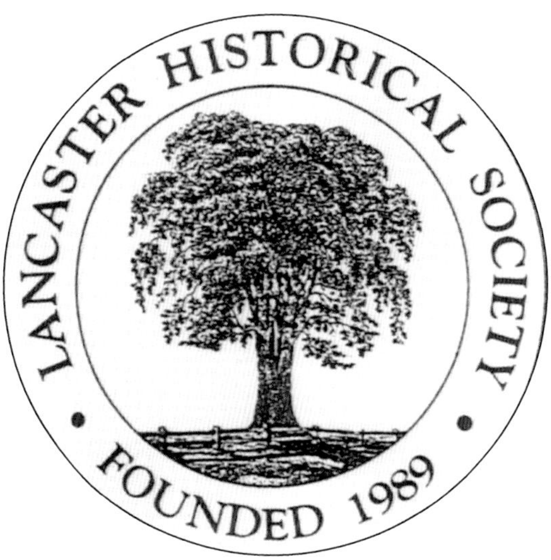

The Lancaster Historical Society and Commission. The Lancaster Historical Society (LHS) was founded in 1989. It is a nonprofit organization, and membership is open to all. The Lancaster Historical Commission (LHC) was established in 1963 by approval at the town meeting. Members are appointed by the town's selectmen. Michael Sczerzen is president of the LHS and chairman of the LHC. Joan Richards is the secretary of the LHS and office coordinator for the LHC.

INTRODUCTION

The decade following the founding of Massachusetts Bay Colony in 1630 included the Great Migration of more than 20,000 Puritans. Pushing west, the English first sought trade with the native people. One such trader was Thomas King of Watertown, who in 1642 was shown a sweeping view from the heights of the Wattaquodoc Range in what is now Bolton, Massachusetts.

The valley below was a series of fertile intervales, or meadowlands, interrupted by forested areas with lofty and ancient trees. The lower land was laced with ponds and softly flowing streams running between the many ranges of gently rolling hills. The native people called the area Nashaway, or "meeting of the waters." Nearby, the sparkling branches of the Nashua River, called the Penecook by early settlers, converged flowing northward to the Merrimack.

Because his people had been ravaged by disease and Mohawk attacks, the Nashaway sachem Sholan sought protection and invited Thomas King to settle in the valley. Accepting his offer, King and his partner Henry Symonds paid 12 pounds sterling and promised to allow the native people to hunt, fish, and plant in their accustomed places. While Sholan had interest in trade and protection for his people, the English had interest in permanent settlement.

As the original proprietors fell away, the tenacious John Prescott took responsibility for setting up a trading post on the south side of George Hill. The location was advantageous because three main Native American trails intersected nearby. One was the Bay Path, which led to the coast. Under Prescott, nine families settled and petitioned the Massachusetts General Court for the right to incorporate. On May 18, 1653, Lancaster became the oldest town in what is today Worcester County.

As the English settlements grew, an inevitable clash of cultures occurred and violence increasingly erupted. In one such incident, the English from three colonies enlisted the aid of the Mohegans to wipe out a Narragansett village of 700. The enraged King Philip, sachem of the Wampanoags, sought retribution.

Lancaster, still in frontier territory and considered unsafe, had about 50 families and a population of about 350 in 1675–1676. Because the snows were deep that winter, perhaps the settlers felt some measure of security. However, on February 10, 1676, the town was brutally attacked. Sacking and burning the garrisons, the natives killed several and took more than 20 hostages. This event was later dramatically described by the minister's wife, Mary White Rowlandson, who was taken captive. Her book A *True History of the Captivity and Restoration of Mrs. Mary Rowlandson* was first published in 1682.

After the burning, Lancaster lay desolate. After King Philip's death, however, some 17 families, headed by none other than John Prescott, petitioned the Massachusetts General Court to rebuild. Resettlement had begun by 1681. However, it would be several more years until all attacks would cease.

In 1701, Lancaster's territory increased to 112 square miles, with an additional grant of land sold by Sholan's nephew George Tahanto. It included what is today Leominster, Sterling, and parts of the two Boylstons. As early as 1706, however, residents among the two thirds of Lancaster's population who were settled on the "safer" high ground east of the Nashua drew up a petition for separation. Travel to the meetinghouse for sabbath worship was difficult, and upkeep on the many bridges spanning the Nashua was burdensome.

Several years later, the "swarming off" began and, in 1732, Harvard became a separate town. Bolton followed in 1738 (including much of what became Berlin in 1784). In 1740, Leominster, farther to the north, became a town. After 60 years of wrangling, the area called Chocksett became Sterling in 1781. Boylston and West Boylston, in the most southerly region, became separate towns in 1786 and 1808, respectively. The last town to break away was Clinton (1850).

Life in Lancaster was not entirely rural and agricultural in the 19th century. Before the coming of the Fitchburg Railroad in 1845, travel through town was heavy, as Lancaster was a thoroughfare to points west and north. In 1838, each week, 32 horse-drawn stagecoaches carrying an average of 48 passengers daily, passed through. Teamsters hauling freight contributed to the long flow of traffic, creating a need for food and lodging. Five hotels operated in town at the time. Travel-related tradesmen—blacksmiths, wheelwrights, wagon makers, and harness makers—found ready employment.

Other local tradesmen did engraving and printing, cabinetmaking, watchmaking, painting, and gunsmithing, as well as hat, comb, soap, and pocketbook making. Lancaster also had a tannery, brickyards, a tin shop, and cider mills. The early sawmills and gristmills at Ponakin gave way to a cotton factory established there in 1861. Not far away, another factory was turning out shoe shanks.

Lancaster—with its clean air, soft water, beautiful trees, and tranquil scenery—was also a tourist destination and a retreat for those seeking relief from the stresses of city life. It also had a reputation as a dwelling place for wealthy gentlemen who enjoyed a quiet country lifestyle.

The Thayer family, first settling in the late 18th century, greatly enhanced this reputation. Dr. Nathaniel Thayer (pastor of the First Church of Christ, Unitarian) was influential in town affairs. His son Nathaniel II continued the tradition. Though prominent in Boston's 19th-century financial world, he always felt a close tie to Lancaster, endowing it in many ways. He, his four surviving sons, and one grandson established large country estates affording an atmosphere of quiet elegance and refinement.

With the 18th and 19th centuries came a diversification of religious belief. Shakers, Swedenborgians, and Universalists were present in the Lancaster area. In reaction to Unitarianism, an Orthodox Evangelical Congregational Church was established. A few decades later, a Roman Catholic church was built. Seventh-Day Adventists, with their roots in the 1840s Millerite movement, founded not only a church but also an educational program including the elementary, secondary, and college levels.

Lancaster, in fact, has been home to many schools. In the early 18th century, Lancaster had grammar schools, as was required by law. In 1784, the town was divided into districts, which changed as populations shifted. Small schoolhouses were established in each. In 1790, the town voted to build a Latin grammar school, which was eventually succeeded by the Lancaster Academy, established in 1815. In 1873, the town started a free high school, which continued until the Nashoba Regional District was begun in 1961.

Other schools have included the short-lived Elizabeth Peabody's academy for young ladies in the early 1820s and Prof. William Russell's Normal Institute, which held sessions from 1853 to 1855. The State Industrial School for Girls, established in 1854, operated for many years on Old Common Road. In the early 20th century, the Dr. Franklin Perkins School, catering to a special needs clientele, began. More recently, the Trivium, a Catholic preparatory school, was founded.

Today, Lancaster is best described as a bedroom town, with many of its residents commuting to jobs in surrounding areas. Overall, there are few stores, businesses, or industries within the town's borders. Pleasant views across pastoral landscapes still exist, and the meandering Nashua River, once heavily polluted, runs clean again. As Lancaster approaches its 350th anniversary, it retains a rural quality and small-town charm enjoyed by all residents.

One

OUT OF THE WILDERNESS

"At length they came and beset our own house, and quickly it was the dolefullest day that ever mine eyes saw." Thus wrote Mary Rowlandson of the attack on her family's garrison on February 10, 1676. Her story is very much a part of Lancaster's early history, and the town today has many reminders of her experience. Following her redemption in Princeton, after an ordeal that lasted almost three months, she and her husband moved to Wethersfield, Connecticut. In 1678, Joseph Rowlandson died. It was long assumed that Mary passed away shortly thereafter, but recent scholarship has revealed her subsequent marriage to a Capt. Samuel Talcott. Mary White Rowlandson Talcott died at the age of 73 on January 5, 1711.

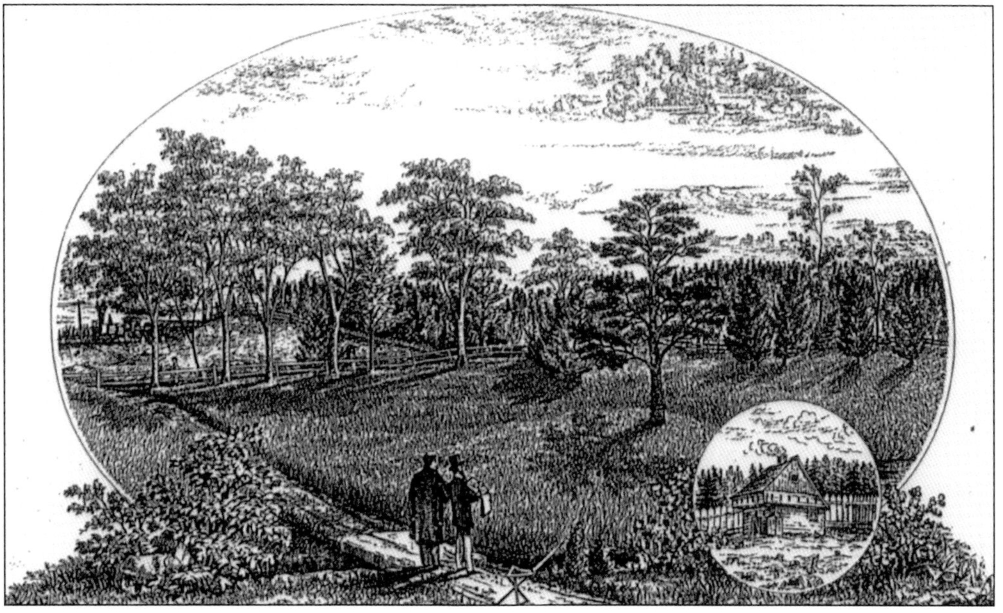

THE GARRISON HOUSES. Although the garrison houses of the early settlers are long gone, the sites for some of them can be identified throughout the town. They are as follows: Cyprian Steven's on Center Bridge Road, Rev. Joseph Rowlandson's on Main Street, Thomas Sawyer's on Main Street in South Lancaster, Ephriam Roper's on George Hill Road at Langen Road, and Capt. Peter Joslyn's on Main Street toward North Lancaster. Pictured here is the Rowlandson garrison site.

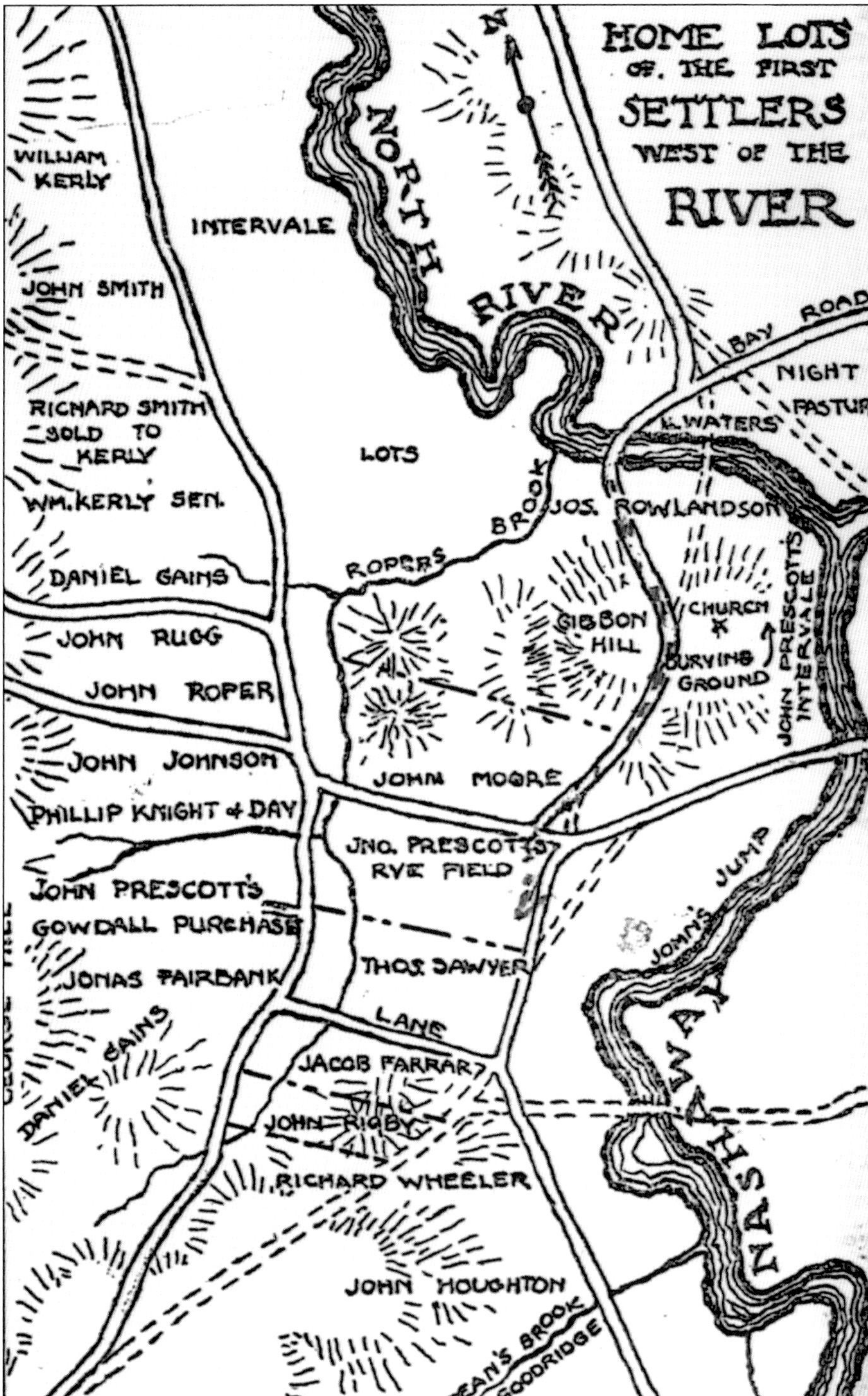

EARLY MAPS OF LANCASTER. These maps originally appeared in H.S. Nourse's *Early Records of Lancaster, Massachusetts*. Later, they were redrawn by Phila Linville Staines and appeared

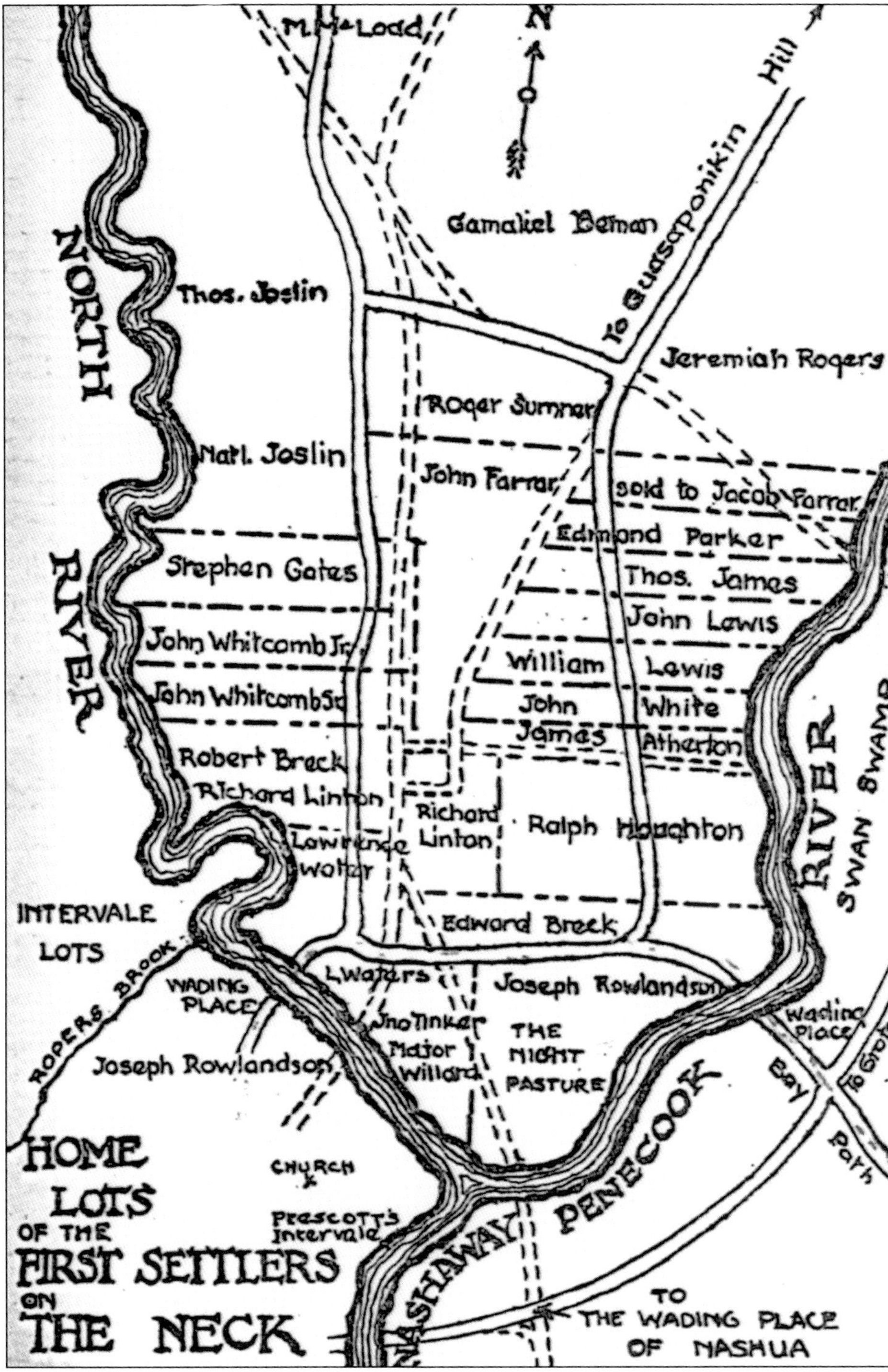

in Marion Fuller Safford's *The Story of Colonial Lancaster*, which was published in 1937. The images are used with permission. (Tuttle.)

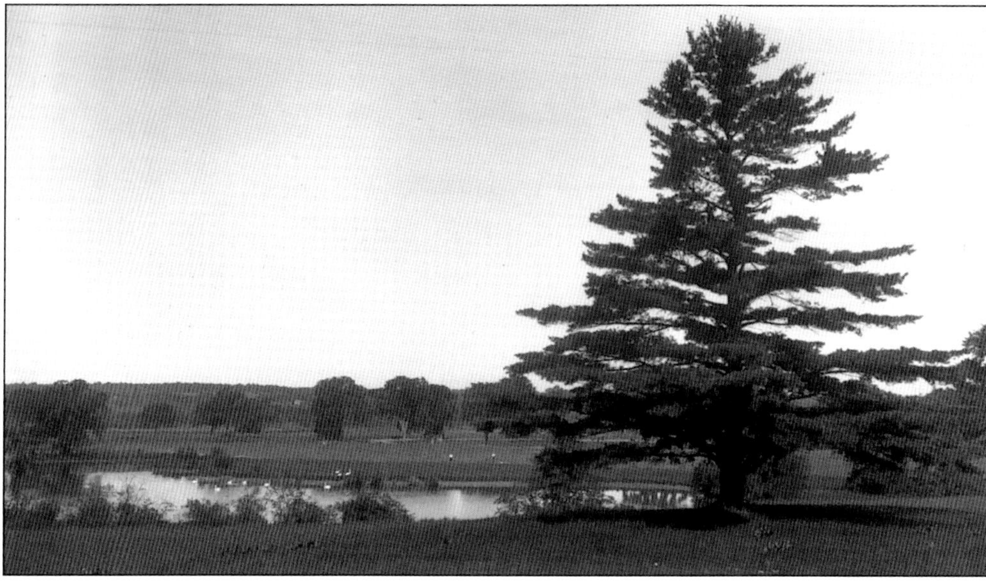

The Rowlandson Pine. When Lancaster was resettled after the attack that destroyed the Rowlandson garrison during King Philip's War in 1675–1676, resident Philip Goss built a house on the same site. It was burned by the French and Native Americans in 1704. Years later, when the field was being plowed, the doorstep and hearthstone of the Goss house were uncovered. The Rowlandson Pine was planted in 1853 to mark the spot and to commemorate the town's 200th anniversary. It is a well-loved local landmark.

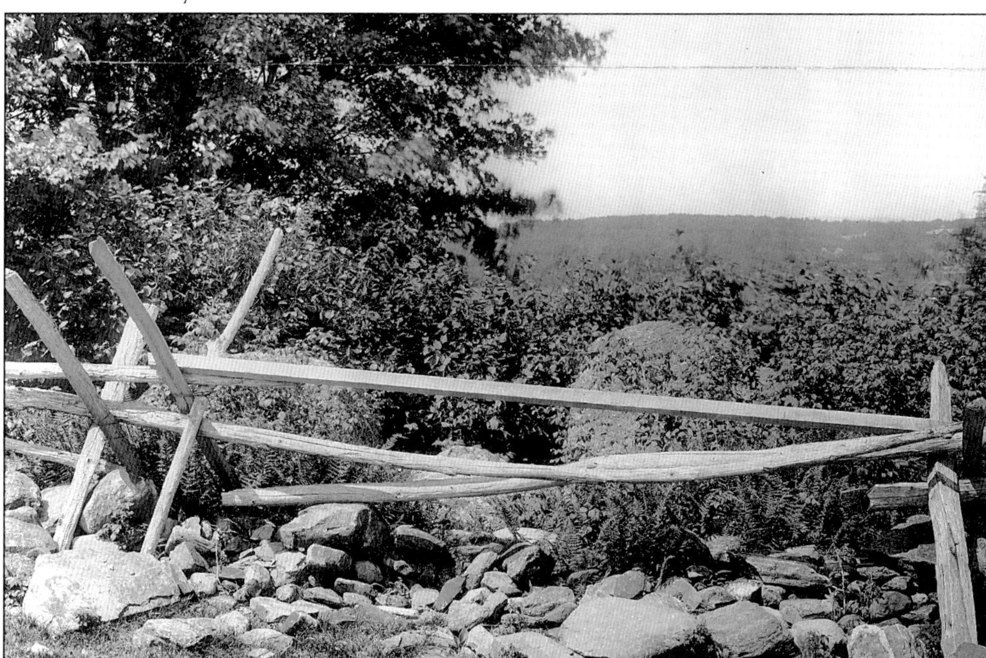

The Rowlandson Rock. This is the spot where Mary Rowlandson and her daughter spent their first night of captivity when Lancaster was burned. It is located on the crest of George Hill in South Lancaster. Today, two large water towers stand nearby. This view shows it as it looked c. 1900.

MARY ROWLANDSON'S BOOK. This front page is from Lancaster's earliest edition of Mary Rowlandson's book (first published in 1682). Some scholars regard it as the first of a uniquely American literary genre, the "captivity narrative." A popular classic of days past, it has seen more than 40 editions. It is also notable as the first American full-length work authored by a woman. (TML, Griffin.)

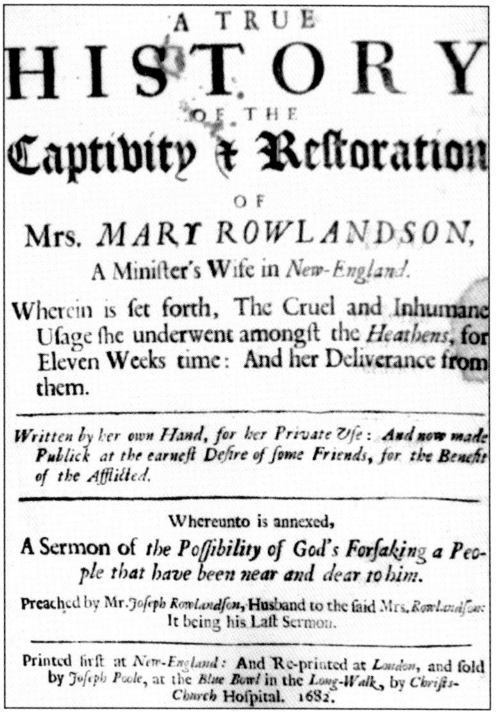

A TRUE
HISTORY
OF THE
Captivity & Reſtoration
OF
Mrs. *MARY ROWLANDSON*,
A Miniſter's Wife in *New-England*.

Wherein is ſet forth, The Cruel and Inhumane Uſage ſhe underwent amongſt the *Heathens*, for Eleven Weeks time: And her Deliverance from them.

Written by her own Hand, for her Private Uſe: And now made Publick at the earneſt Deſire of ſome Friends, for the Benefit of the Afflicted.

Whereunto is annexed,
A Sermon of *the Poſſibility of God's Forſaking a People that have been near and dear to him.*

Preached by Mr. *Joſeph Rowlandſon*, Husband to the ſaid Mrs. *Rowlandſon*: It being his Laſt Sermon.

Printed firſt at *New-England*: And Re-printed at *London*, and ſold by *Joſeph Poole*, at the *Blue Bowl* in the *Long-Walk*, by *Chriſts-Church* Hoſpital. 1682.

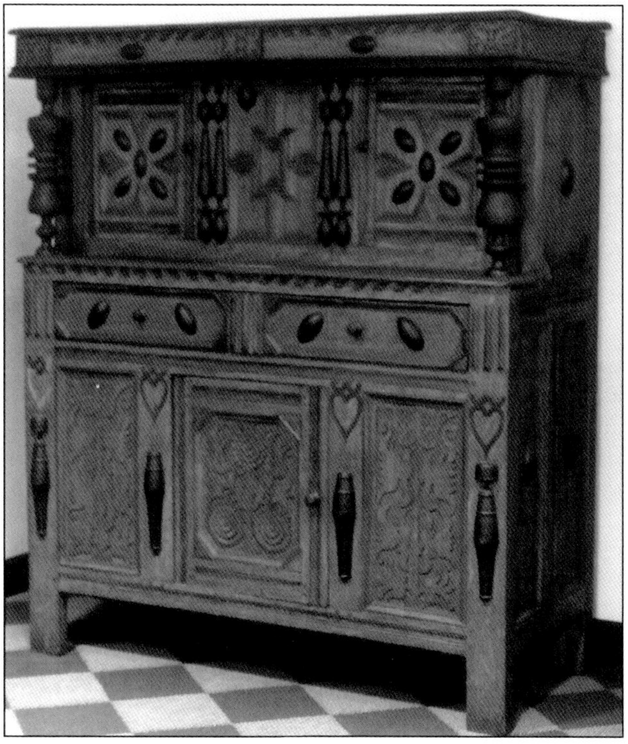

THE ROWLANDSON LOCKER. This locker was never part of the Rowlandson family's Lancaster furnishings. According to one tradition, it was brought from England by Mary's parents and came into her possession after she left Lancaster. Other research indicates that the chest may have been made in Connecticut and was part of the Talcott family's possessions. In 1876, the Lancaster Town Library purchased it with money donated by Lancaster native Mary Whitney. (TML, Griffin.)

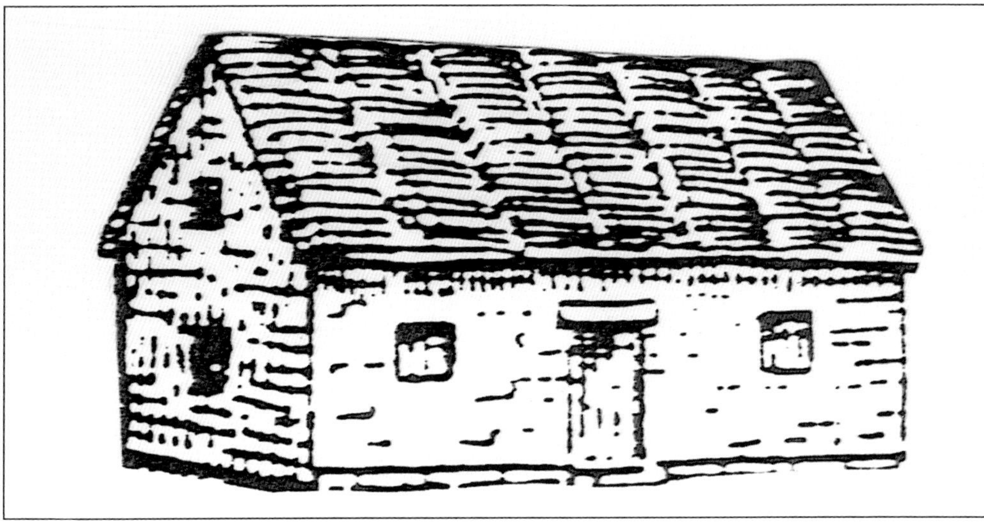

The Early Meetinghouses. None of Lancaster's early meetinghouses remain. The first two, built *c.* 1654 and 1684, were located near the Old Settler's Burial Field and were burned by the Native Americans. The third meetinghouse, located on the Old Common, was built in 1706 and taken down in 1743. The fourth, located near 634 Main Street and built in 1743, was used for worship until the fifth meetinghouse was erected in 1816. After that, it was used for a town hall until it was replaced in 1823. Shown is an artist's conception of what the earliest meetinghouses may have looked like.

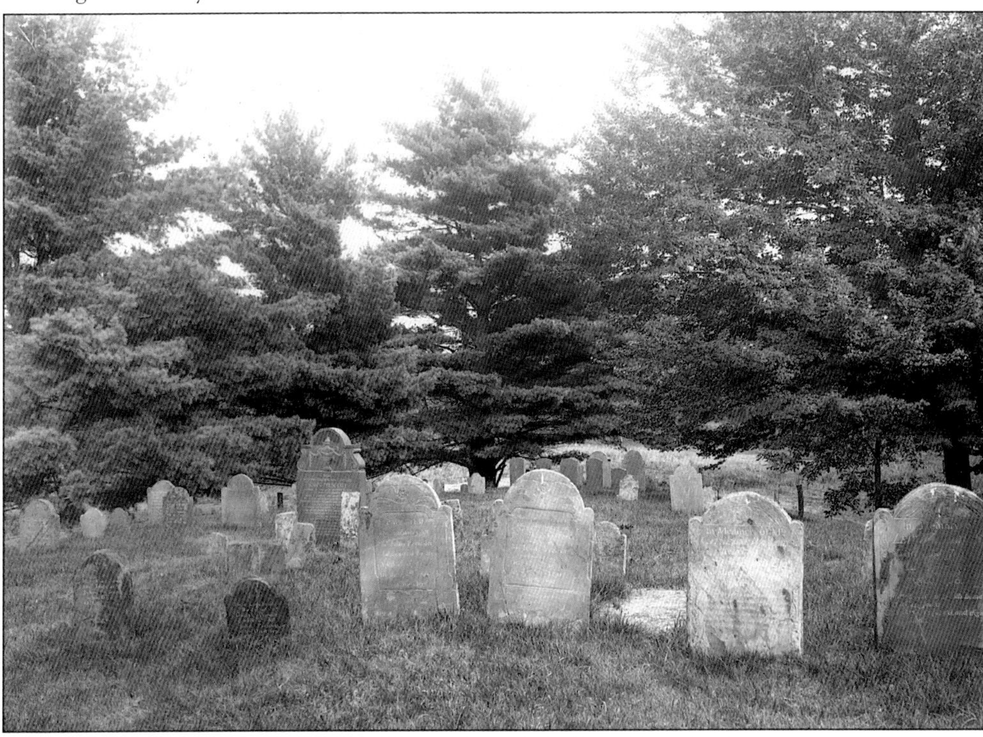

The Old Settler's Burial Field. The Old Settler's Burial Field is located on a long narrow knoll not far from the banks of the Nashua and below the hill where the first and second meetinghouses were constructed, east of the Middle Cemetery.

THE PRESCOTT MEMORIAL STONE. This commemorative marker in the Old Settler's Burial Field was erected to recognize the many contributions of Lancaster's most persevering settler, John Prescott, a blacksmith by trade. His coat of arms bore the legend "He conquers who endures or bears."

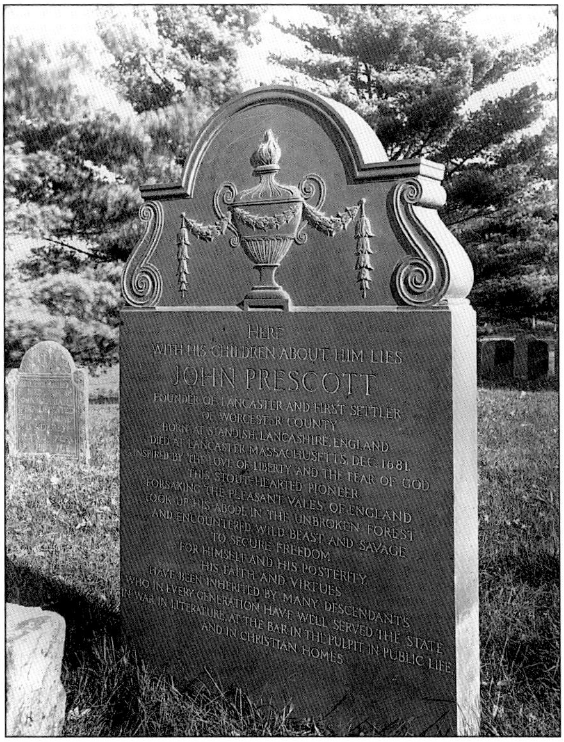

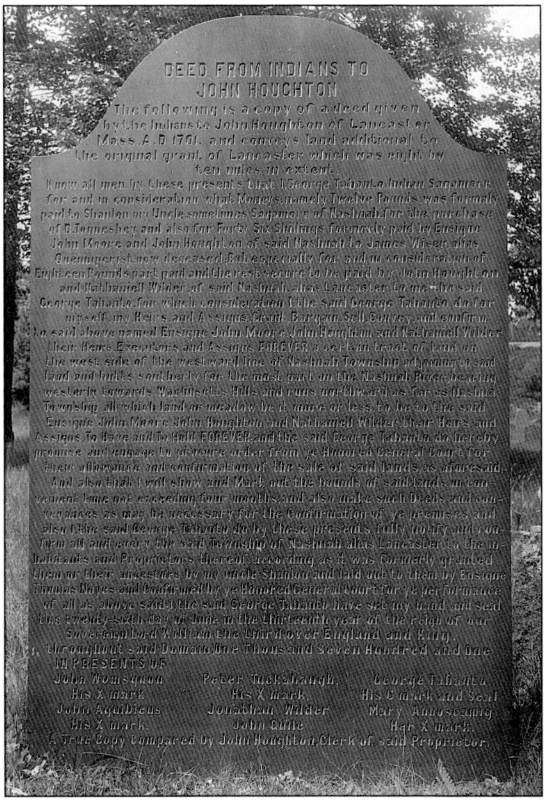

THE ADDITIONAL GRANT. Written in stone in the Old Settler's Burial Field is a copy of the 1701 deed for the grant of land from the Native Americans to the town clerk, John Houghton. It increased Lancaster's size from 80 to 112 square miles. Out of this territory later came Leominster, Sterling, and a large part of Boylston and West Boylston. (TML.)

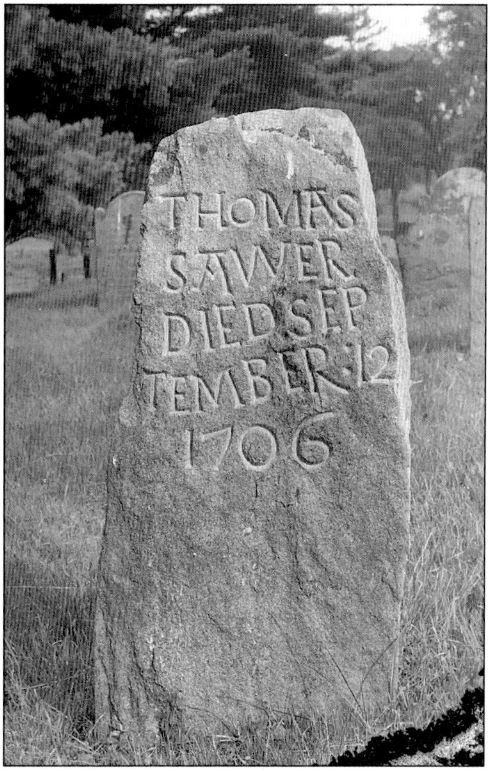

A Rough-Hewn Marker. Shown here is a rough-hewn early grave marker from the Old Settler's Burial Field. The earliest stones in this cemetery were granite slabs crudely inscribed using a blacksmith's chisel.

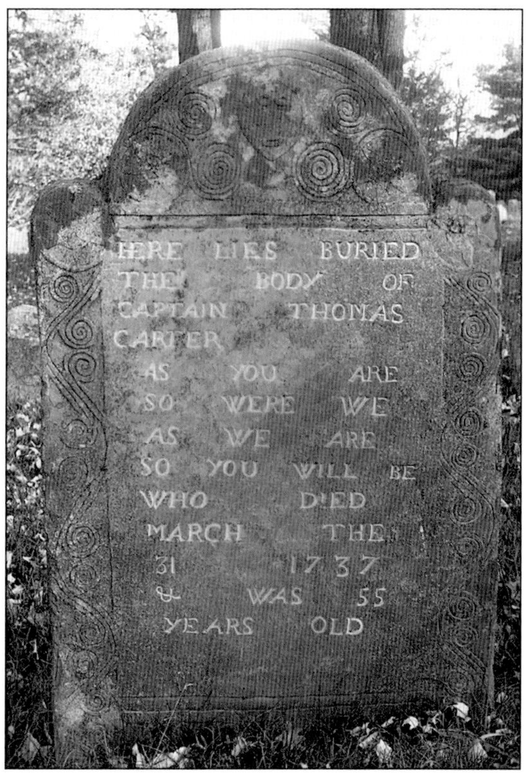

An Unusual Epitaph. This tombstone, like many from the town's burial grounds, has an unusual epitaph. Other burial grounds in Lancaster are the North Lancaster Burial Yard, the Middle Cemetery, the Old Common Cemetery, the North Village Cemetery, and Eastwood Cemetery. There is also an old Shaker cemetery near the Lancaster-Shirley line.

Two

The Town Green, Churches, Schools and Other Notable Buildings

Lancaster has actually had three town greens. The first was the Night Pasture, an expansive enclosed area between Neck Road and the Meeting of the Waters. The first and second meetinghouses and Old Settler's Burial Field were close by. The second common was in the quaintly named Bridecake Plaine area. The meetinghouse was opposite the small cemetery on Old Common Road. The present town green grew up around the fifth meetinghouse, First Church, erected in 1816. Of the green, architect Thomas Mutrux said in *Great New England Churches*, "The church is only a single element in what is a superb exercise in urban design. It cannot be separated from the library, the town offices and its relation to the access avenue. All the elements . . . are part of an eminently satisfying whole."

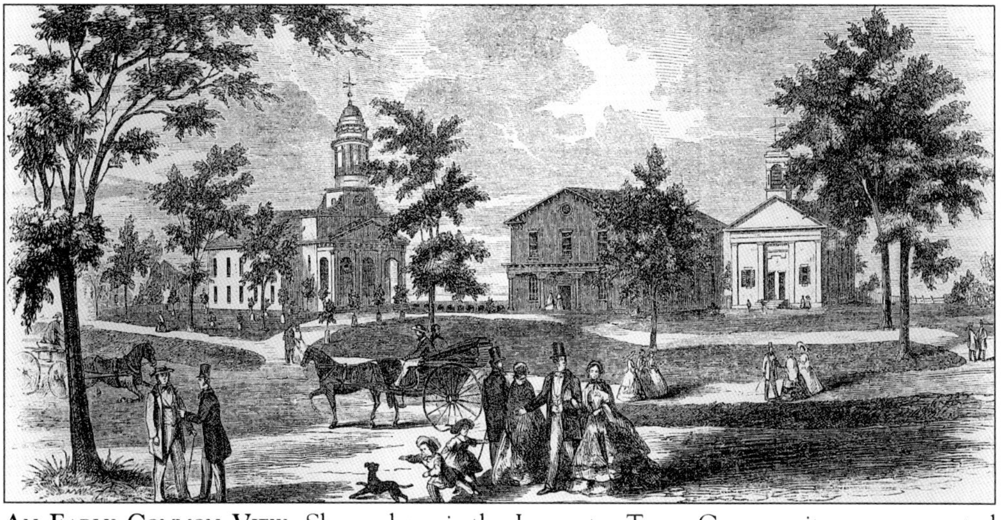

An Early Common View. Shown here is the Lancaster Town Green as it was represented in *Ballou's Pictorial Drawing-Room Companion* in 1856. Shown from left to right are the First Church, the Lancaster Town House, and the Lancaster Academy.

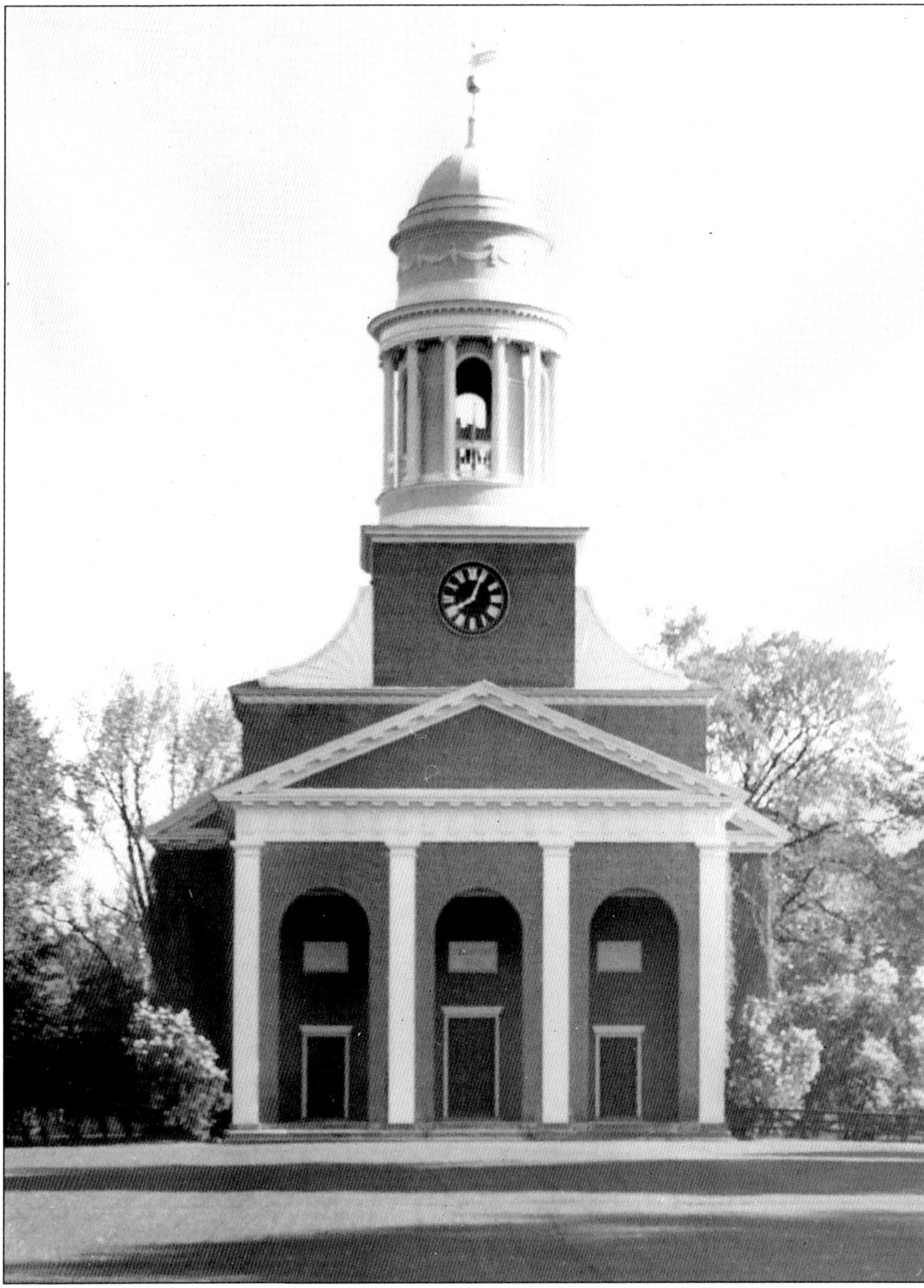

AN AMERICAN MASTERPIECE. Called an "American masterpiece" by William Pierson in *American Buildings and Their Architects*, the fifth meetinghouse (First Church of Christ, Unitarian), on the Lancaster Town Green, is one of the town's finest architectural jewels. Designed by Boston architect Charles Bulfinch and erected in 1816, it is regarded as his greatest ecclesiastical work. It was constructed from local materials under the direction of local master builder Thomas Hersey in 157 working days. The building is a National Historic Landmark.

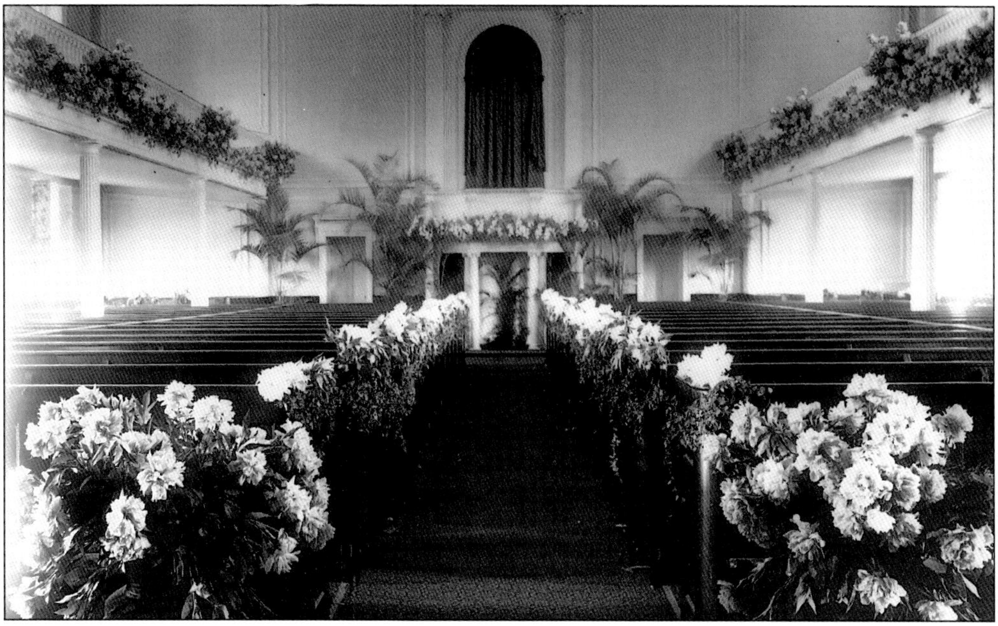

THE FIRST CHURCH INTERIOR. This view shows the interior of the First Church elaborately decorated for a wedding in a style popular *c.* 1900.

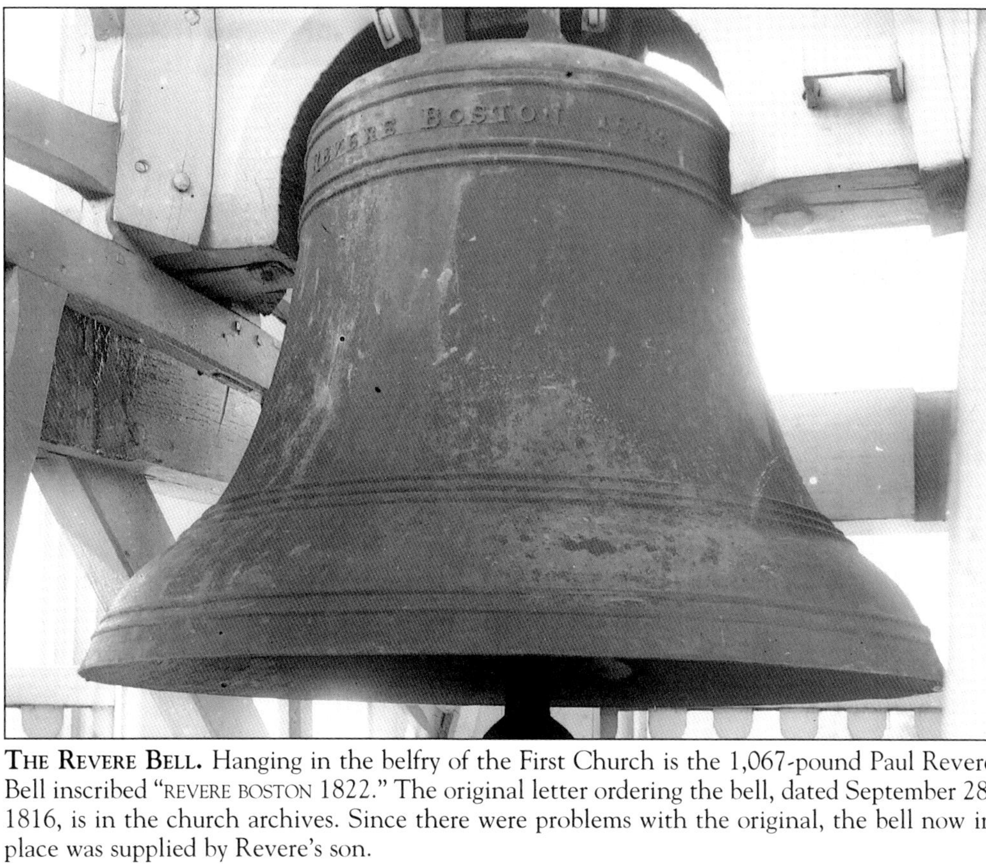

THE REVERE BELL. Hanging in the belfry of the First Church is the 1,067-pound Paul Revere Bell inscribed "REVERE BOSTON 1822." The original letter ordering the bell, dated September 28, 1816, is in the church archives. Since there were problems with the original, the bell now in place was supplied by Revere's son.

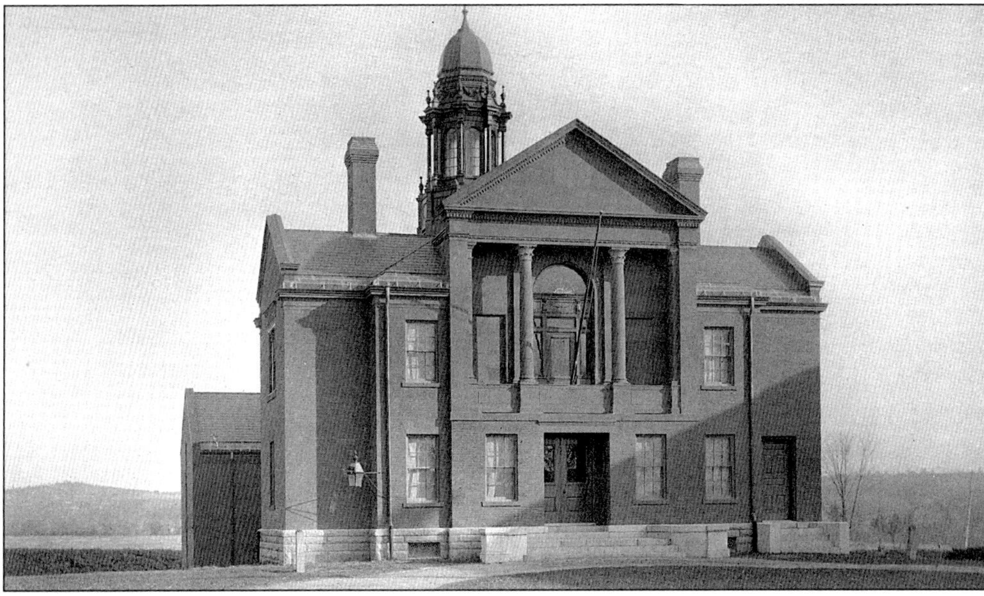

Memorial Hall. Built at a cost of $30,000 (most of which was a gift from Nathaniel Thayer II), Memorial Hall, on the Lancaster Town Green, was dedicated in 1868 to the 39 townsmen lost in the Civil War. In 1929, a north children's wing was added by Mrs. Bayard Thayer in memory of her son. In 1999, a multimillion-dollar renovation was made adding a south reference wing. This view shows the library as it looked in 1890.

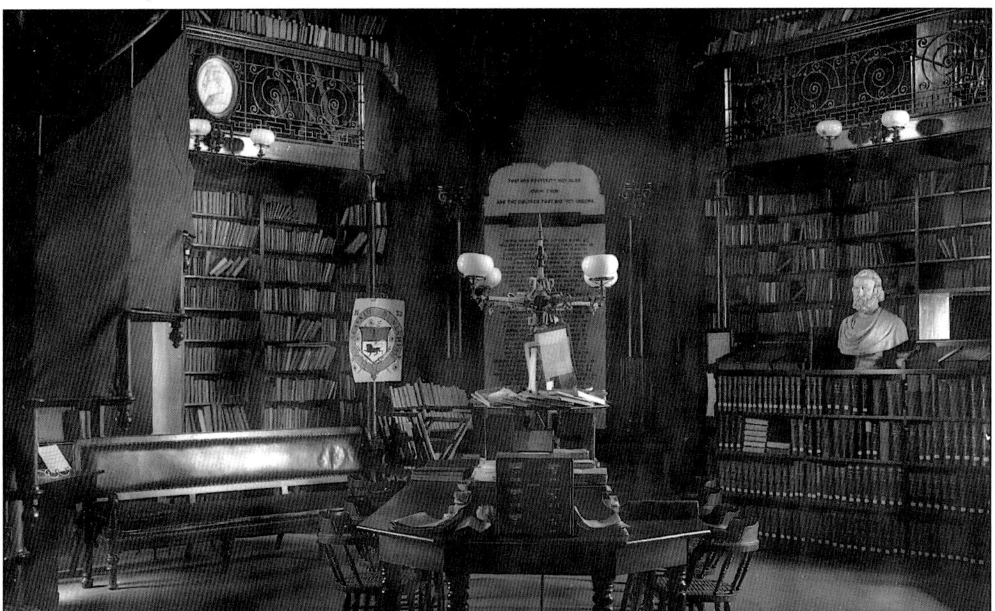

The Reading Room. Here is an early view of the handsome and finely appointed former reading room of the town library. On the back center wall is a plaque honoring the town's Civil War dead. During the recent renovation, the plaque and reading table were relocated to the library's new south wing. Note the circular staircase on the left draped to accommodate the modesty of female patrons.

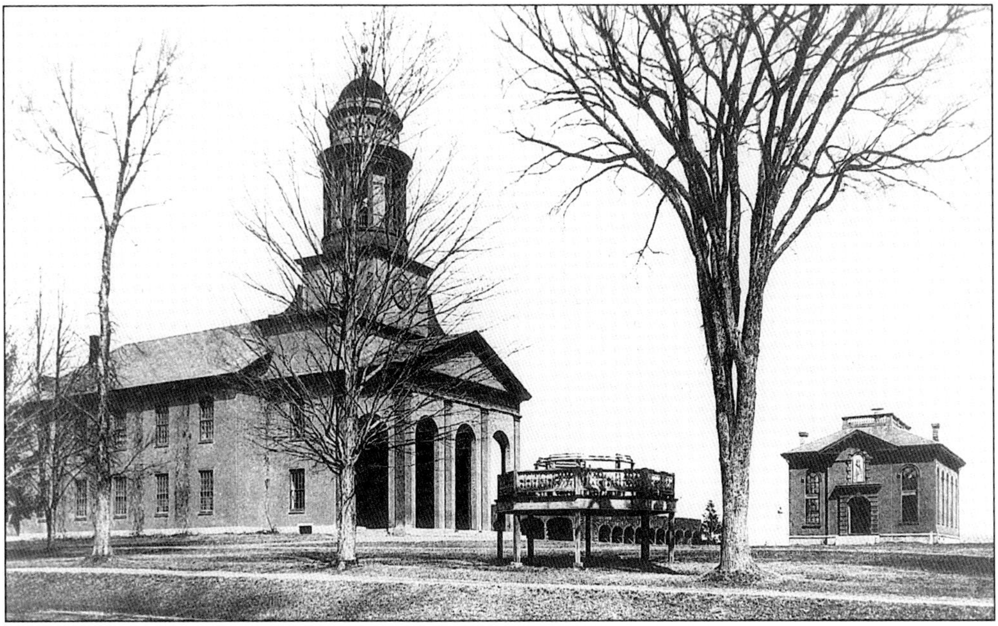

AN EARLY VIEW OF THE GREEN. This is the Lancaster Town Green as it looked in the latter half of the 19th century. Note the drab trims on the First Church and Memorial Hall as it looked before any additions were made. The extra horsesheds and the bandstand have long since been removed. (TML.)

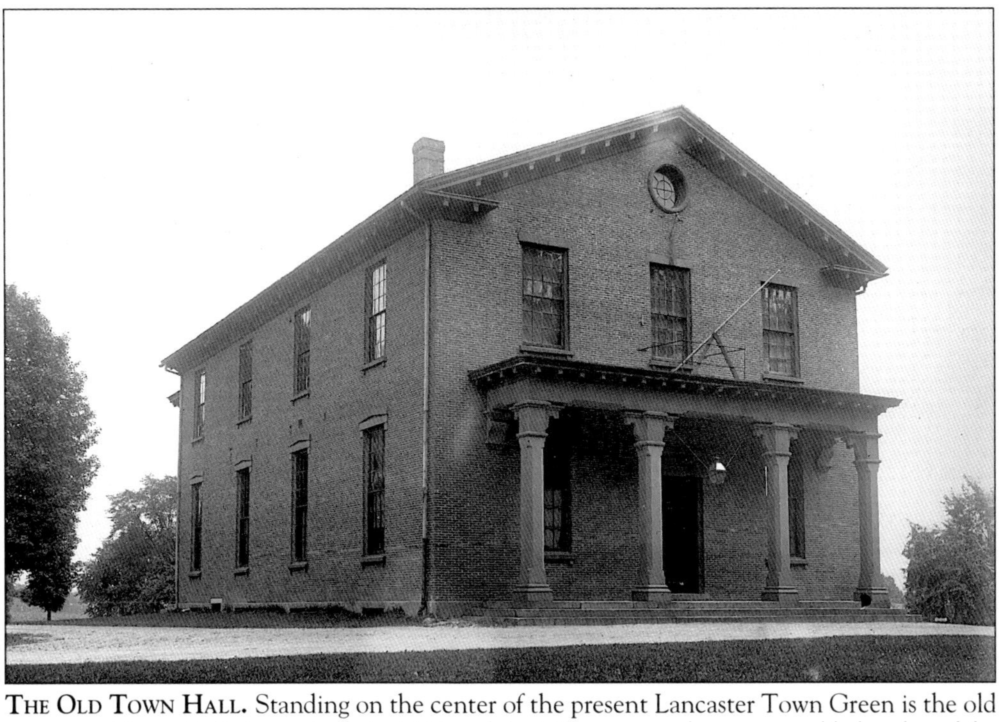

THE OLD TOWN HALL. Standing on the center of the present Lancaster Town Green is the old Lancaster Town Hall. It was built in 1848 and, in 1852, a second story was added and used for schoolrooms. The building was demolished *c.* 1907 and a "new" Lancaster Town Hall, which is now almost 100 years old, took its place.

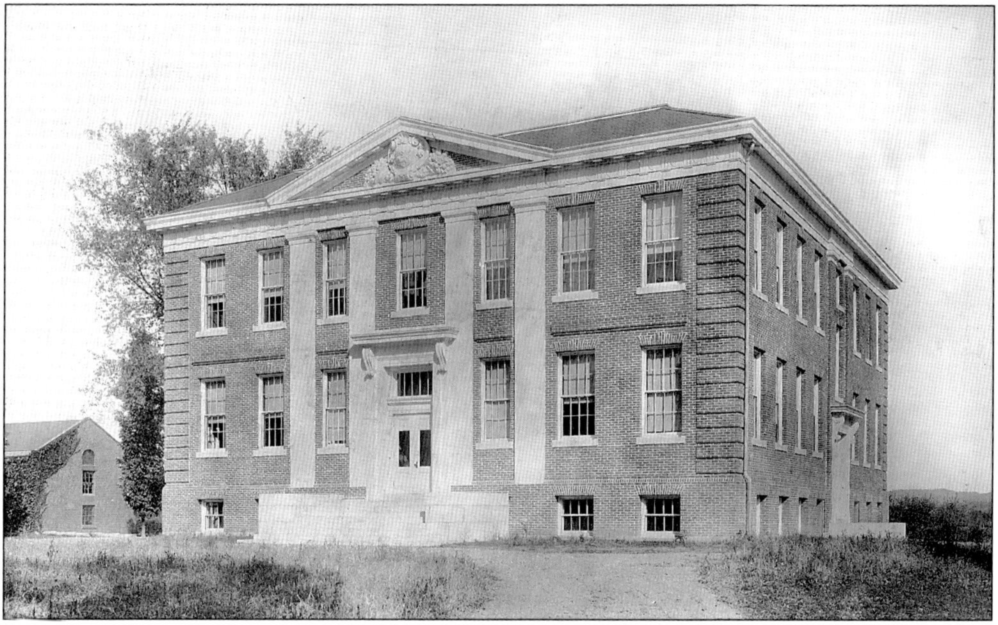

The Center School. Designed by Herbert D. Hale of Boston, the Center School was constructed in 1903–1904 at a cost of more than $35,000. In keeping with the architectural style on the Lancaster Town Green, it was recommended that it be Bulfinch Colonial. When it first opened, the second story was used for high school students and the first story for lower grades. Most recently, the entire building has been used to house the elementary grades.

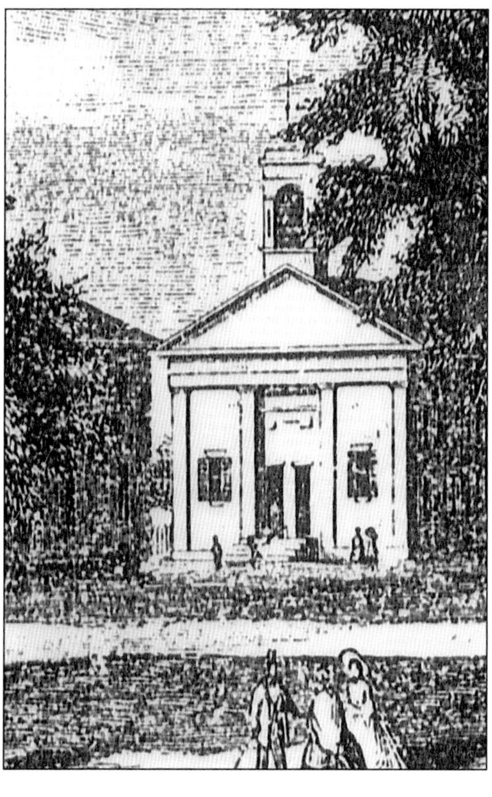

The Lancaster Academy. The Lancaster Academy building was built on the Lancaster Common in 1825 on land donated by Horatio and George Carter of the Carter and Andrews printing and engraving firm. It was replaced with another building, which was used until the Center School was built in 1903–1904.

THE TOWN SEAL. The present town seal was adopted at the annual town meeting in 1900, the year all towns were requested to do so by the state. The seal adopted was the ancient coat of arms of Lancaster, England, substituting for the Latin motto the legend "Lancaster on the Nashua, 1653." In the center, a golden "rampant" lion with paw raised is shown on a shield with a background of blue and red.

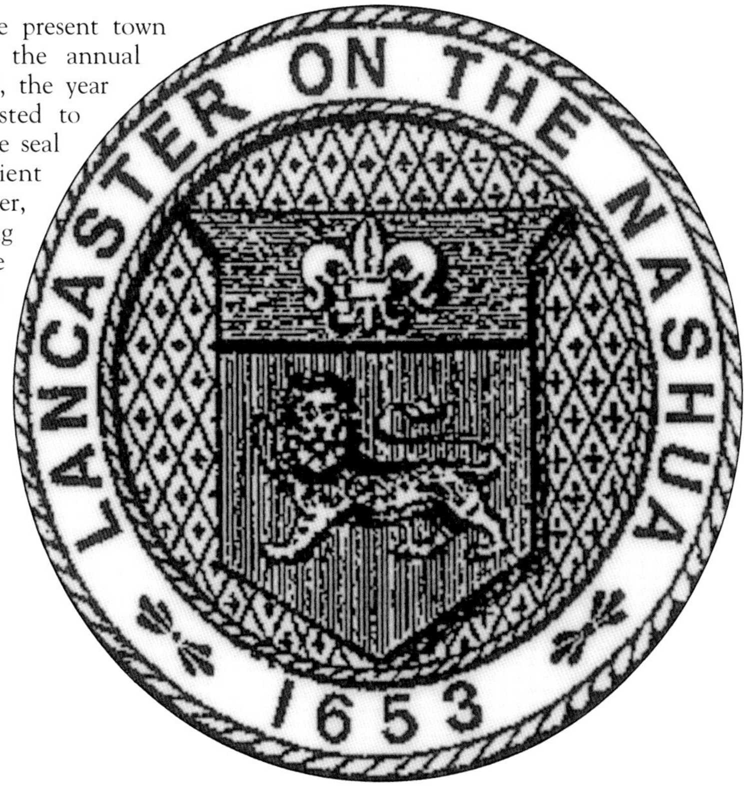

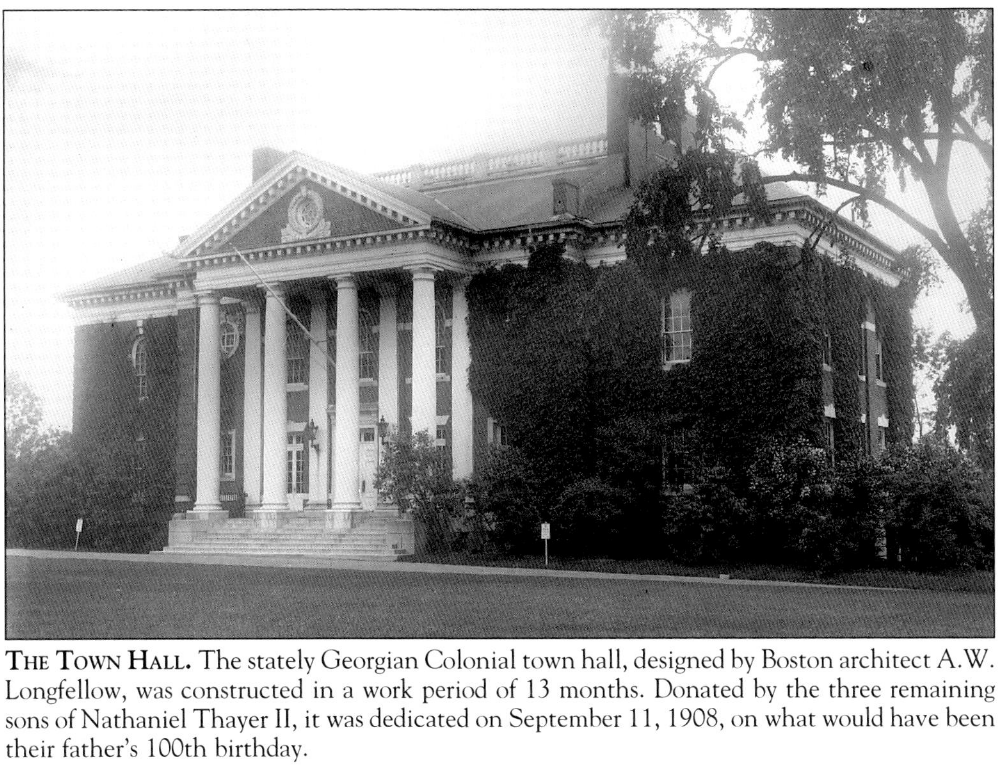

THE TOWN HALL. The stately Georgian Colonial town hall, designed by Boston architect A.W. Longfellow, was constructed in a work period of 13 months. Donated by the three remaining sons of Nathaniel Thayer II, it was dedicated on September 11, 1908, on what would have been their father's 100th birthday.

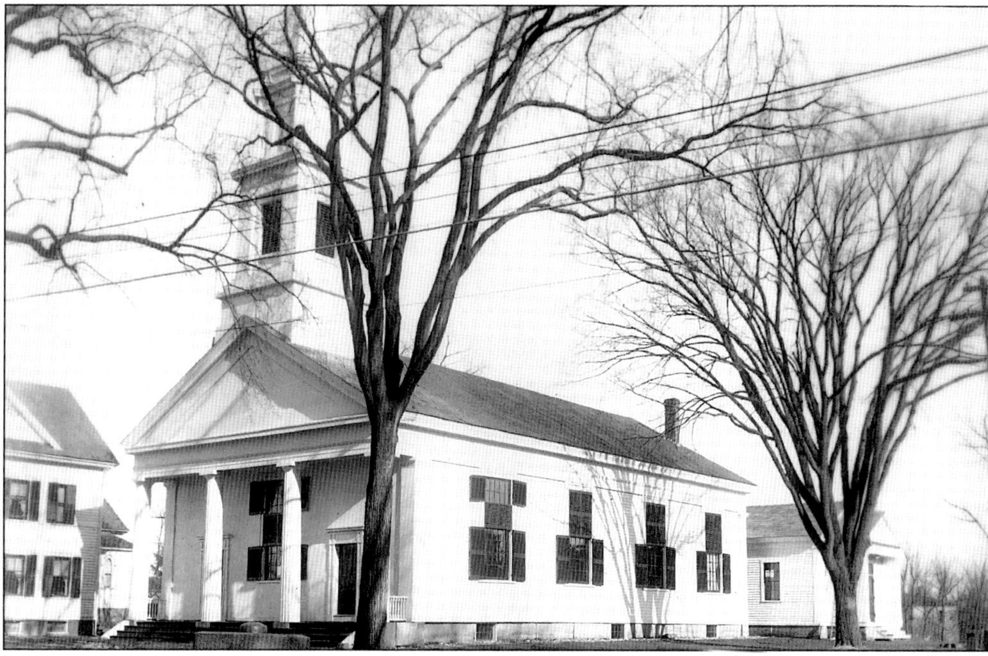

The Evangelical Congregational Church. The Evangelical Congregational Church (once referred to as the Orthodox Congregational) was built in Lancaster Center in 1841 at an approximate cost of $4,500. It was enlarged in 1868. An adjoining parsonage was added in 1902. This classic white-pillared church was destroyed by fire in 1950 but was rebuilt shortly thereafter using a similar design.

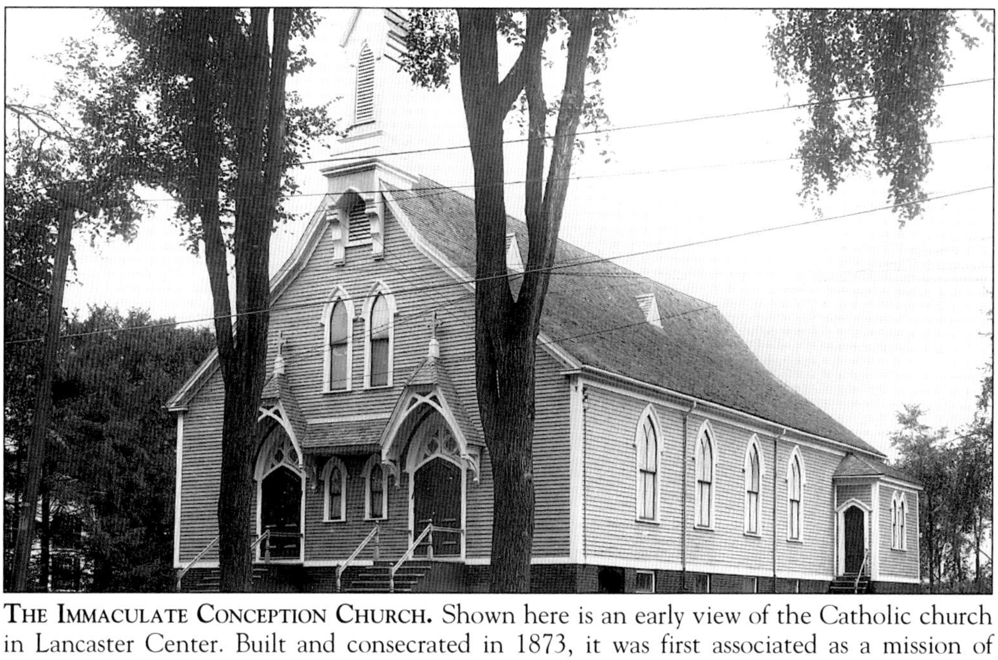

The Immaculate Conception Church. Shown here is an early view of the Catholic church in Lancaster Center. Built and consecrated in 1873, it was first associated as a mission of St. John's in Clinton. In 1915, it became the Immaculate Conception Church with Fr. John F. Boyle serving as the first parish priest. Destroyed by fire in 1941, the building was soon rebuilt using a more modern yet Colonial style.

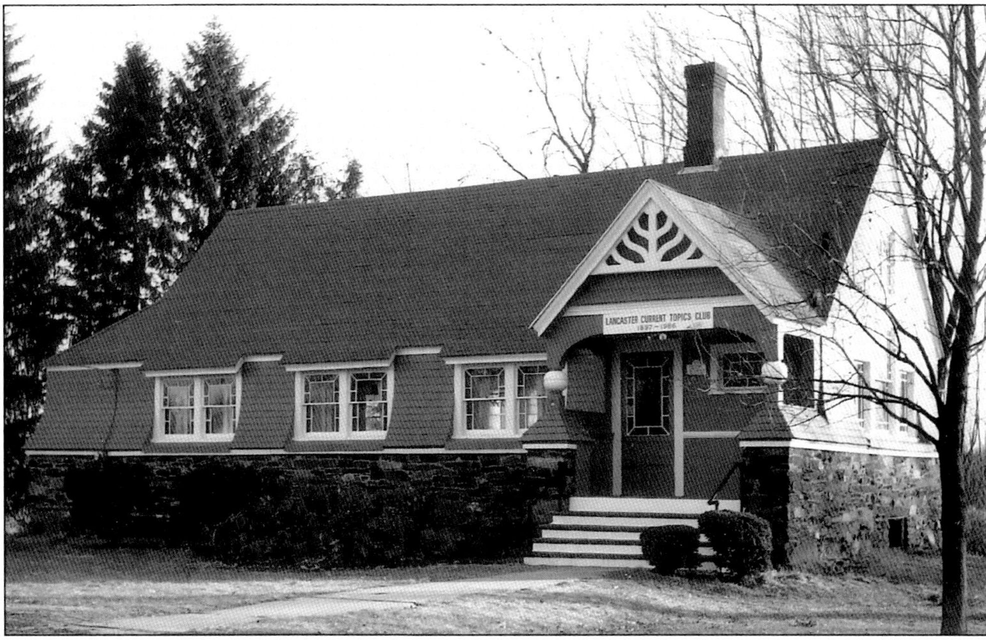

The Swedenborgian Chapel and Current Topics Club. Built in 1881 as a Church of the New Jerusalem, this unique Swedenborgian chapel was designed as a reproduction of an English chapel, Queen Anne style. The building's rich interior was constructed using the wood of a large black cherry tree that once stood on the grounds. In 1923, the building was purchased by members of the Current Topics Club, which has been meeting there ever since. (Watson.)

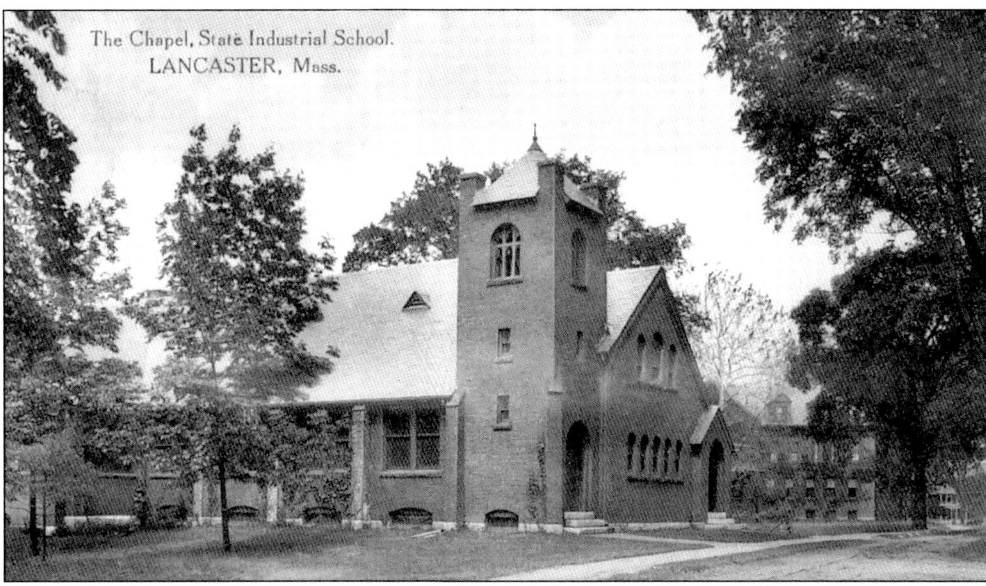

The First Universalist Society. In 1838, a First Universalist Society organized in New Boston (as South Lancaster was known) and a brick church was built near Bennett Lane across from the junction of Sterling Road and Main Street. After Clinton incorporated in 1850, the group disbanded and, in 1858, the building was sold and relocated to what was then the State Industrial School for Girls for use as a chapel. It is still on the grounds today. (Schumacher-Hardy.)

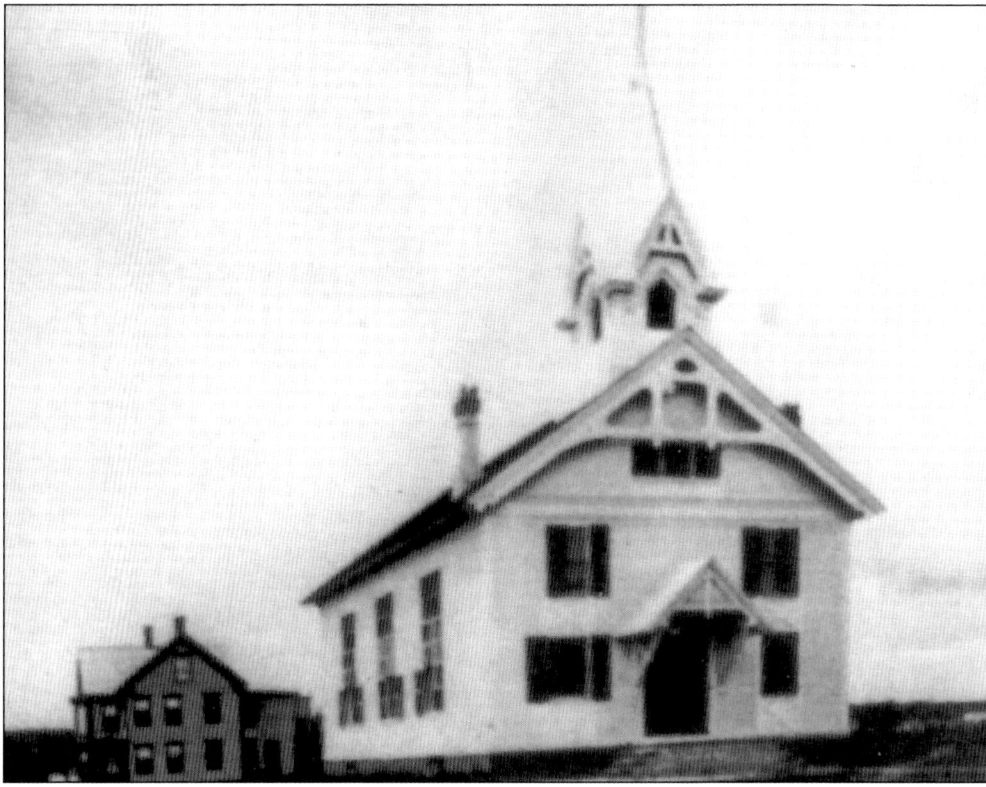

The South Lancaster Village Church. Although Advent believers had been meeting in homes and various other locations in South Lancaster as early as 1856, it was several years before they had a designated meetinghouse. To accommodate their growing numbers, a frame structure was built and dedicated in May 1878. Several additions have subsequently been made to the building, which stands at the corner of Sawyer Street and Narrow Lane. (VC.)

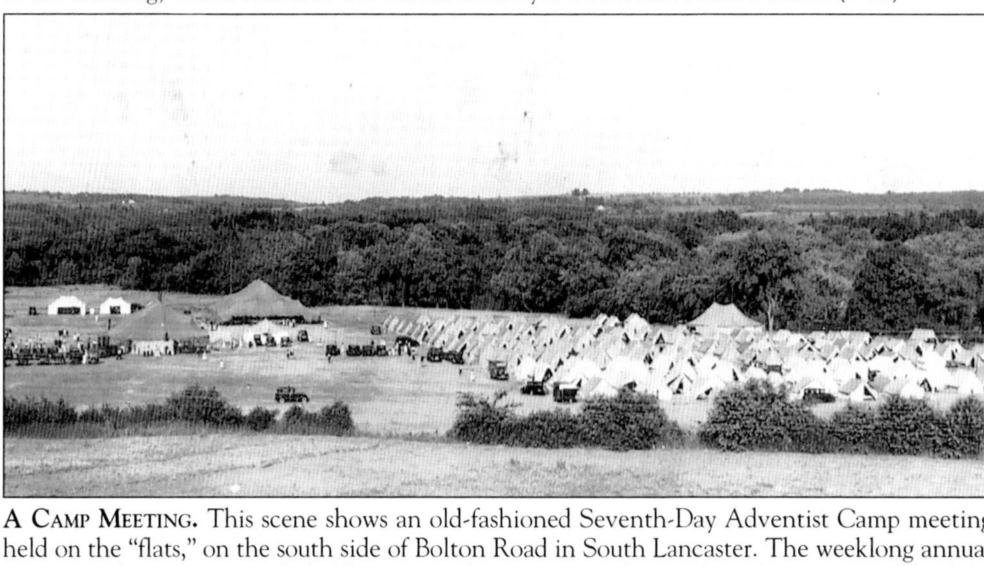

A Camp Meeting. This scene shows an old-fashioned Seventh-Day Adventist Camp meeting held on the "flats," on the south side of Bolton Road in South Lancaster. The weeklong annual summer gathering, previously held in various locations, is today conducted on the grounds of the Southern New England Conference of SDA on Sawyer Street in South Lancaster. (Ponte.)

The Peabody School. This announcement appeared in an 1821 issue of the *Massachusetts Spy*. At the time, Mrs. Peabody and her 16-year-old daughter, Elizabeth, were about to open a school in Lancaster. Unfortunately, the school proved unsuccessful and the Peabody family moved away not long thereafter. Elizabeth (1804–1894) was prominent in the 19th century as an educator, writer, and first woman publisher in Boston. Her younger sisters, Sophia and Mary, married writer Nathaniel Hawthorne and educator Horace Mann, respectively.

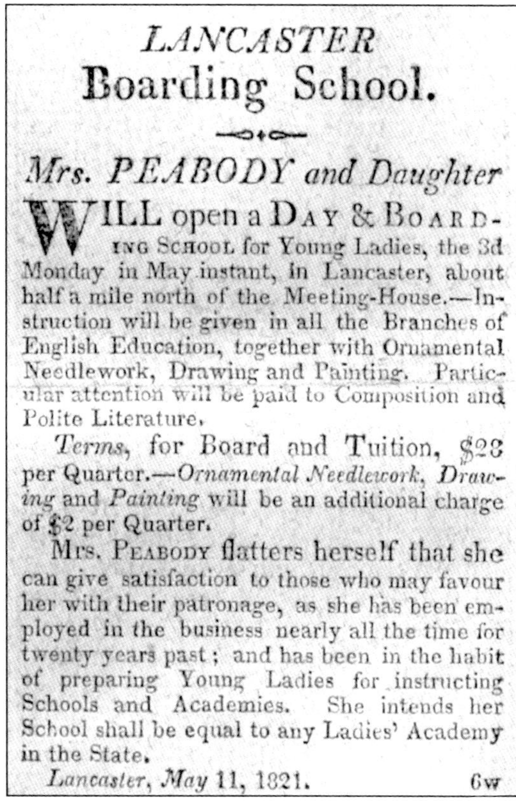

LANCASTER

Boarding School.

Mrs. PEABODY and Daughter

WILL open a Day & Boarding School for Young Ladies, the 3d Monday in May instant, in Lancaster, about half a mile north of the Meeting-House.—Instruction will be given in all the Branches of English Education, together with Ornamental Needlework, Drawing and Painting. Particular attention will be paid to Composition and Polite Literature.

Terms, for Board and Tuition, $23 per Quarter.—*Ornamental Needlework, Drawing* and *Painting* will be an additional charge of $2 per Quarter.

Mrs. Peabody flatters herself that she can give satisfaction to those who may favour her with their patronage, as she has been employed in the business nearly all the time for twenty years past; and has been in the habit of preparing Young Ladies for instructing Schools and Academies. She intends her School shall be equal to any Ladies' Academy in the State.

Lancaster, May 11, 1821. 6w

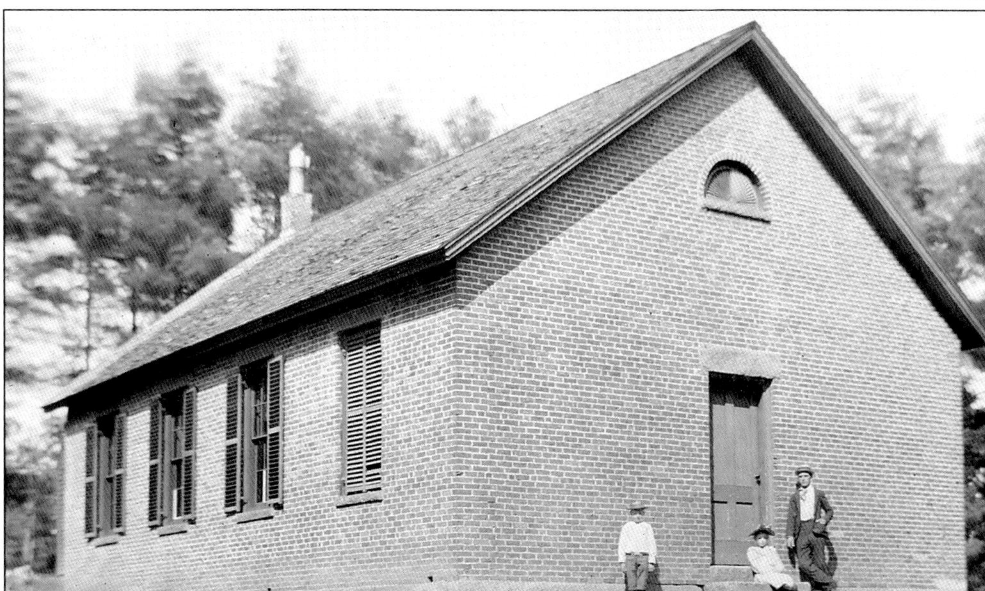

The Pine Grove School House. Shown here is the old Pine Grove School House (no longer standing), which was located on Shufelt Road in the Harvard Road area. Luther Burbank attended this school as a young boy. The building stood on land taken over by Fort Devens in 1938.

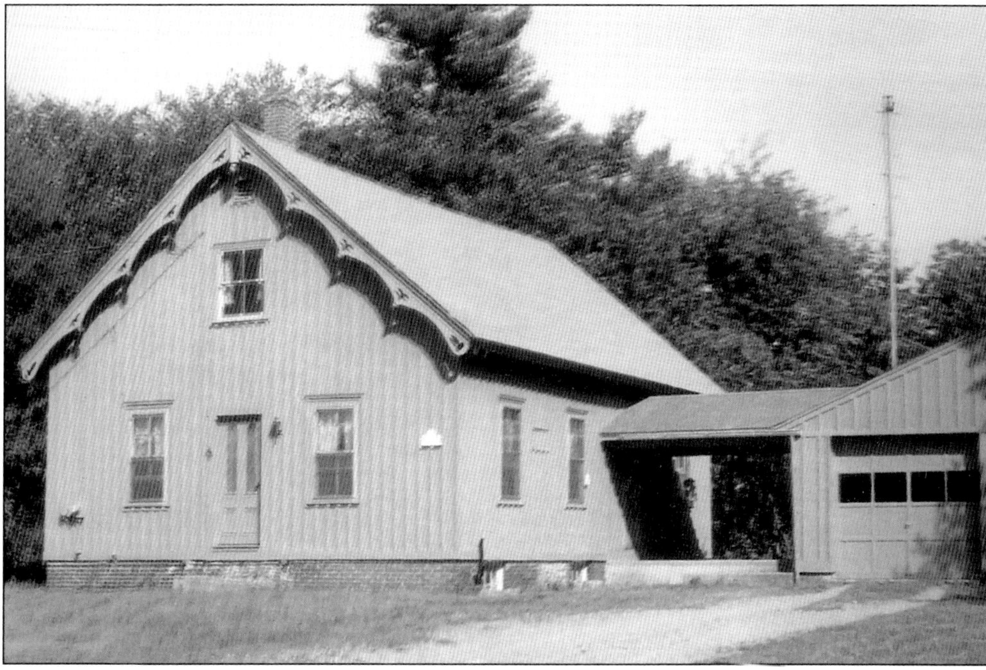

The Deershorn School. This is the former Deershorn School, built in 1852. Located near the Four Ponds area, it was the last one-room schoolhouse in town and was used as such until the 1920s. It was then adapted for use as a private dwelling and, in the early 1970s, was restored to its former Victorian Gothic style.

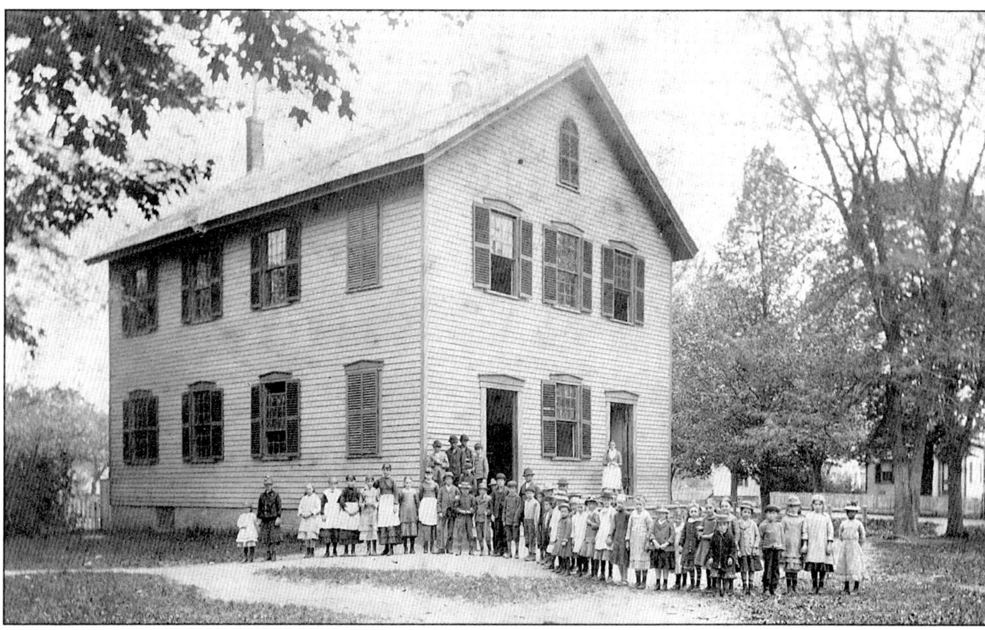

The Ward Park School. Located near the South Lancaster Fire Station and the intersection of Main Street and Bolton Road is the Ward Park School (no longer standing). It was used for public elementary education in the late 19th century until the Narrow Lane School was opened in 1897. (TML.)

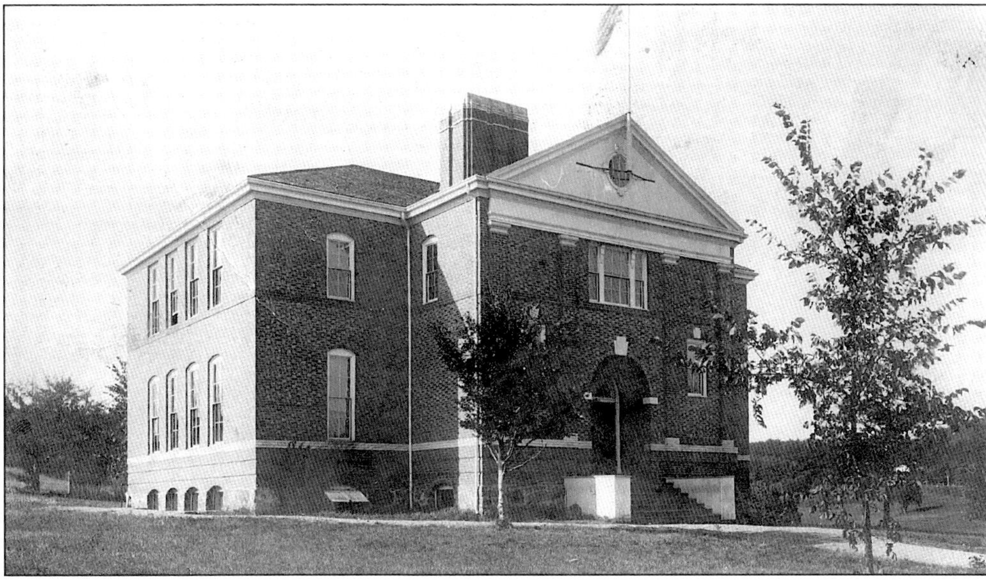

The Narrow Lane School. The Narrow Lane School in South Lancaster was built in 1897 at a cost of $12,000. It was located on a two-and-a-half-acre parcel of land procured from the Turner family. The school housed elementary grades for many years until the Memorial School in Lancaster Center opened in 1957. In 1969, the school department turned the building over to selectmen. Costs for upgrading the building for town use proved prohibitive and, in 1973, it was demolished.

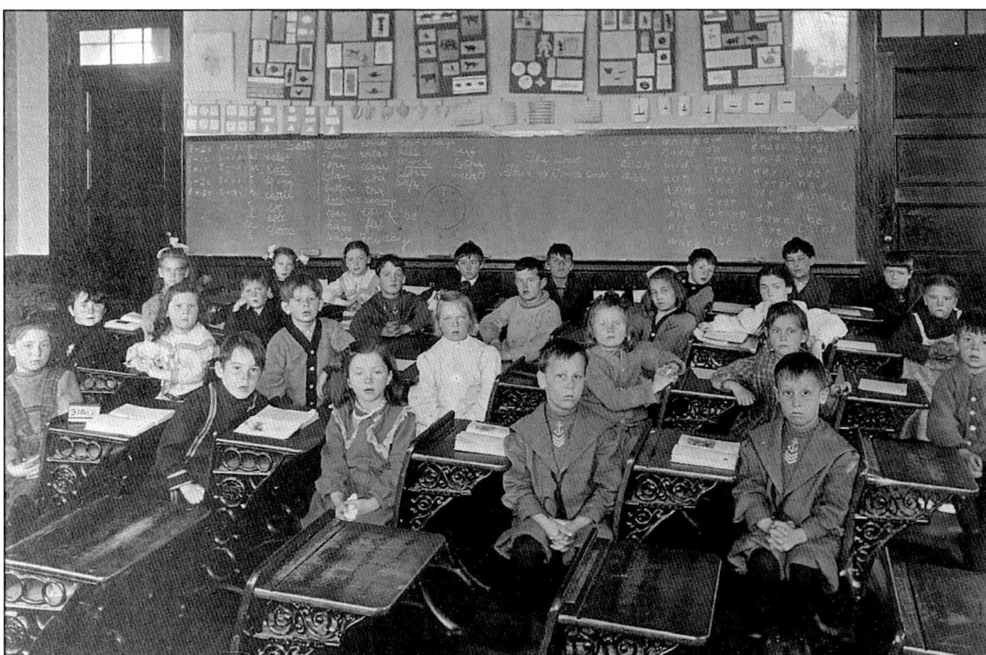

A Well-Behaved Class. A well-behaved first- and second-grade class at the Narrow Lane School sit up straight with hands folded. The photograph was taken c. 1906–1908. Longtime Lancaster resident Marion F. Ancill Robinson was a member of this class. Her father, Henry Ancill, was Col. John E. Thayer's head groom. (Kilbourn.)

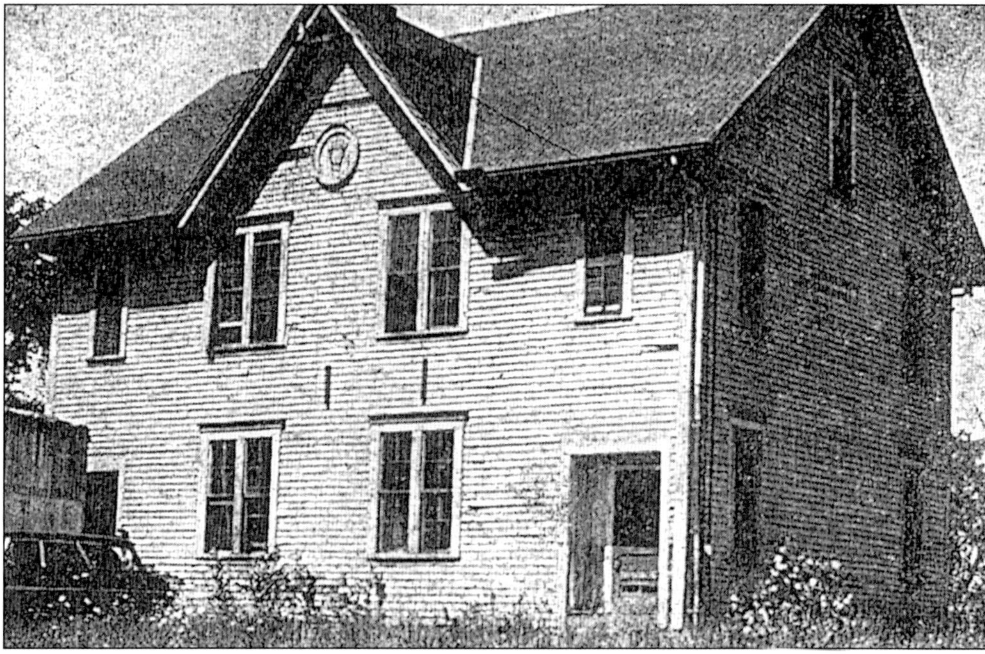

THE BALLARD HILL SCHOOL. This is the Ballard Hill School, which was used in the latter part of the 19th century until the Center School was built in 1903–1904. After it was no longer needed as a school, it was purchased by the Lancaster Sportmen's Club. At one time, there were plans to use it as a Baptist church. Finally, because the building had become a hazard, it was burned down under the supervision of the local fire department. (Item, Ponte.)

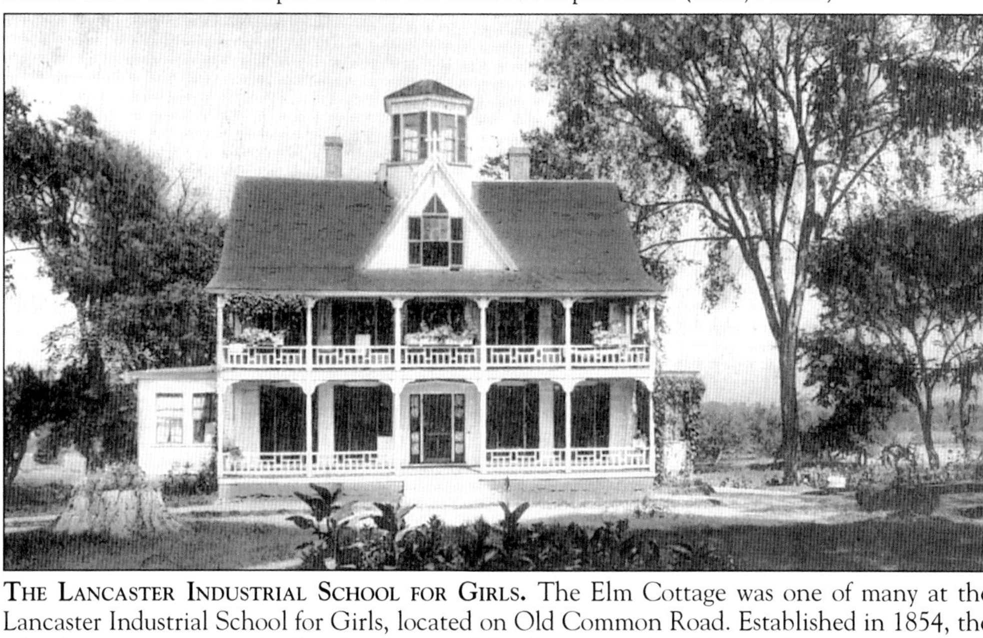

THE LANCASTER INDUSTRIAL SCHOOL FOR GIRLS. The Elm Cottage was one of many at the Lancaster Industrial School for Girls, located on Old Common Road. Established in 1854, the school was very progressive for the times and the first correctional institution to give the girls private rooms in a cottage system. The Bridecake Plaine area has been designated as a National Historic District since the 1970s. The facility is currently a coeducational, minimum-prerelease security prison. (Colley.)

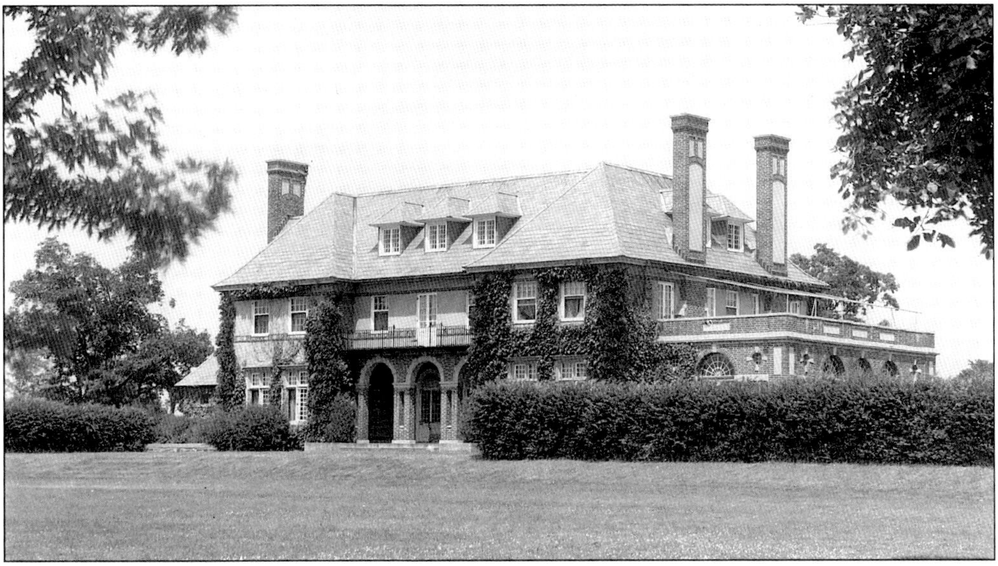

THE DOCTOR FRANKLIN PERKINS SCHOOL AND FORMER MRS. IVER JOHNSON ESTATE. This elegant estate on North Main Street was built in 1910 as a country home for Mrs. Iver Johnson. Her late husband was well known for the manufacture of firearms and bicycles and, in 1894, had opened a retail sporting-goods store in Fitchburg. In 1934, the estate became the Dr. Franklin Perkins School, serving a wide range of clientele in a nurturing and homelike environment. The facility has been expanded several times over the years.

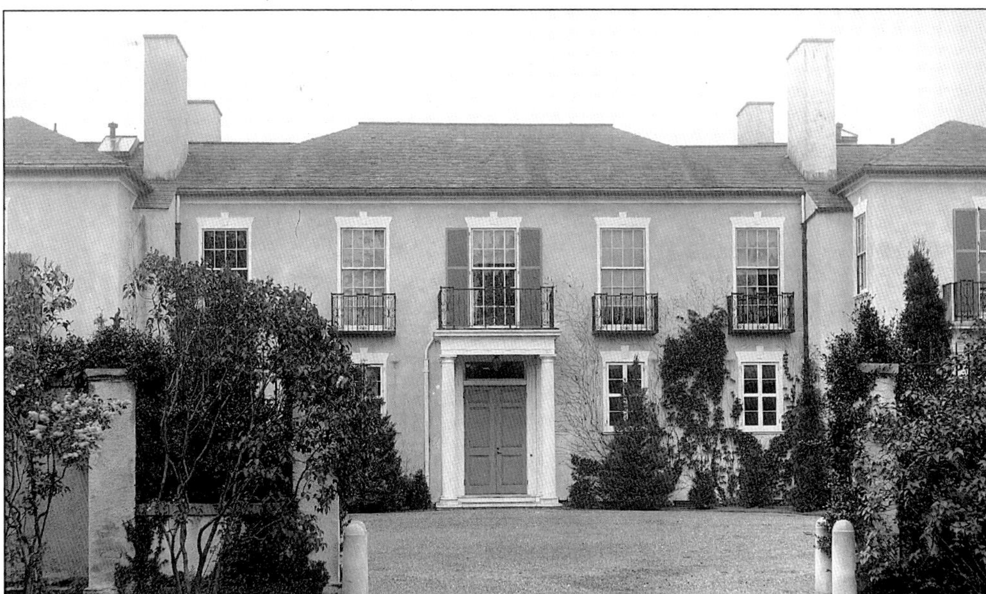

THE TRIVIUM SCHOOL. The Trivium School, a small independent Catholic preparatory school, was founded in 1979 by Mr. and Mrs. John Schmitt. Offering an integrated program of studies and activities, the school takes its name from the classical curriculum in the liberal arts: grammar, logic, and rhetoric. Shown here is the courtyard entrance. The facility, located on Back (Langen) Road, was originally called Crownledge and was the country home of Eugene van Rensselaer Thayer II. (Kilbourn.)

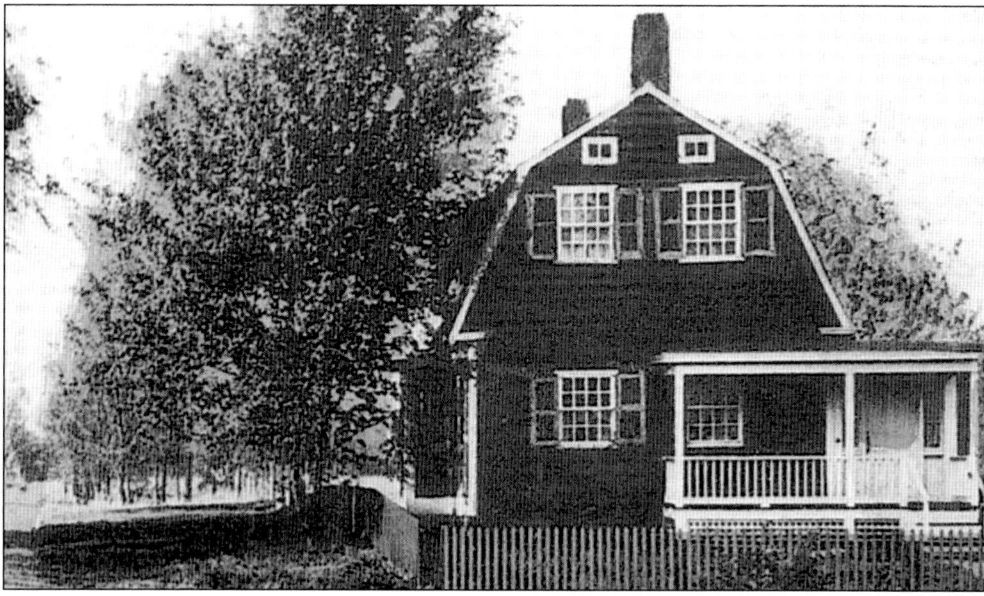

THE OLD SHAKER INFIRMARY. This dwelling on the Old Union Turnpike near Route 2 was originally used as an infirmary by the nearby Shirley Shaker Community. It was moved to a site across from the Old Brick Tavern to serve as a caretaker's cottage *c.* 1905–1909. The Shaker Village was begun when Mother Anne Lee visited the area in the late 18th century. A small Shaker cemetery and their Holy Hill are located north of Route 2 on the Lancaster-Shirley line. (Ponte.)

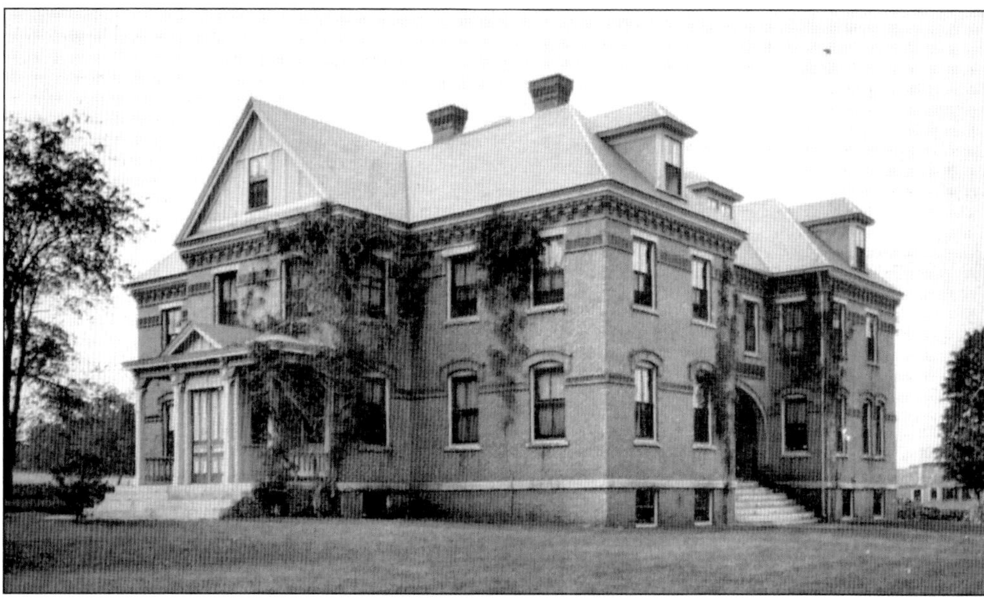

A TOWN FARM. Lancaster's first almshouse, established in the early 19th century, was located in a remote section of town near the Old Slate Quarry. Later, it was moved to the Ballard Hill area. This card shows the last "poor farm" facility, which was built there in 1884. Eventually, the building was sold and, in 1947, was converted into the Rest Haven Nursing Home. In 1968, the out-dated building was razed and the River Terrace Healthcare facility was put in its place. (Colley.)

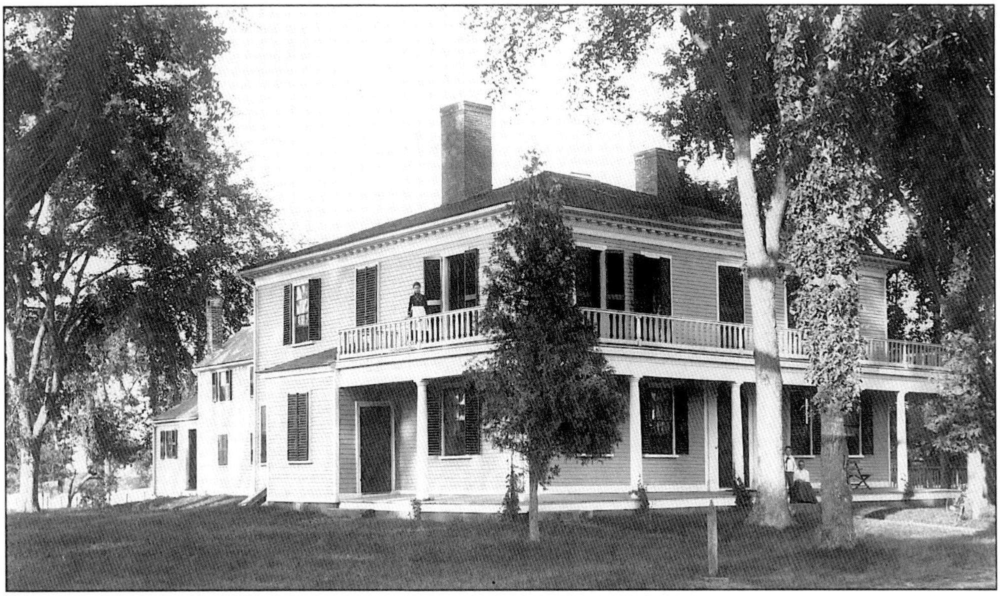

Goodrest. Built in 1800, this stately home on Old Common Road was the dwelling of Thomas Safford, who was a baker. Beginning in 1890, and for many years afterward, the philanthropic Pauline Revere Thayer maintained the place as Goodrest, a vacation home for working women and girls from Boston.

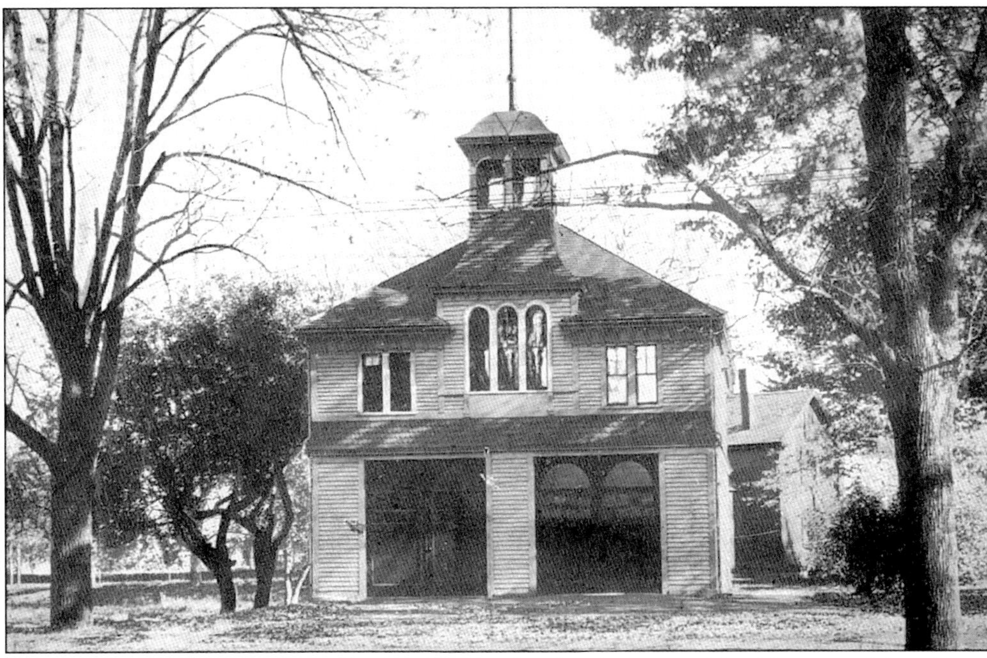

The South Lancaster Hose House. This is the South Station Fire House on Main Street in South Lancaster. Through a motion made by Nathaniel Thayer III at the town meeting in 1887, it was voted to spend $3,500 for its construction. The building has been used according to its original purpose ever since. It is on the National Register of Historic Places. Hose houses constructed at about the same time in the North Village and Deershorn area have since been converted into private dwellings. (AUC.)

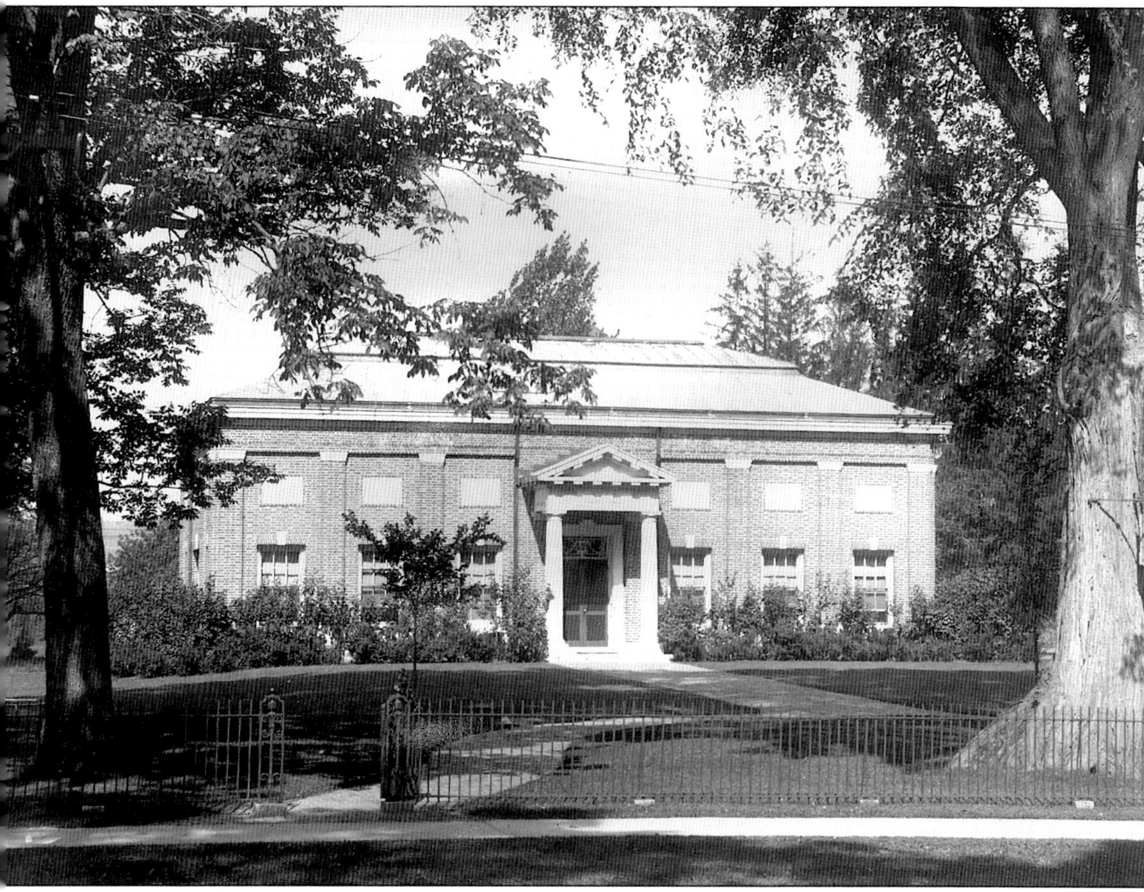

FORMER THAYER BIRD MUSEUM AND AUC ART GALLERY. The Thayer Bird Museum, on Main Street in South Lancaster, was designed by architect Henry Forbes Bigelow and built in 1903 for ornithologist John Eliot Thayer II, who needed a place to house his vast collection of North American bird specimens. Even though Lancaster was off the beaten path, the museum attracted more than 10,000 visitors in its first six years. In 1974, the building was sold to Atlantic Union College and is now the Mabel Bartlett Art Gallery. Much of the Thayer collection was donated to the Museum of Comparative Zoology at his alma mater, Harvard University.

Three

A Heritage of Homes

"Lancaster is a beautiful township. The surface is extremely pleasant, and even elegant. It consists of hills, valleys, and plains, finely interspersed with groves and orchards, and a succession of intervales. The houses in Lancaster are, in many instances, very good; and appear obviously to be the habitations of gentlemen. A greater degree of taste is conspicuous than in various other places, where the buildings are equally expensive. A number of polished people have always resided here; and the inhabitants at large have been distinguished for industry, sobriety, and good order." So wrote Timothy Dwight, a president of Yale College, in the early 19th century in his *Travels in New-England and New-York.* Nearly 200 years later, the impression still lingers. Although some of Lancaster's fine old homes have been lost through the years, many others remain as elegant reminders of earlier times. Some of these are shown on the following pages.

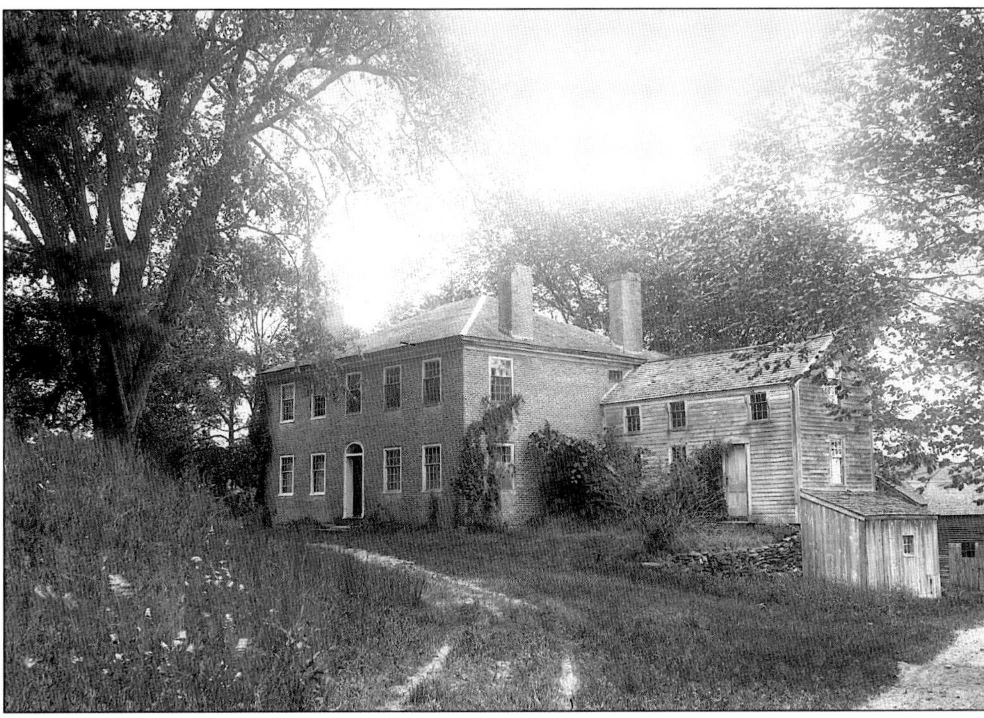

The Burbank Homestead. The Burbank Homestead was built c. 1800 by Simon Willard. "Plant wizard" Luther Burbank, born in 1849, lived here until he was about 21. In the 1930s, Henry Ford came to Lancaster and negotiated with the Dexter family, who then owned the house, to move the ell to his museum in Dearborn, Michigan. The U.S. Army acquired the land as part of the South Post of Fort Devens and demolished the remaining brick structure.

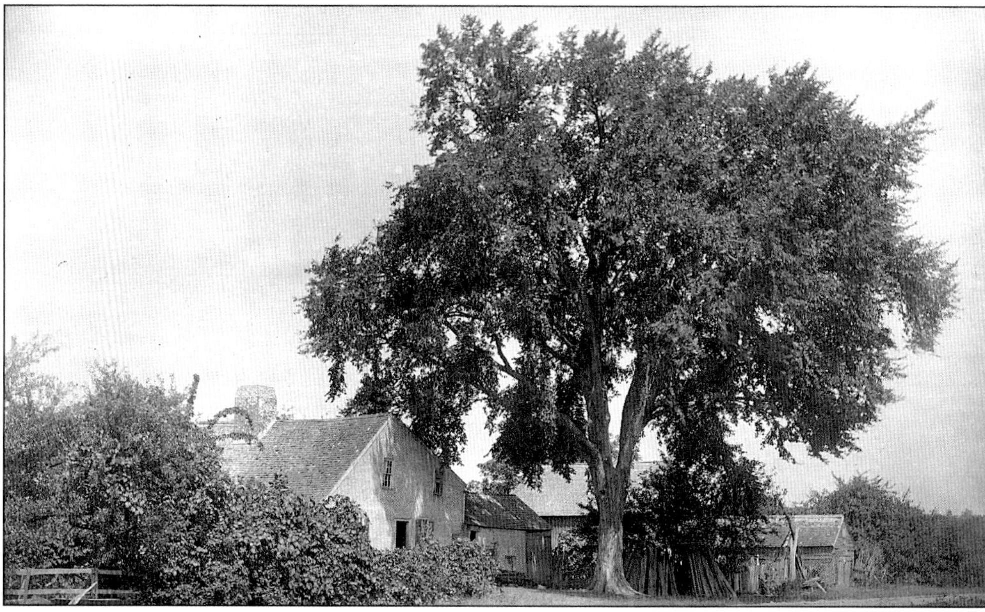

The Old Phelps House. The old Phelps House was built *c.* 1720 on Harvard Road. Originally, the exterior was plastered in imitation of granite. With exposure to the elements, it developed a discolored and weather-beaten look, making it appear very ancient. The last of the family to occupy the house was William Phelps. Born there in 1805, he lived to be over 90 years of age.

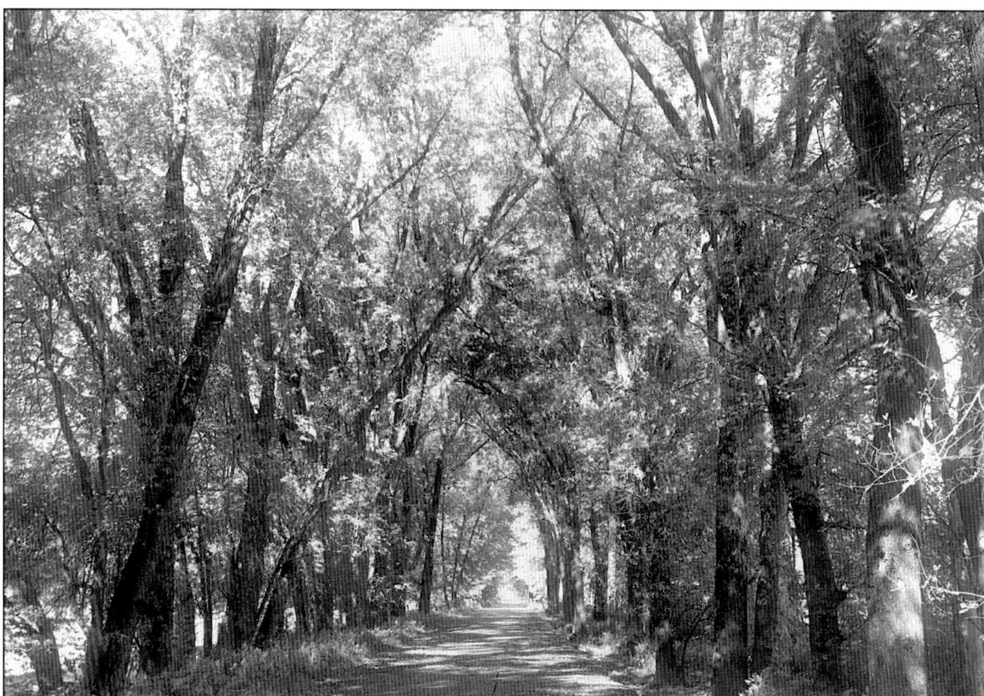

The Seven Bridge Road. Shown is an early view of Seven Bridge Road, or present-day Route 117, heading east toward Bolton.

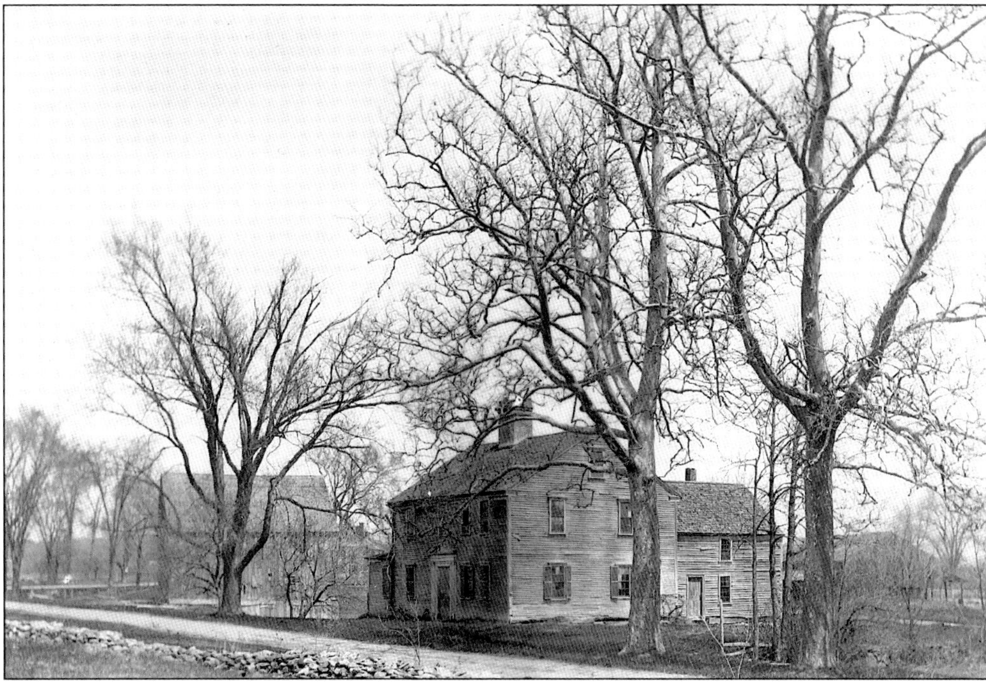

The Deacon Jonas Lane House. Between Harvard Road and the railroad tracks near the Route 117 intersection was the Deacon Jonas Lane House, which was built in 1786. Deacon Lane (1761–1848) was said to have been a "man of influence" in town and church affairs. This photograph shows the house, with buttonwood trees in front, as it looked in 1893. Many years later, the house and barn were burned down.

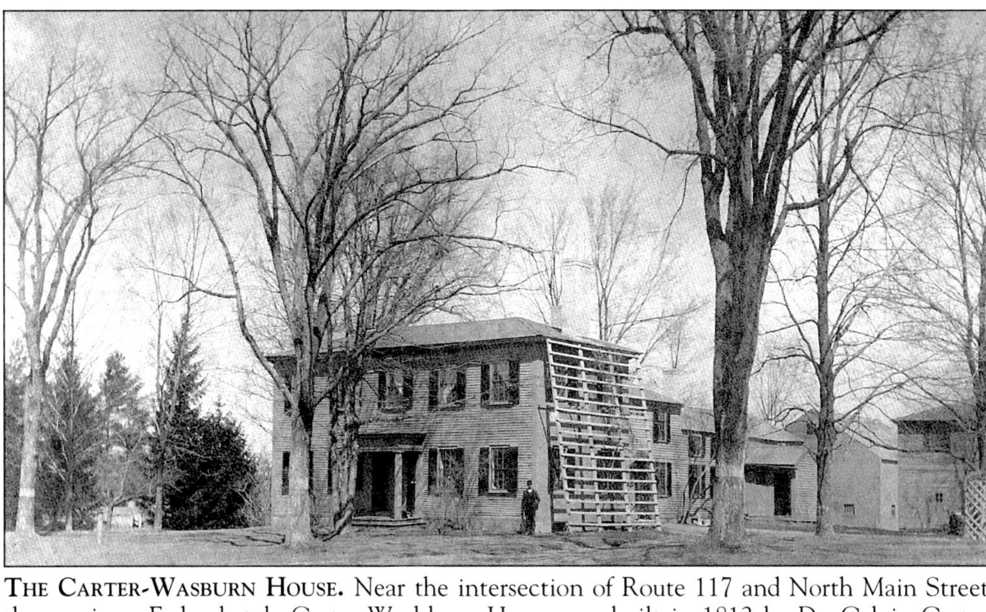

The Carter-Wasburn House. Near the intersection of Route 117 and North Main Street, the gracious, Federal-style Carter-Washburn House was built in 1812 by Dr. Calvin Carter. It was later occupied by retired Boston businessman John M. Washburn. Washburn, who resided in Lancaster until his death in 1861, lost two sons in the Civil War—Capt. Edward R. Washburn and Col. Francis Washburn. This photograph was taken in 1891.

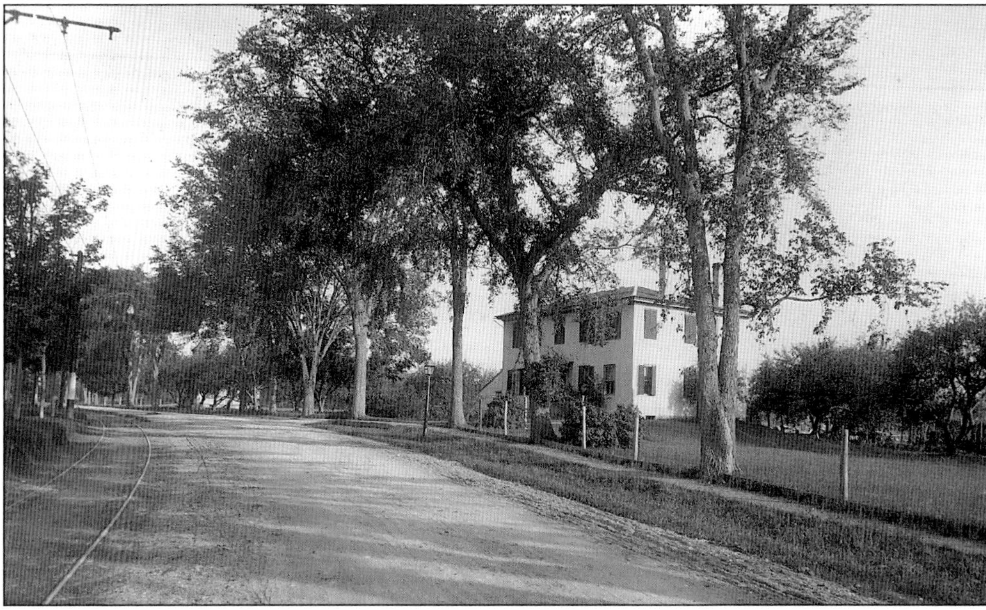

THE MAJOR JACOB FISHER HOUSE. This is the Major Jacob Fisher House, built in 1794 in the North Village. A watchmaker, surveyor, and cabinetmaker, Fisher was known as a shrewd businessman. The area, then called Union Village, began to flourish with the arrival of this prominent man.

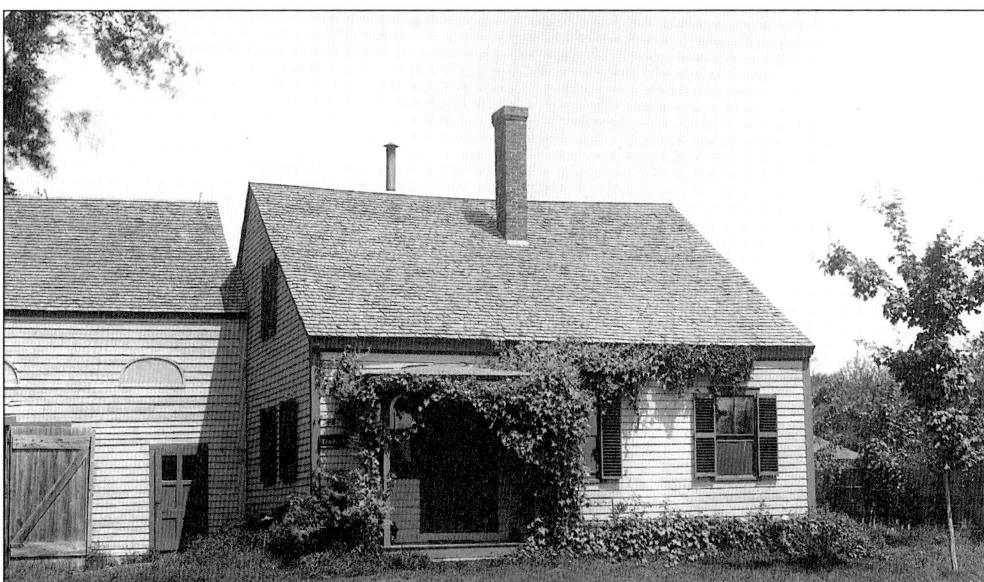

THE JACOB FISHER JR. HOUSE. This house, located on present-day Route 117, was built in 1817 on a one-and-a-half-acre parcel of land purchased from his father. By 1830, he had built a larger home nearby.

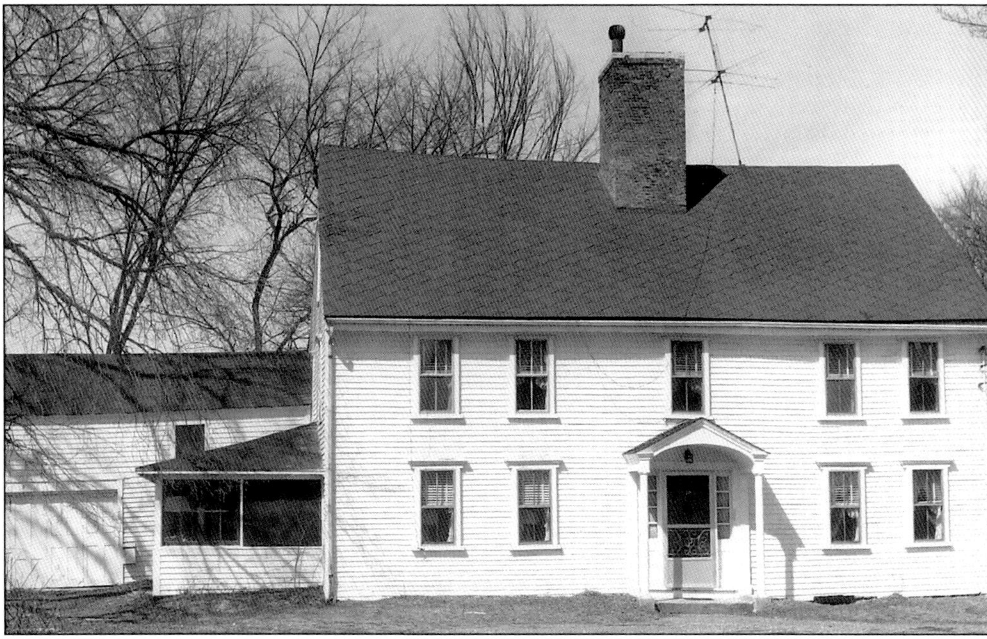

THE CAPTAIN JOHN BENNETT HOUSE. The Captain John Bennett House, near the Nashua River on Route 117 in North Lancaster, was built in 1717. Local legend identifies this house as a stopping place on the Underground Railroad for runaway slaves escaping to Canada. This, however, has never been substantiated. From 1872 to 1874, the house was occupied by the first Adventist missionary, J.N. Andrews, who revised his *History of the Sabbath* while living there. (AUC.)

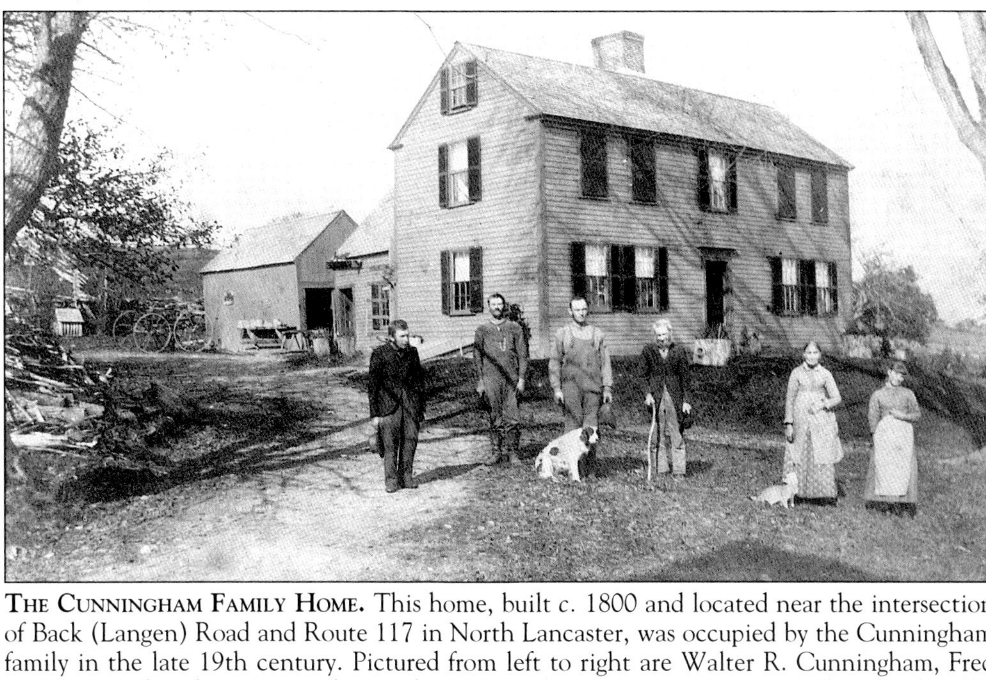

THE CUNNINGHAM FAMILY HOME. This home, built c. 1800 and located near the intersection of Back (Langen) Road and Route 117 in North Lancaster, was occupied by the Cunningham family in the late 19th century. Pictured from left to right are Walter R. Cunningham, Fred L. McGee, Edward T. Cunningham, John Cunningham, Louisa Rice Cunningham, and Nellie Barbour (Mrs. Albert Carr). This photograph was taken c. 1880.

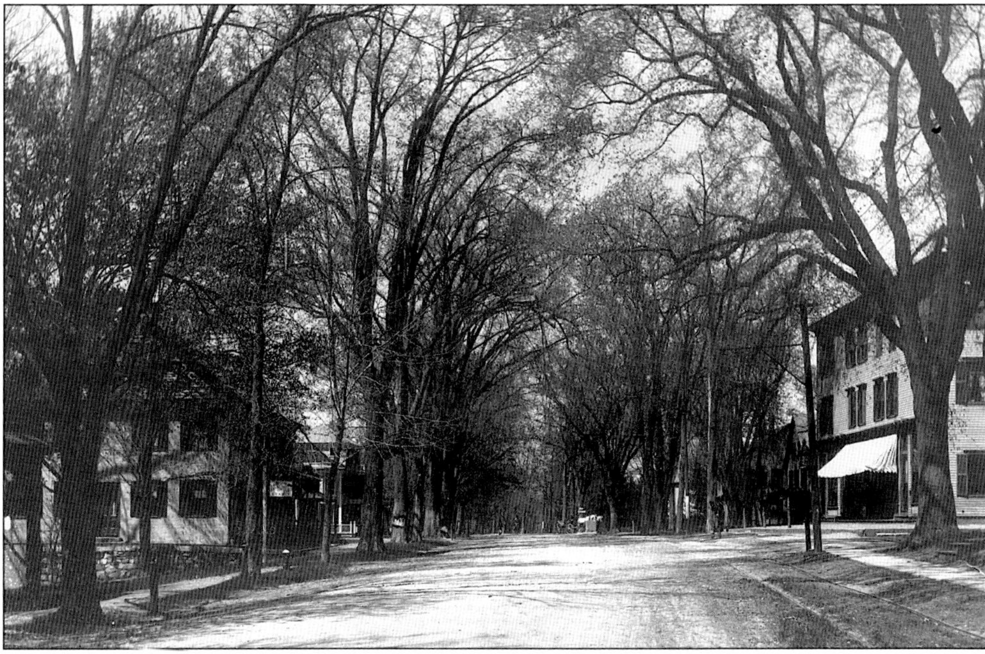

A View of Main Street Looking North. Luxuriously foliated trees create a canopied view of Main Street looking north from the Center Village c. 1900.

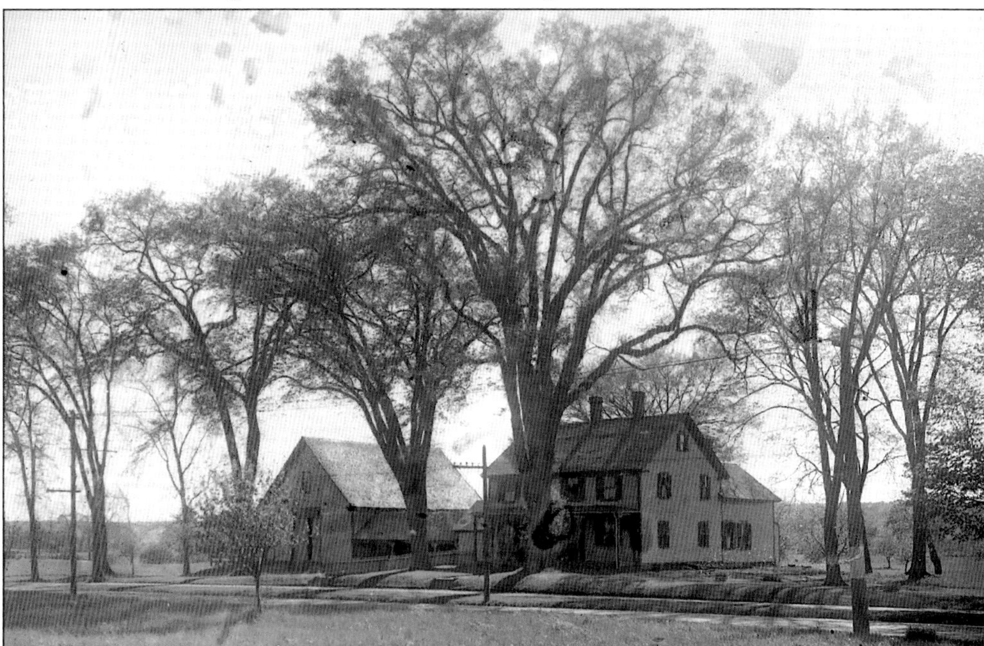

The General John Whiting House. The General John Whiting House, c. 1775, is on North Main Street across from Creamery Road. Whiting, who died in 1810, served through the Revolutionary War. He was lieutenant colonel of the 4th U.S. Infantry and held a commission as brigadier general in the militia. This view shows the house with a porch and barn, which have both been removed since. Whiting is buried in the Middle Cemetery.

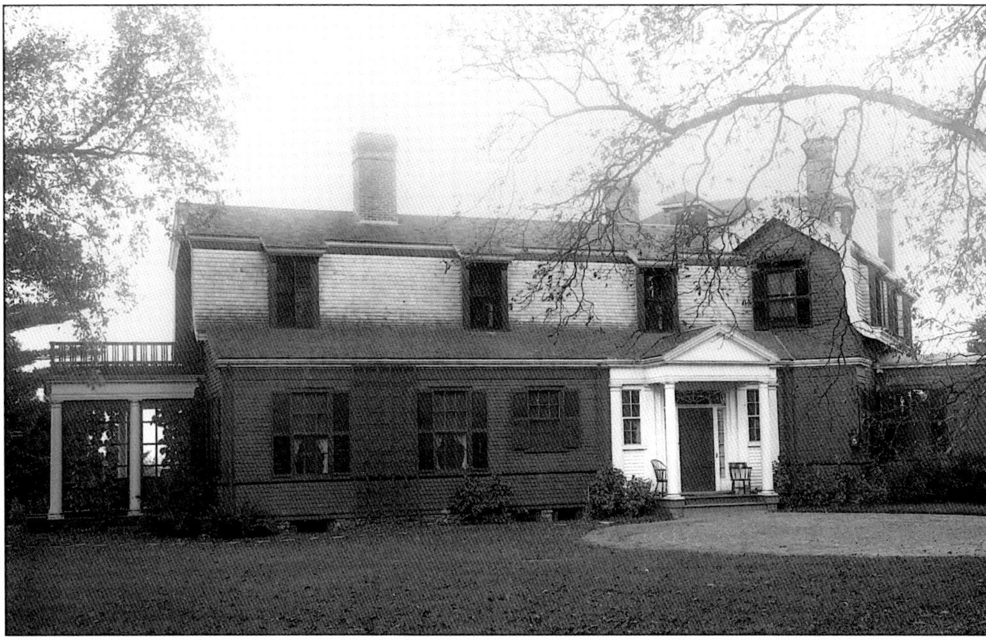

THE REVEREND AMOS LAWRENCE RESIDENCE. This residence, on Main Street in Lancaster Center, was built in 1861 for Rev. Amos E. Lawrence, who was the pastor of the Evangelical Congregational Church. It later became the home of Rev. George M. Bartol, D.D., of the First Church of Christ, Unitarian.

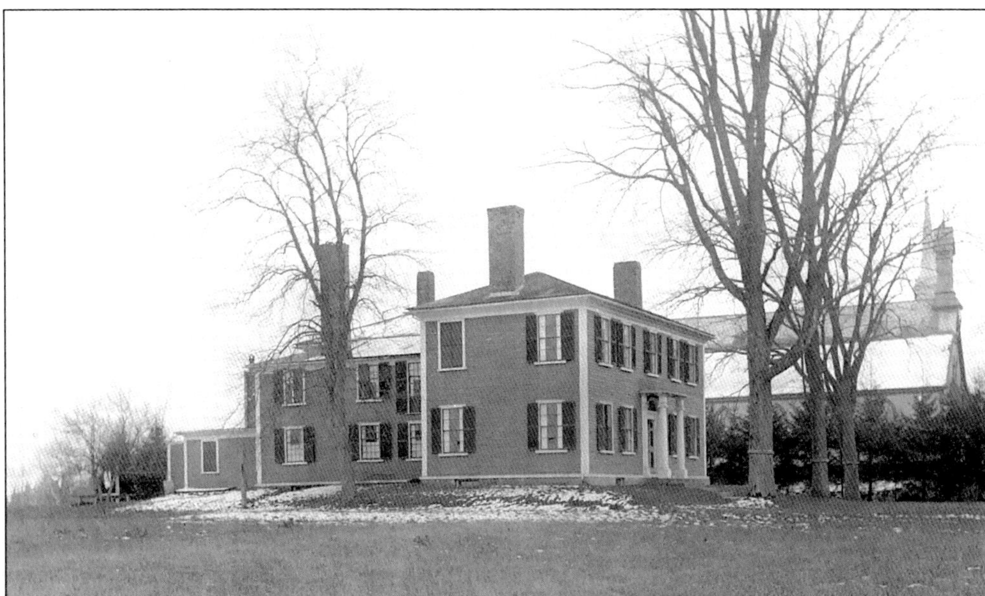

THE RICE-PICKMAN MANSION. Located on the east side of Main Street just north of the Immaculate Conception church, this dwelling was built in 1794 by Maj. Merrick Rice, who was a lawyer. Having built the place for a woman he hoped would become his wife, he sold it and left town when the marriage failed to take place. In 1814, Benjamin Pickman of Salem greatly enlarged the structure, turning it into an elegant Salem-styled mansion. This photograph shows the place as it looked in 1892.

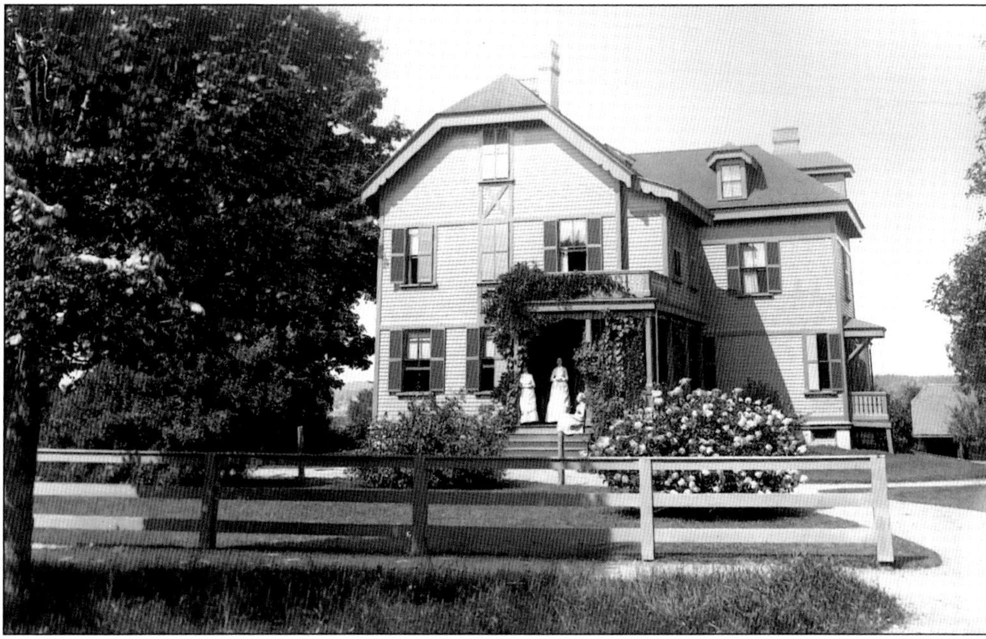

The Chandler Residence. This residence, located at 918 Main Street, was built in 1867 by retired Boston lithographer John Greene Chandler (1815–1879). Chandler was a wood engraver who trained at the Carter and Andrews firm in Lancaster. His most famous toy book was an adaptation of the *Chicken Little* folk tale. His daughter Alice Greene Chandler (1851–1935) was a librarian for the town and a talented photographer. Many of her photographs appear in this book.

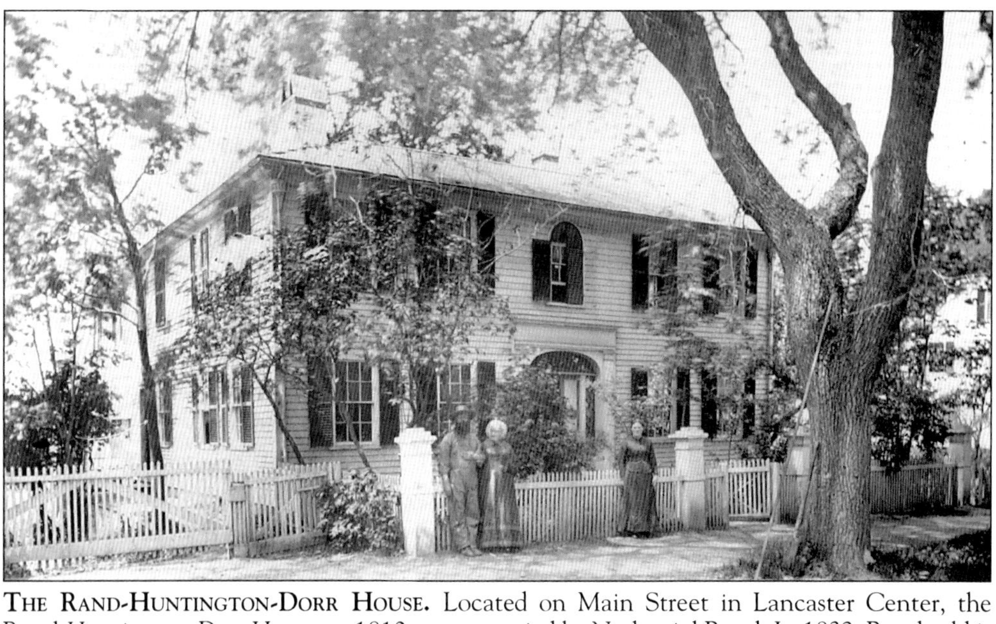

The Rand-Huntington-Dorr House. Located on Main Street in Lancaster Center, the Rand-Huntington-Dorr House, *c.* 1810, was occupied by Nathaniel Rand. In 1832, Rand sold it to Joseph Huntington. His daughter Julia married Mr. Dorr; their son, prominent Boston lawyer Dudley Huntington Dorr, later inherited it. After 127 years, it was sold out of the family. The place was remodeled *c.* 1900 and again *c.* 1959.

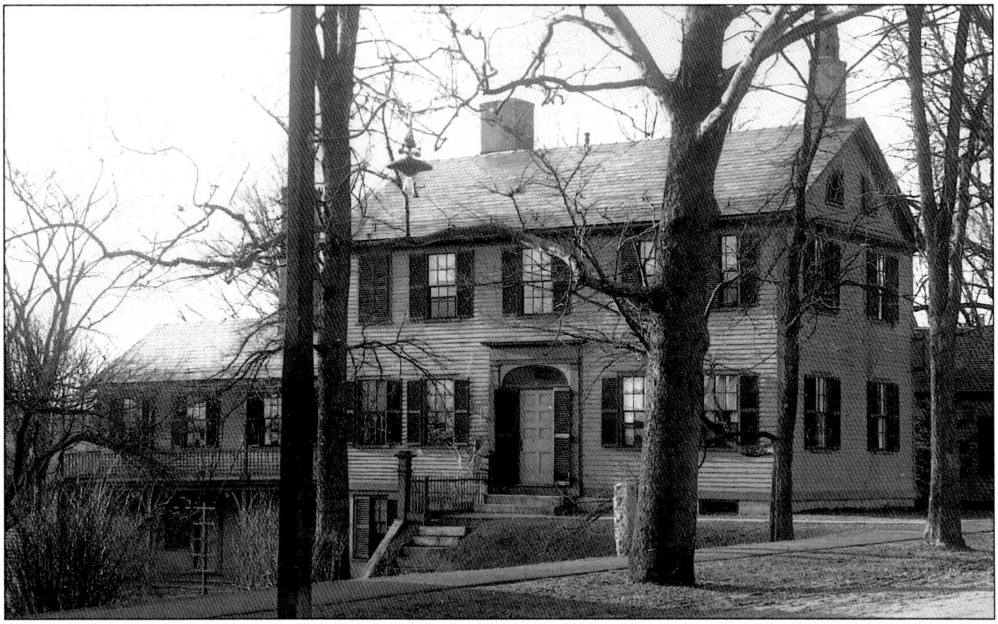

THE GEORGE CARTER RESIDENCE. The George Carter residence was built in the 1820s. Facing south, it is located near Barnes Court and Main Street in Lancaster Center. Carter was one of the partners in the successful Carter and Andrews firm, which was established in Lancaster in the early 19th century.

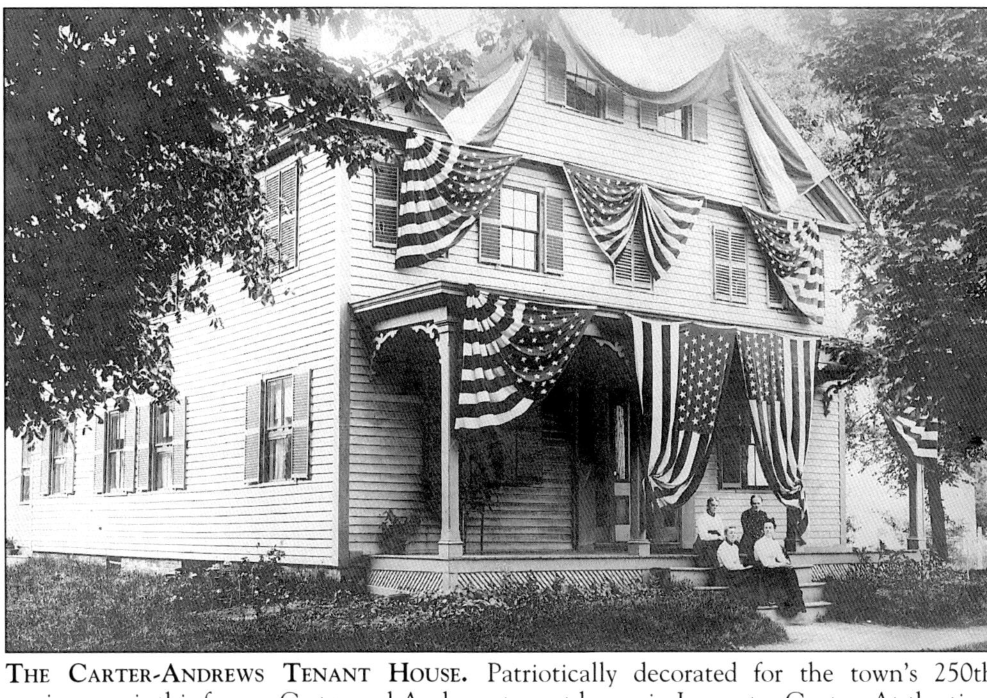

THE CARTER-ANDREWS TENANT HOUSE. Patriotically decorated for the town's 250th anniversary is this former Carter and Andrews tenant house in Lancaster Center. At the time this photograph was taken in the early 1900s, it was called the Club House. Seated from left to right are the following: (front row) Emma Floyd and Alice Carr MacDonald; (back row) Isabella Lyman and Sarah Thurston.

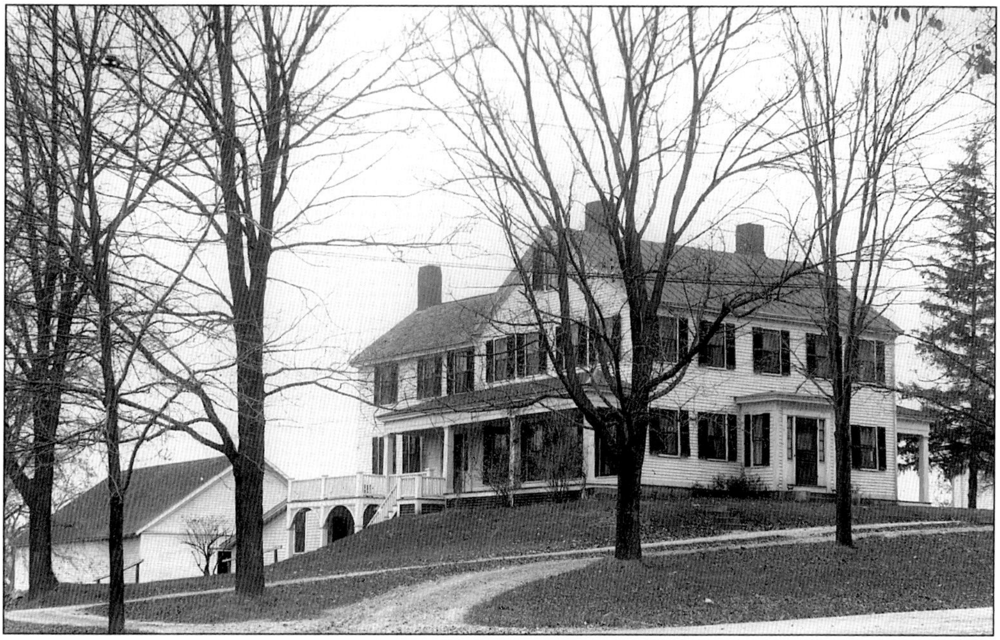

The Elias Danforth House. Originally the Elias Danforth House (built in 1833), the dwelling at 634 Main Street is very close to the site of the town's fourth meetinghouse, which was constructed *c.* 1743. Later, it was the home of Mrs. Edward F.W. Bartol, daughter-in-law of Rev. George M. Bartol.

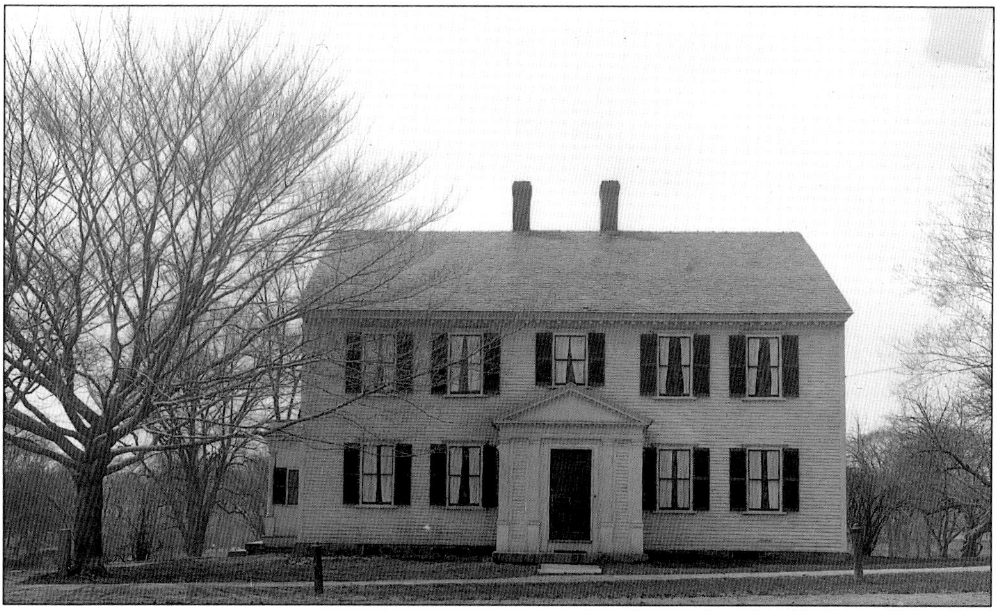

The Unitarian Parsonage. Located on the west side of Main Street near the Nashua River, this home was built in 1785 for Judge John Sprague, who served the town 10 years as a representative, 2 years as a senator, and 3 years as a sheriff. His grandson S.J. Sprague Vose was the last of the family to live in the house. Later, it was purchased and given as a parsonage "fully furnished and equipped" by Col. John E. Thayer, who maintained it for 25 years. In 1933, the year Thayer died, it was bequeathed to the church.

THE MANSION HOUSE. Built *c.* 1750 by carpenter Aaron Willard, the Mansion House, as it has been called, is located not far off Main Street on Neck Road. A third story was added to the structure in the mid-19th century, and it was used for many years as a boarding school by Mrs. Southwick, Rev. M.C. Stebbins, and William A. Kilbourn, A.M.

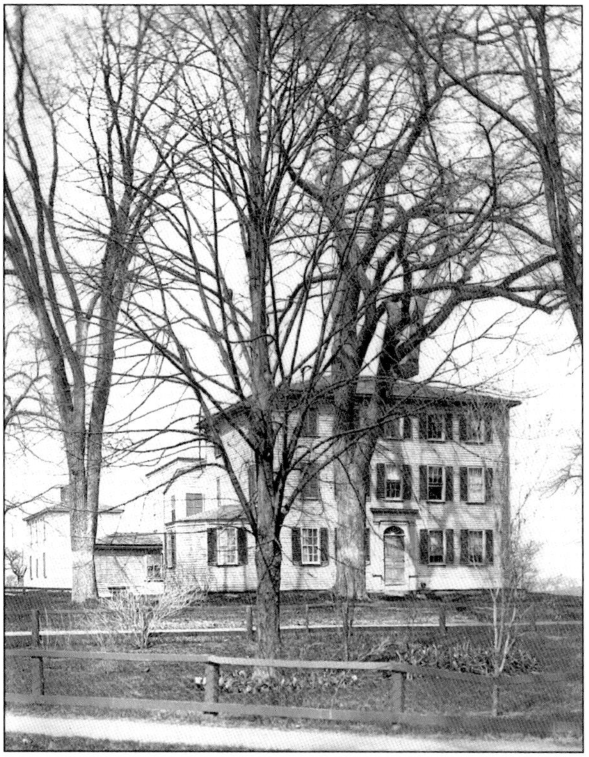

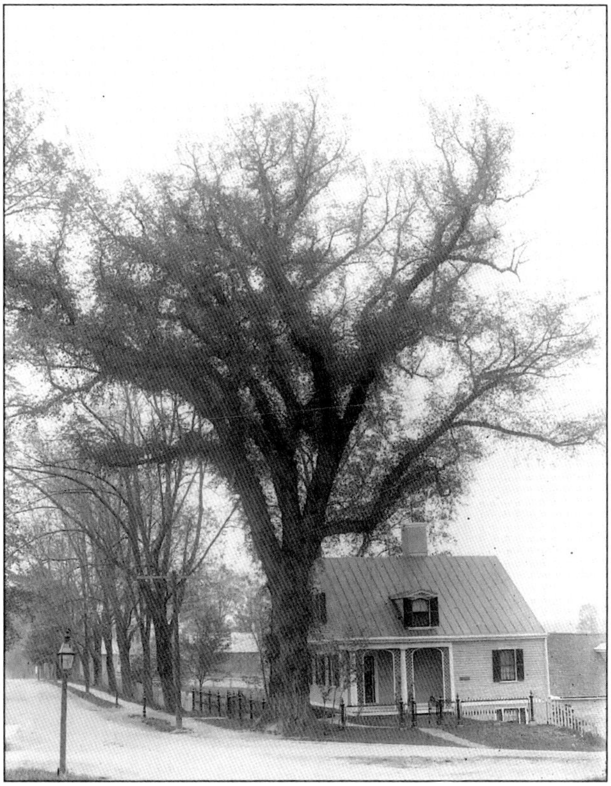

THE JOSEPH BRECK HOUSE. This dwelling, near the junction of Neck and Center Bridge Roads, was built in 1831 for Joseph Breck, who was the superintendent of the Lancaster Horticultural Gardens and founder of the Breck Seed Company. It is also very near the site of the early Cyprian Stevens garrison. The feathered elm was one of the largest of its kind in the area. At one point, it measured 18 feet in circumference, just 5 feet from the base.

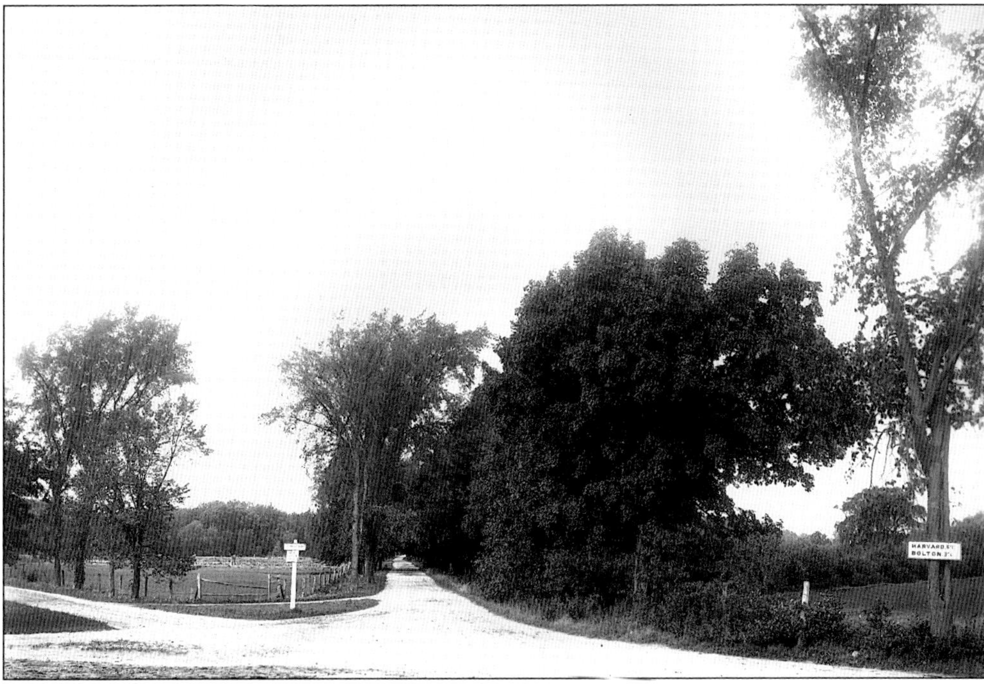

The Five Corners. Shown here without a buggy in sight is a late-19th-century view of the well-traveled Five Corners intersection in the Old Common area of town.

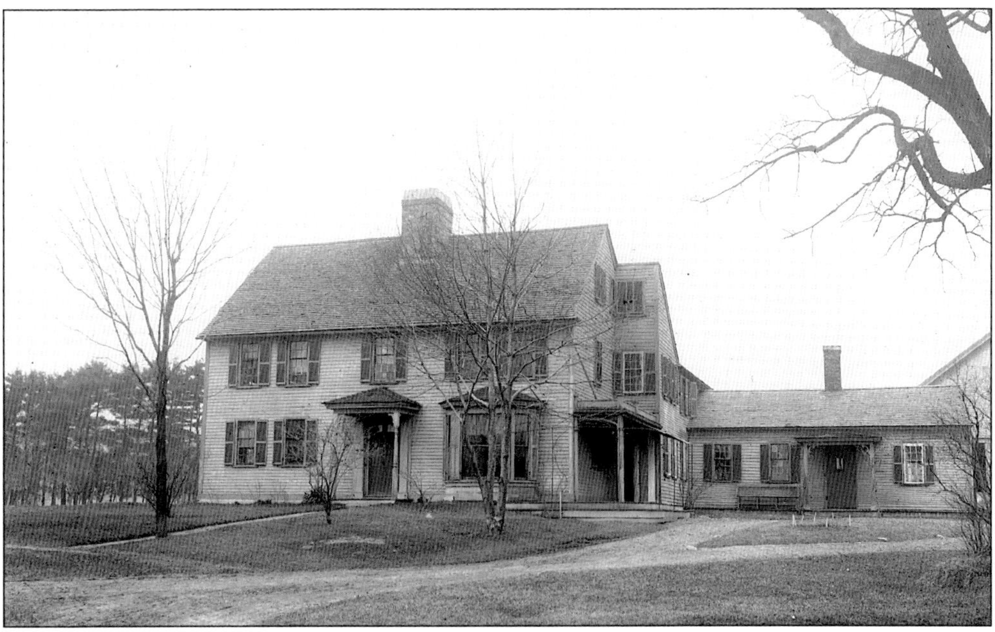

The Capt. Samuel Willard Home. This dwelling is on Neck Road near the railroad tracks and Current Topics Club in Lancaster Center. It was built in 1727 by Capt. Samuel Willard. During the Revolutionary War, a descendant, Col. Abijah Willard, remained a loyalist, or Tory, and went to Nova Scotia. The government confiscated the Lancaster property, but family members were allowed to remain. The last family member to live in the house was his granddaughter Anna (Goodhue) Wilder, who died in 1862.

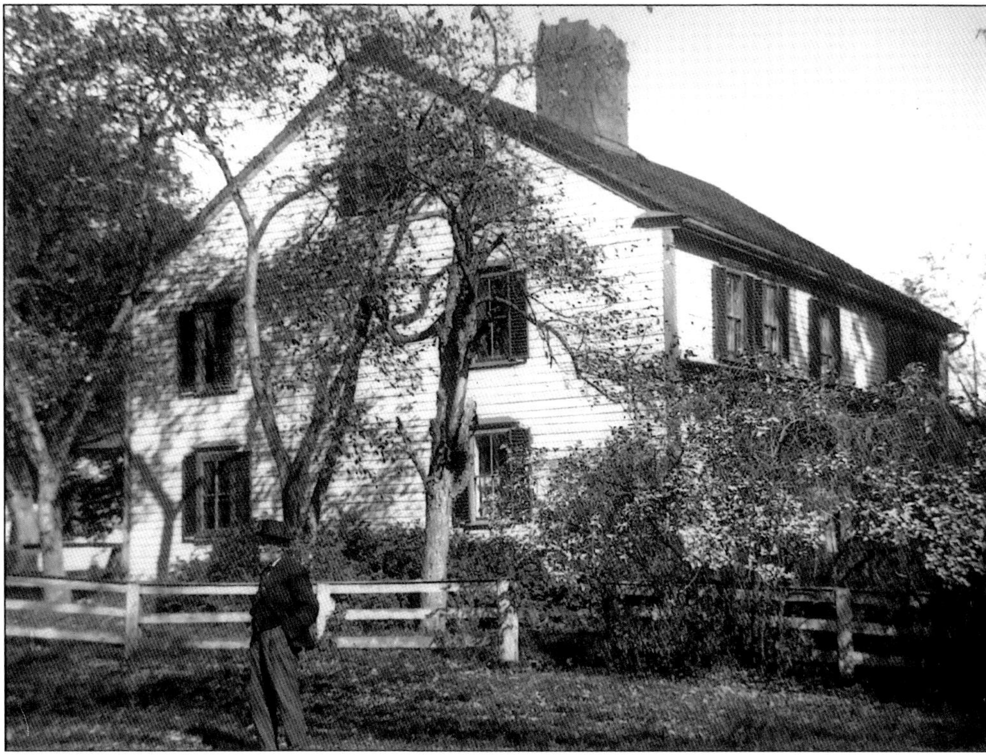

The White-Hawkins House. The oldest dwelling in Lancaster is the White-Hawkins House, on Neck Road. It dates from *c.* 1684, when the town was being resettled after the Indian Massacre during the winter of 1675–1676. It was built by John White, brother to Mary Rowlandson.

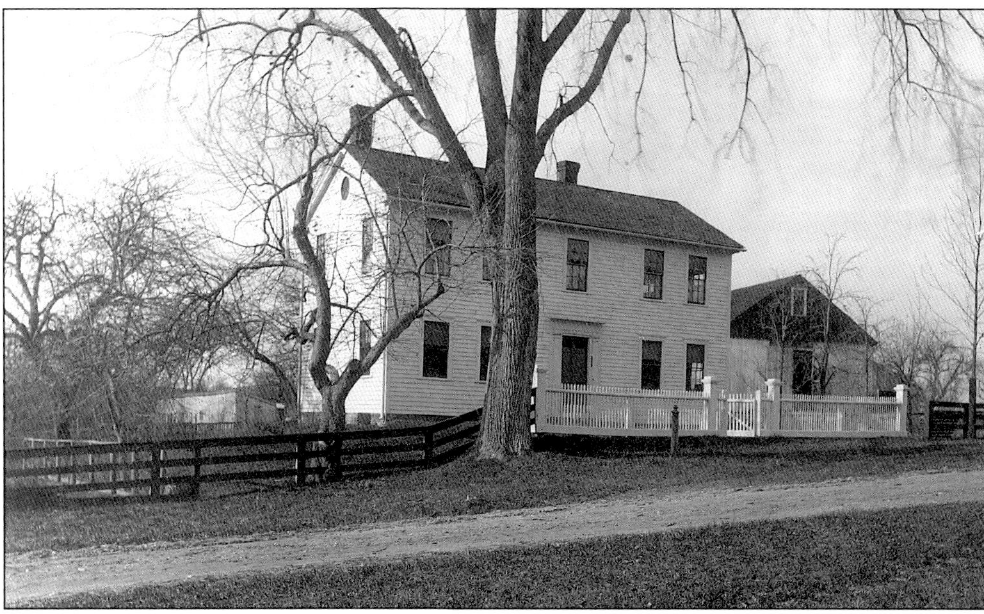

The Deacon Samuel F. White House. This is the Deacon Samuel F. White House, located on Neck Road. It was built in 1816 near the home of his ancestor John White. Members of this family, including Mary White Rowlandson, were among the town's earliest settlers. (TML.)

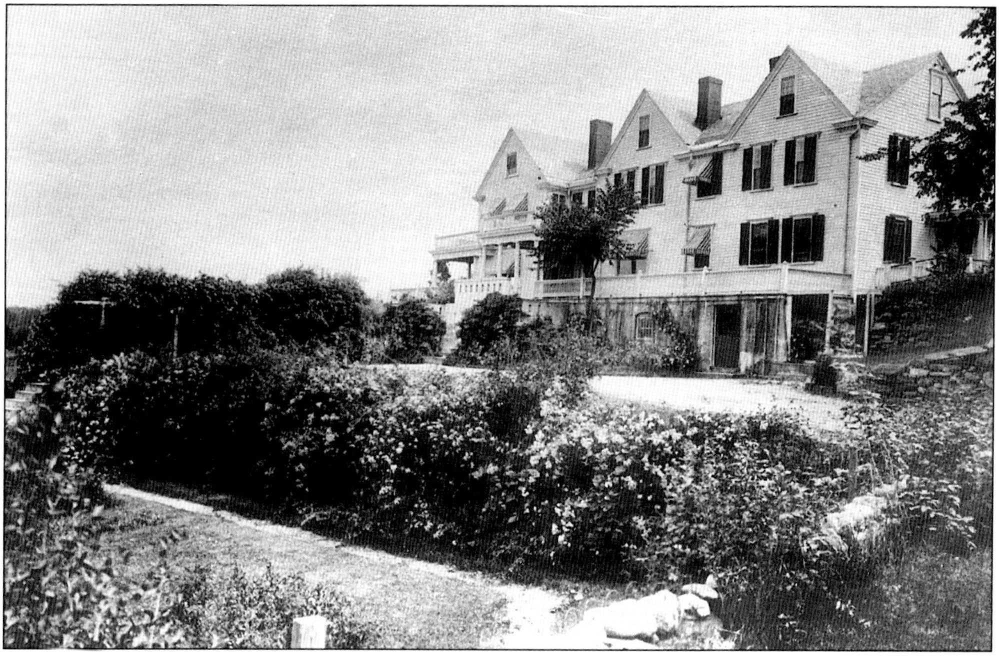

The Hagop Bogigian Estate. This large Neck Road home was built by wealthy Armenian-born rug merchant Hagop Bogigian (1856–1931), who is said to have been the first native importer of Oriental goods in America. The estate, which he maintained from 1905 until his death, originally included an 80-acre tract of land with a formal garden, pond, and orchard. Considered an authority on issues relating to Armenian emigration from Turkey, Bogigian was instrumental in helping many of his fellow countrymen gain entrance to America.

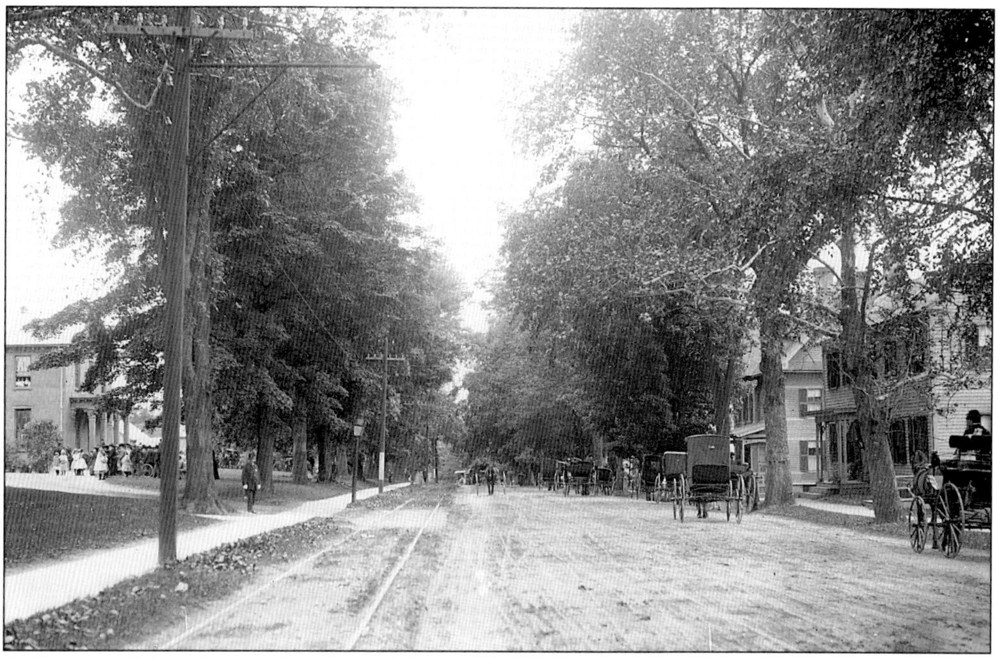

A View of Main Street Looking South. This view shows a tree-canopied Main Street in Lancaster Center in the early 1900s.

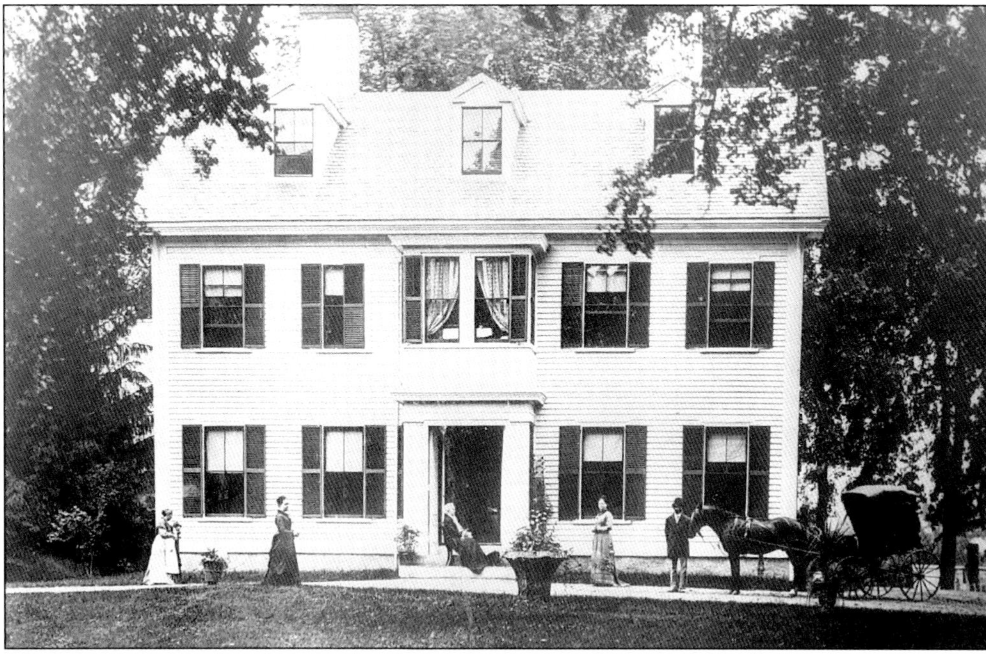

The Colonel Francis B. Fay House. The home of prominent Lancaster citizen Col. Francis B. Fay (1793–1876) was once located in an Elm Grove near the corner of Main Street and East George Hill Road in South Lancaster. After his death, the property, with its beautiful trees, was acquired by the Thayer family and the Eugene van Rensselaer estate, Fairlawn, was built on the site. The Fay residence was relocated to a site on George Hill. (Lawler.)

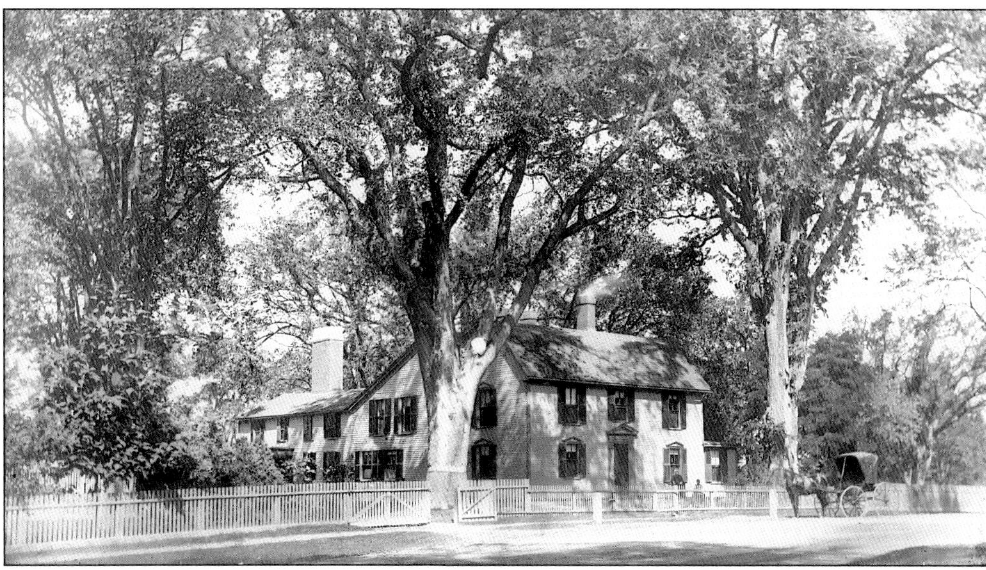

The Captain Samuel Ward House. This house (no longer standing) was already an old place when acquired by Capt. Samuel Ward of Worcester in 1768. In Lancaster, he ran a large mercantile establishment and was a prominent citizen of the town for 59 years. Much later, the dwelling, located on the corner of Main Street and George Hill Road in South Lancaster, was owned by the Hosmer family, who sold the property to Atlantic Union College. A new men's dormitory, Lenheim Hall, was built on the site and dedicated in 1956.

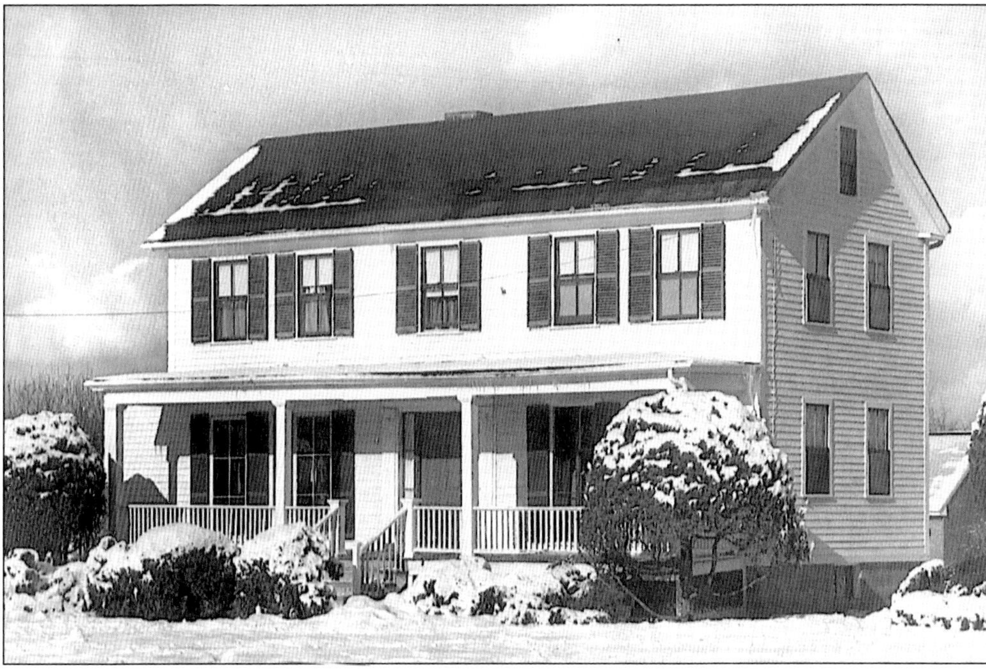

The Sears Home. This was the home of Rev. Edmund Hamilton Sears, D.D., who wrote the well-known Christmas carol "It Came upon a Midnight Clear." Sears was the seventh pastor of the First Church on the Lancaster Town Green, serving from 1840 to 1847. The house was originally located on the corner of Flagg and Main Streets in South Lancaster. In 1944, it was divided in two and moved to the north side of George Hill Road. The dwellings have since been used to house faculty and students from Atlantic Union College. (AUC.)

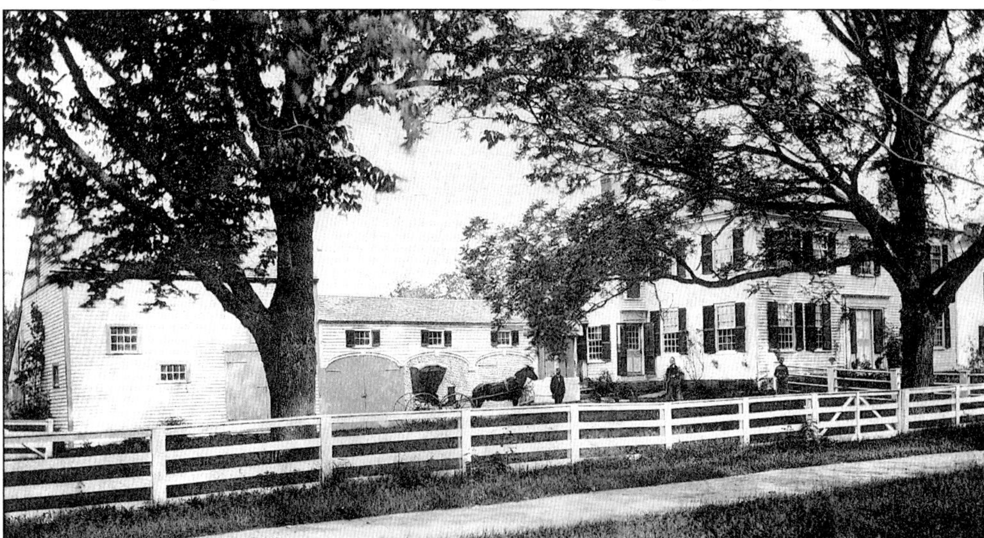

The Hosmer Family Home. This home (no longer standing) was situated on the site of Atlantic Union College's Preston Hall on Main Street in South Lancaster. The house was occupied by members of the Hosmer family. Henry F. Hosmer, great-uncle to the late town historian Herbert Hosmer, was the South Lancaster postmaster and ran a general store located just to the south. This photograph is from the mid-19th century.

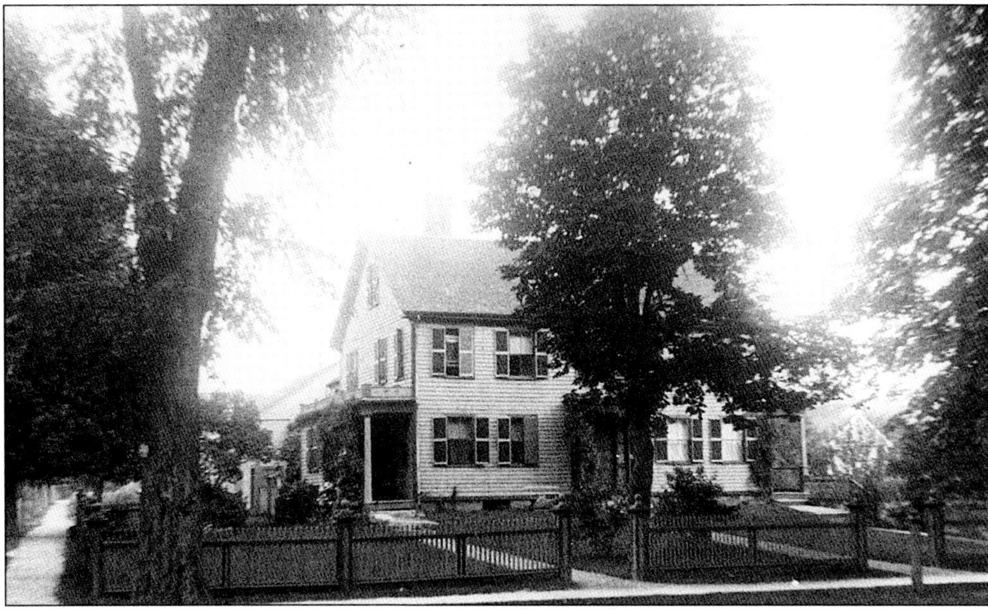

The Stephen Haskell House. This house (no longer standing), built in the 1850s, stands on the north corner of Main Street and Narrow Lane. It was one of the homes lived in by Adventist pioneer Stephen Haskell in the 1870s. At one time, Haskell was the owner of all the land fronting Main Street between Prescott Street and Narrow Lane and extending west to Goss Lane.

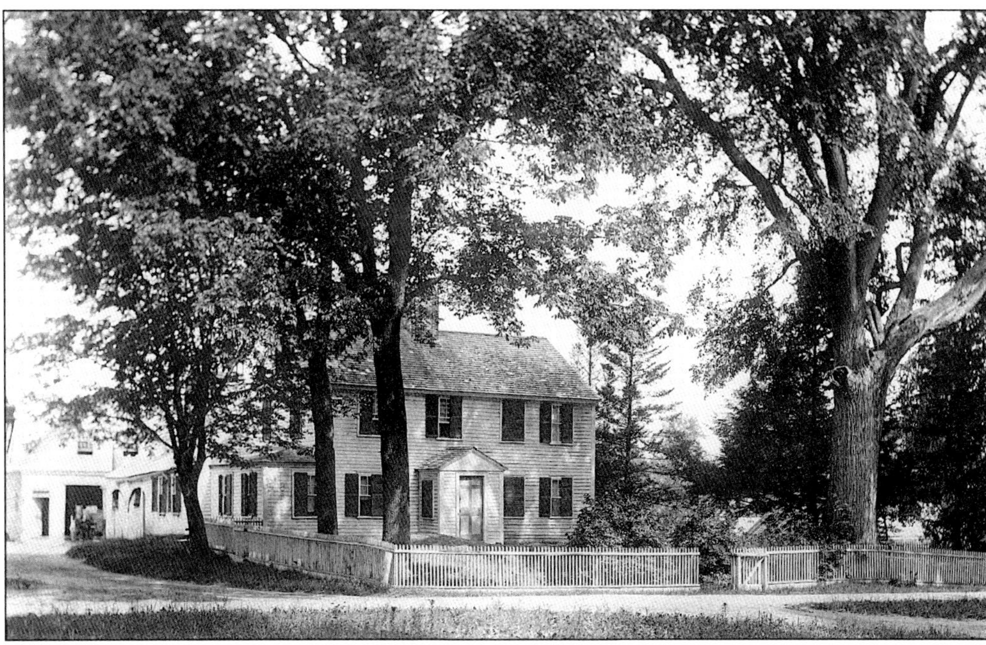

The Honorable John G. Thurston House. Thurston, who lived in Lancaster during the 19th century, was said to have kept the largest store in the county. Known as a man of superior ability, he excelled in business and was very active in community affairs. He held many town offices and served as a member of the general court. The house is presently located on Kilbourn Street. This view shows the residence as it looked in 1894.

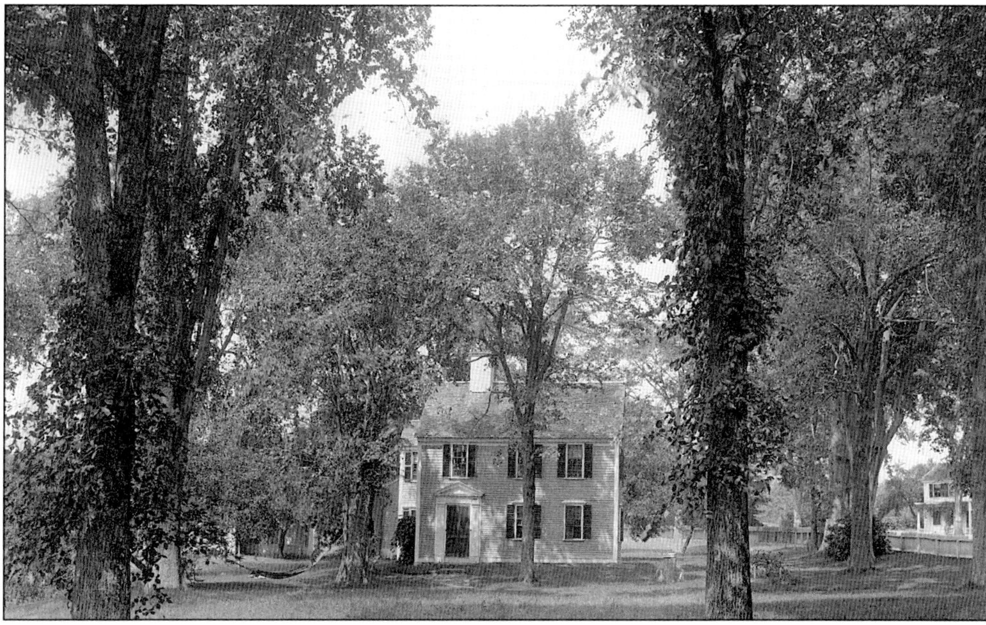

THE PETER THURSTON HOUSE. Located on the south side of Mill Street near the Main Street intersection in South Lancaster is the Peter Thurston House, built in 1784. Thurston, who was a hatter, bought a portion of farmland from his father. Originally, that farmland extended south to the Clinton line and up Sterling Road to the Deershorn area. The house remained in the family for more than 200 years. In more recent times, it was the home of Walter Miles. This photograph shows it as it looked in the late 19th century.

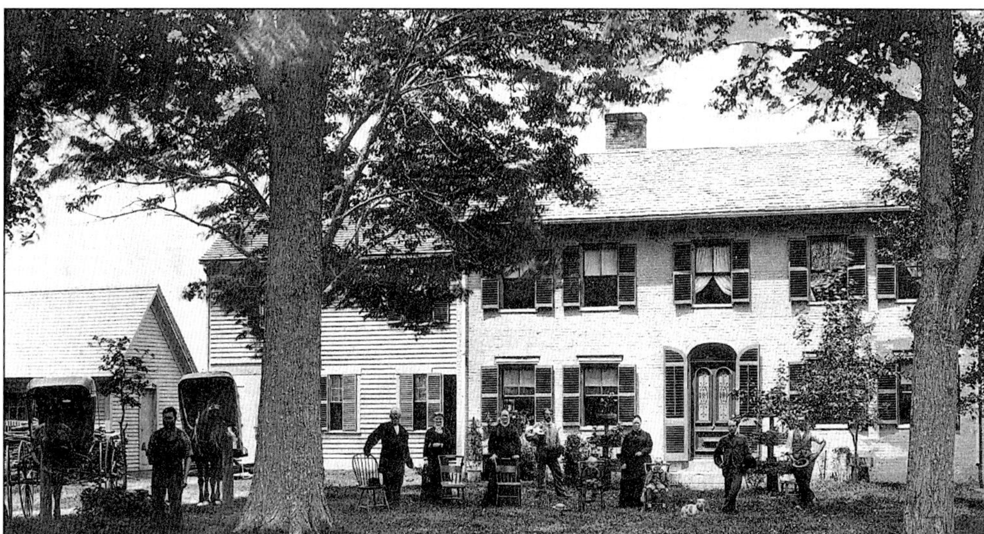

THE TURNER FAMILY HOMESTEAD. Posing in front of their house are members of the Turner family. The house (no longer standing) was located on the south corner of Sterling Road and Sawyer Street. From left to right are the following: an unidentified blacksmith, J.H. Turner, Fanny (Turner) Wallace, Sarah (Carter) Turner, Nathan Turner, Sarah (Turner) Sampson, Charlie or Joseph Sampson, Fred Turner, and Walter Turner. The Turners, blacksmiths by trade, settled in South Lancaster in 1832.

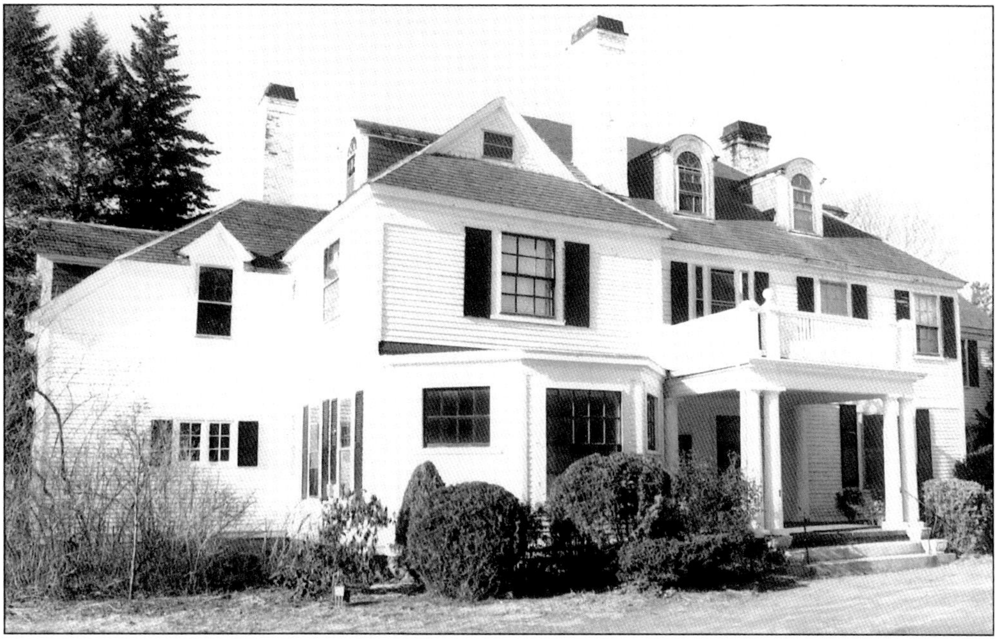

The Honorable Herbert Parker Estate. This 19th-century estate, located on Sterling Road toward the Deershorn area, was the residence of the Honorable Herbert Parker (1856–1939). A son of civil engineer George A. Parker, he was a prominent trial lawyer and also served as an attorney general for the state of Massachusetts. Having a great interest in the migration of birds, he built an extensive aviary behind his estate. The property is currently owned by Edmond Plante. (Griffin.)

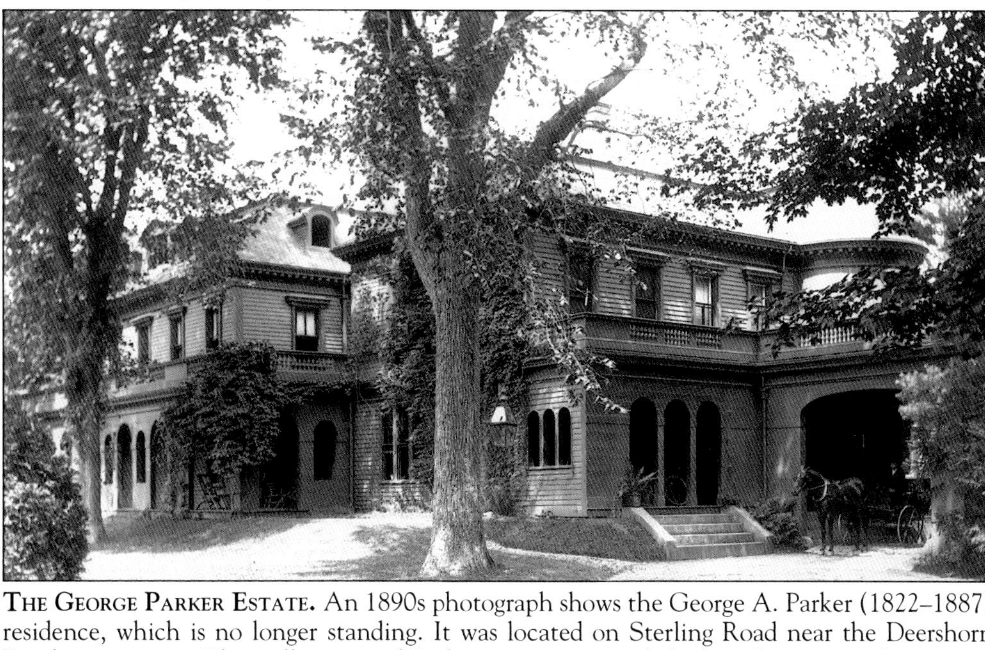

The George Parker Estate. An 1890s photograph shows the George A. Parker (1822–1887) residence, which is no longer standing. It was located on Sterling Road near the Deershorn Road intersection. The well-respected Parker was an accomplished civil engineer who, among other things, acted as superintendent of military railroads at the request of Secretary Stanton during the Civil War.

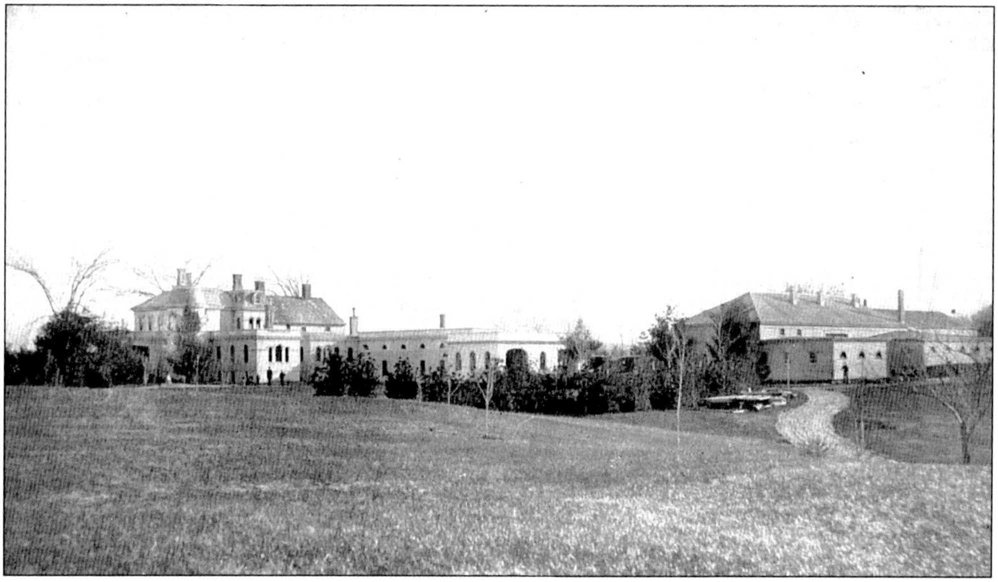

A Panorama of the Parker Estate. Here is a broad view of the former George A. Parker Estate. It was later occupied by his son Harold Parker (1854–1916), who was the chief engineer on the Clinton Dam project in the late 19th century. The buildings have long since been taken down, with the exception of a "bowling alley" section (toward the middle of the photograph). That section was converted into a home occupied for many years by Harold's daughter Cornelia (Connie) Parker.

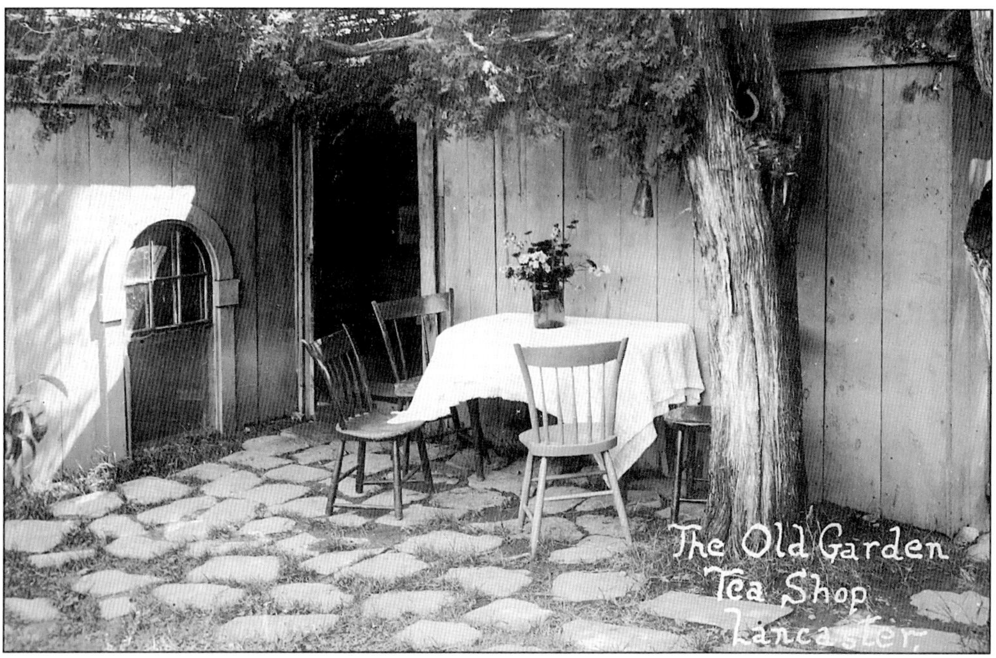

The Parker's Tea Shop. Located on the family's Sterling Road estate was the Tea Shop, once operated by Cornelia and Elizabeth Parker, daughters of Harold Parker. The ladies were well known as gracious hostesses and for their love of fine entertaining. (Schumacher-Hardy.)

Four

The Inns, Shops, Businesses, and Transportation

Lancaster consists of three villages—the northern, central, and southern parts of town. At one time, the North Village was called Union Village and the South Village was called New Boston. In the early 19th century, all three were bustling places, as Lancaster was a thoroughfare of travel from points north and west. Taverns and stores were busy places, and blacksmiths, wheelwrights, and cart makers found call for services. Industrious villagers were employed as comb makers, hatters, and pocketbook makers. At one time, the town even had a copper pump factory and an establishment that made piano keys. Later, railroads and trolleys added to the hum of village life. Many of these places have long since disappeared, but traces of others still remain.

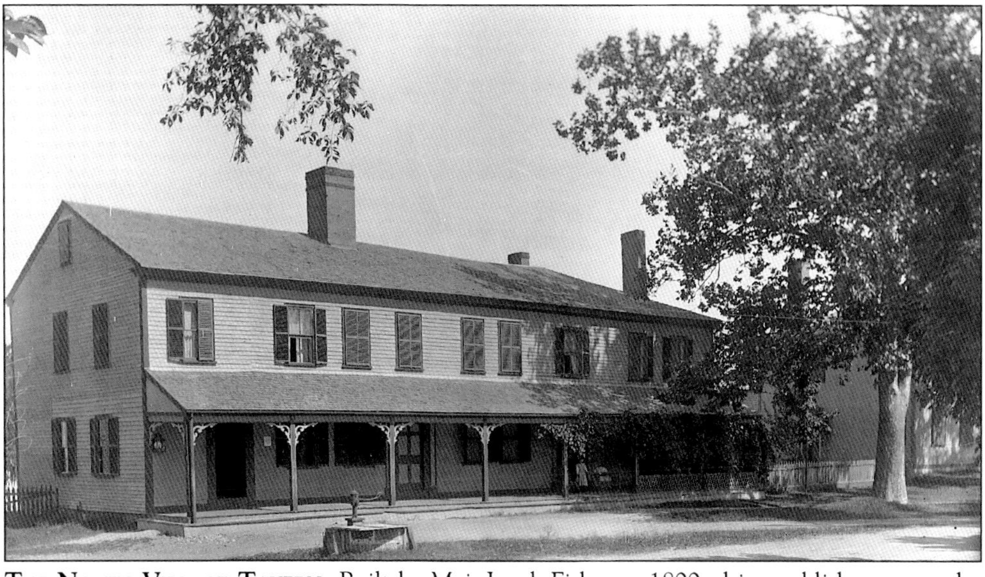

The North Village Tavern. Built by Maj. Jacob Fisher *c.* 1800, this establishment on the south corner of North Main Street and Lunenburg Road was later known as Fairbank's Inn and as Dwyer's Tavern. In the 1930s, it was a single-family dwelling for descendants of the Fuller family who ran a lumbermill near the Lancaster-Clinton line. This image shows the place as it looked in the late 19th century.

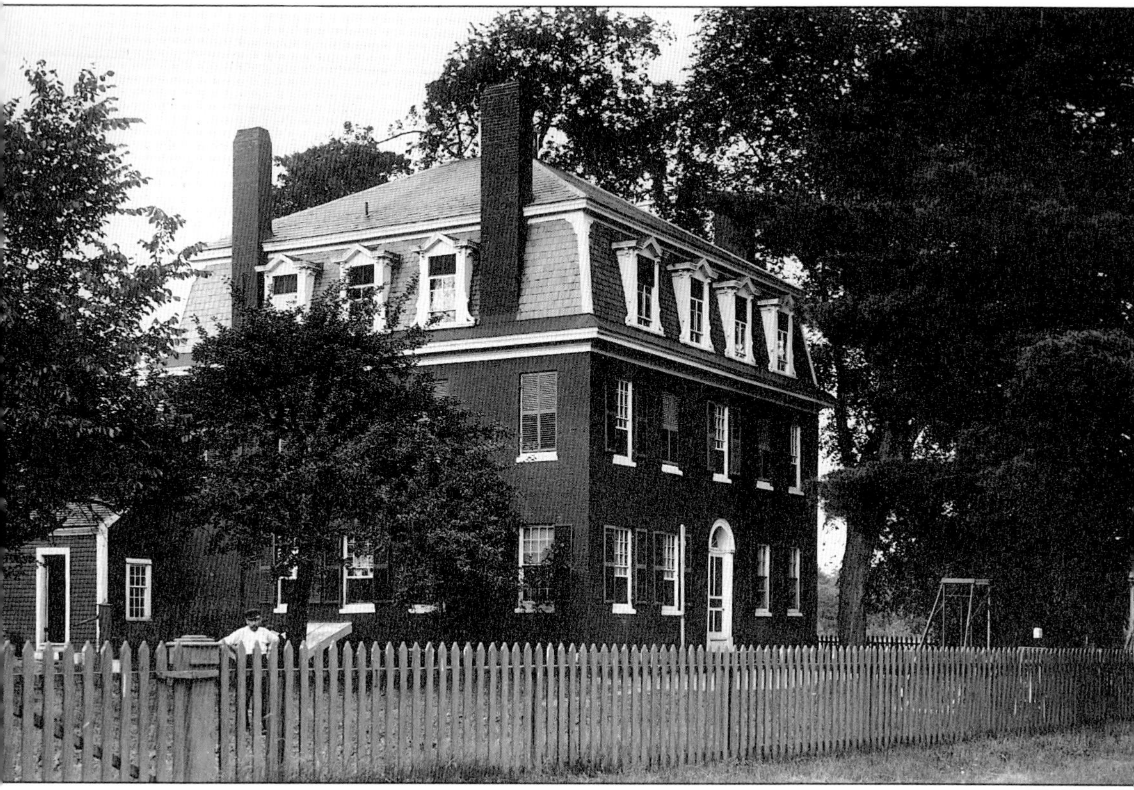

THE OLD BRICK TAVERN. No doubt anticipating a brisk business, Paul Willard, in 1804, built the Old Brick Tavern near Route 2 and Shirley Road. About the same time, the Union Turnpike Company planned and built a road providing a link for travel from Boston to Albany, Greenfield and Brattleboro. The road passed by the tavern. In fact, a tollhouse was established at its crossing of Shirley Road. Within a year, however, the Bolton and Lancaster Turnpike, with its easier grades, opened. That route, through the North Village, received more traffic. In the 1870s, the Shakers bought the property and added the mansard roof. They did not occupy the building themselves but leased it to others to be run as a boardinghouse. Through the years, the building has been used as a retreat house, as quarters for officers during World War I, and as a private convalescent hospital. Today, it is a private residence.

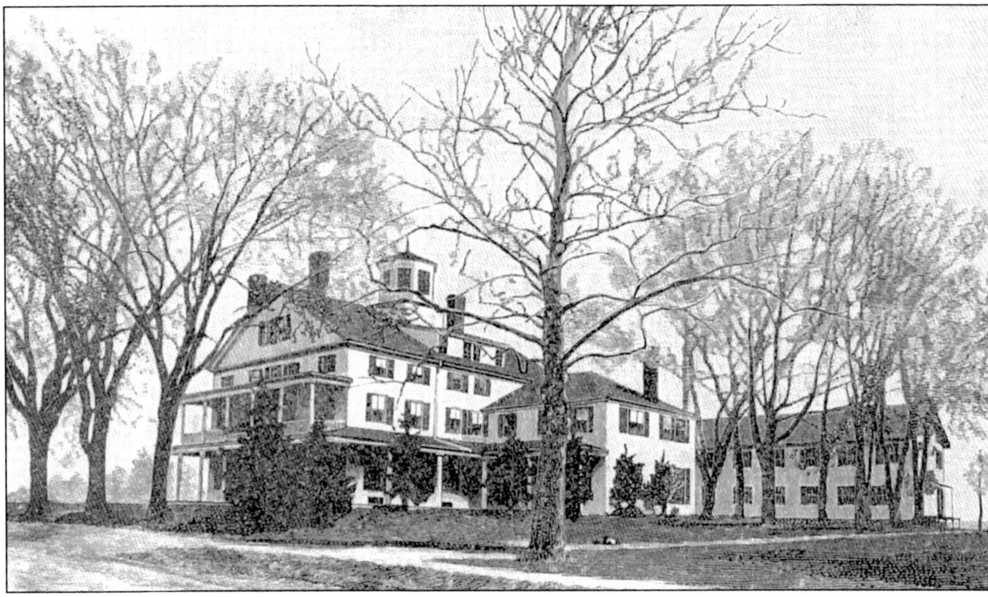

THE LANCASTER HOTEL. Built in 1786, the Lancaster House (also known as Lancaster Hotel or Lancaster Inn) was located on the east side of Main Street just north of the First Church. The handsome building was four stories high, surmounted by an observatory, and had piazzas on three sides and a front balcony. After providing food and lodging in a relaxed country setting for more than 100 years, the place burned down on July 18, 1906. This view shows the building from the south.

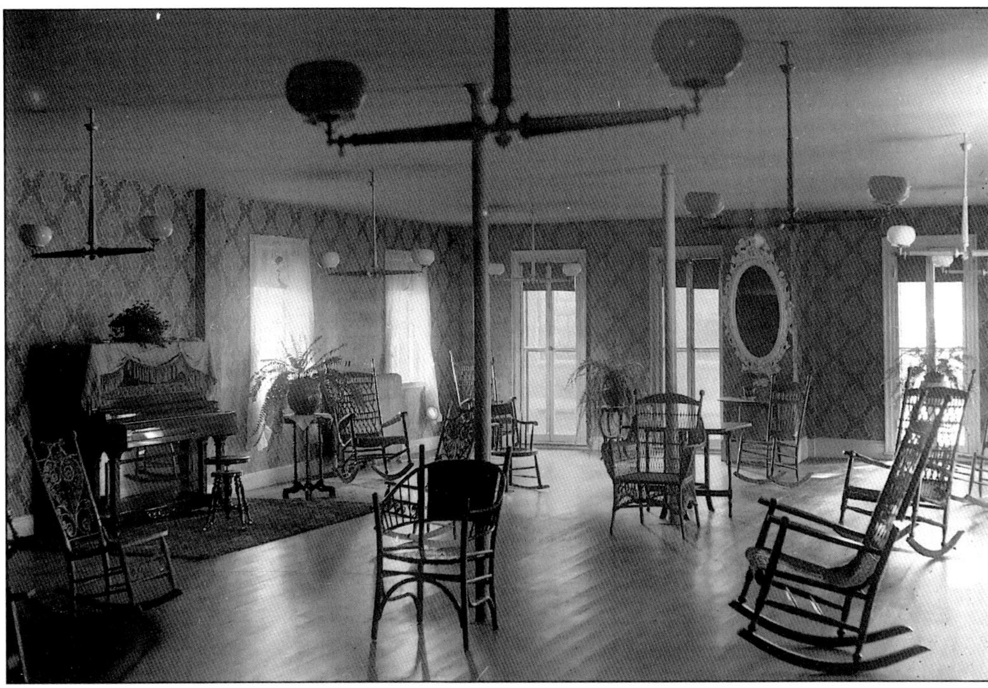

THE MAIN PARLOR. Numerous rocking chairs furnish the spacious main parlor of the Lancaster Hotel on Main Street. An abundance of natural light floods through many floor-to-ceiling windows.

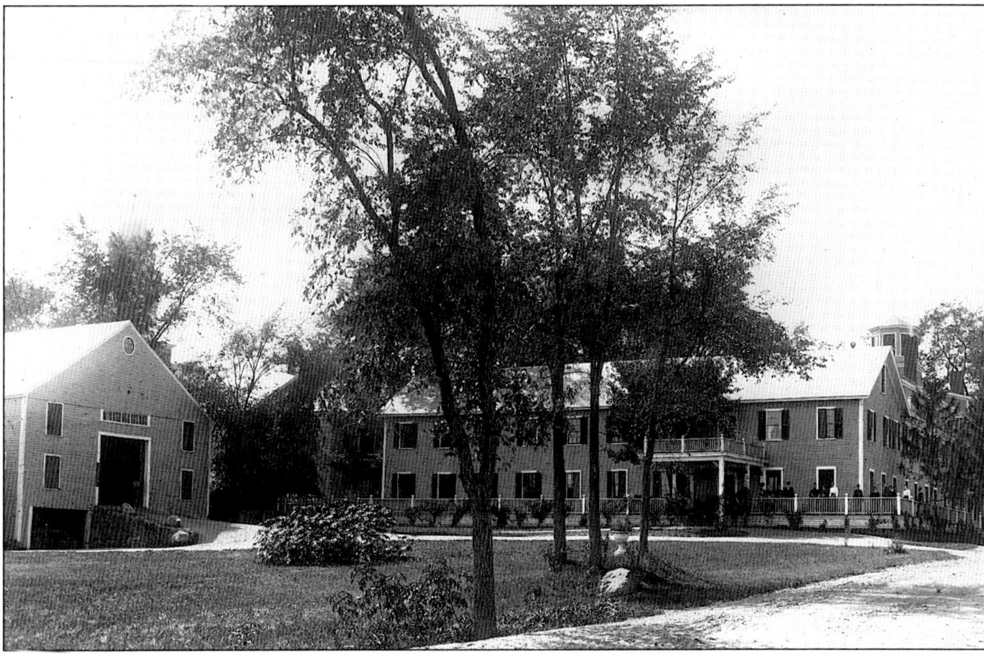

THE LANCASTER HOTEL (REAR VIEW) AND GYMNASIUM. This is an east, or rear, view of the Lancaster Hotel from the Harvard Road side. On the left is the stable, which was later converted into a gymnasium by the Thayer family for use by the townspeople.

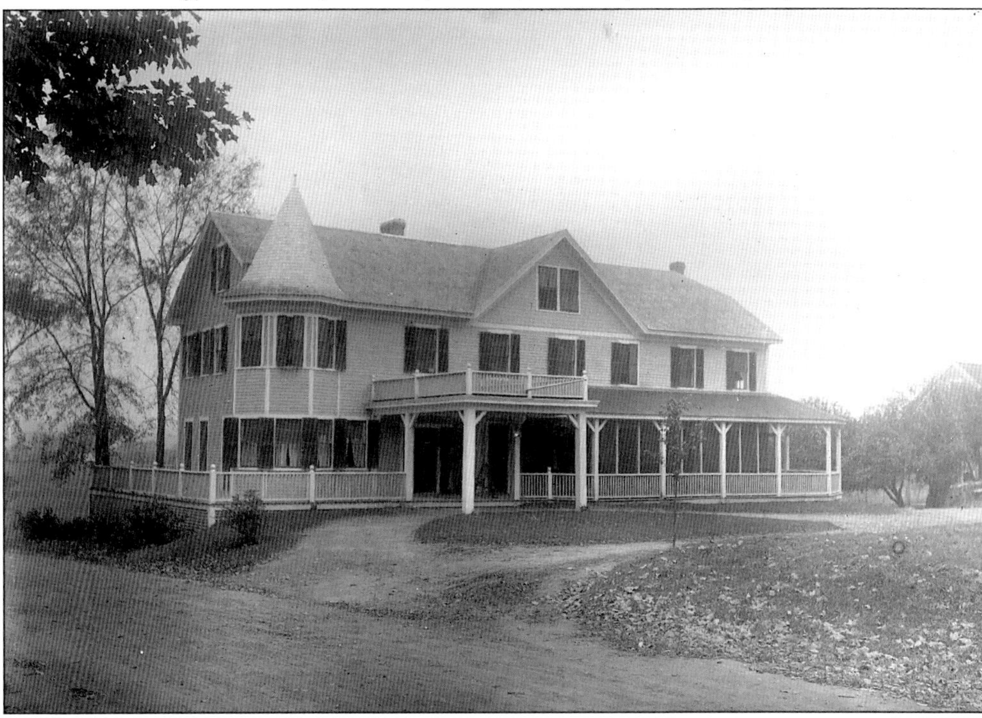

THE HOTEL ANNEX. Built after 1898, this annex to the Lancaster Hotel was located on Harvard Road in Lancaster Center. For a time in the 1930s, it was used by the town as a public health clinic. In the late 1970s, the building was taken down.

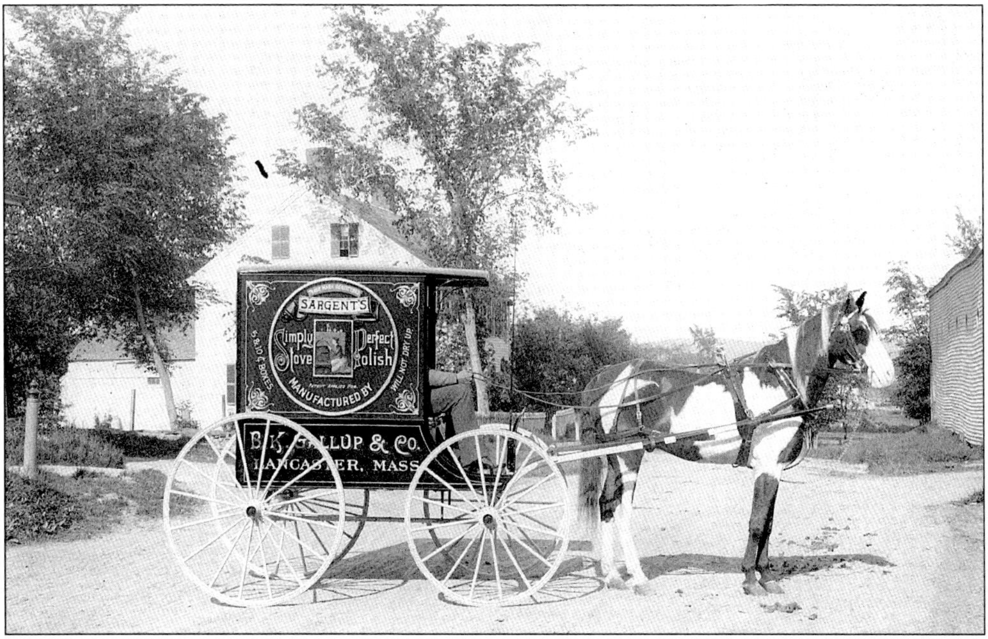

B.K. Gallup and His Calico Horse. Ready to go out on the road are B.K. Gallup (in wagon) and his horse. They are seen here in Lancaster Center, just off Main Street and near the Lancaster Hotel stable. Gallup was, at one point, associated with Safford in the running of the general store. This photograph was taken *c.* 1886.

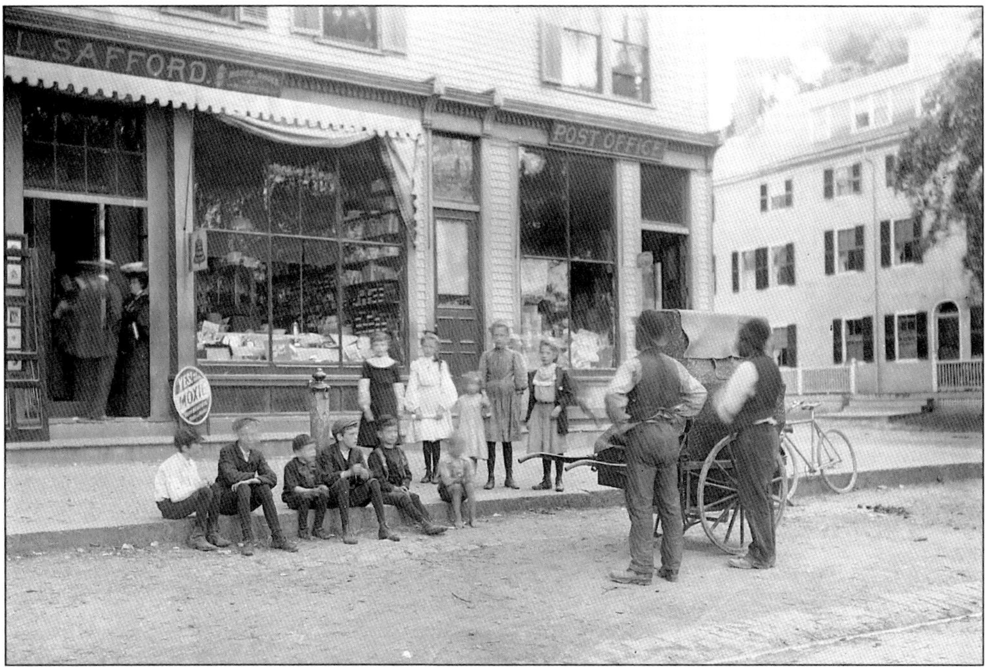

A Street Scene in Lancaster Center. Children are pictured face to face with two vendors and a cart outside the A.L. Safford Store and Post Office, located on Main Street. Note the cobblestone street and trolley tracks in the foreground. The elegant Lancaster Hotel is on the right. The store burned down in 1913.

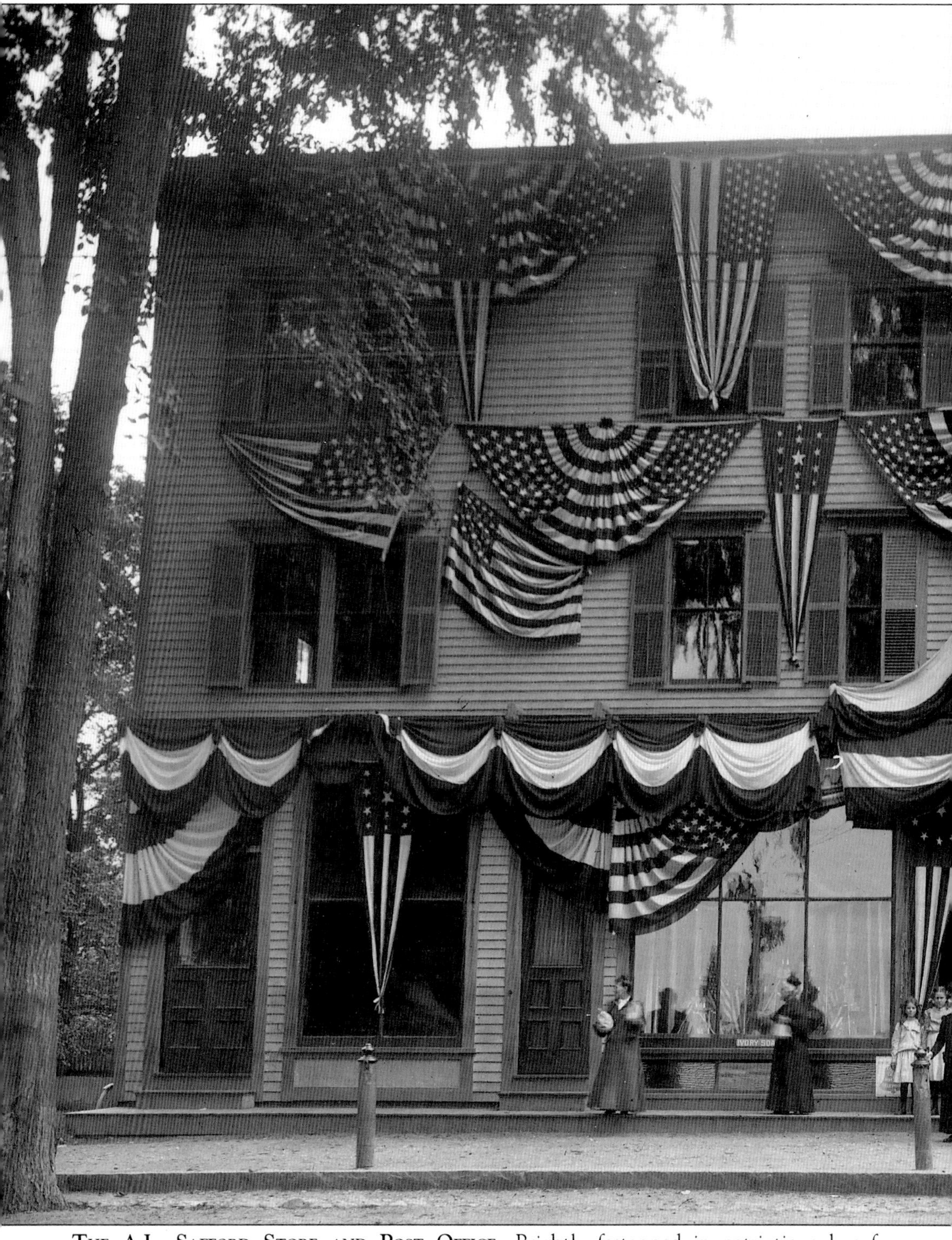

The A.L. Safford Store and Post Office. Brightly festooned in patriotic colors for Lancaster's 250th anniversary in 1903, the A.L. Safford Store and Post Office is shown here in full view on Main Street in Lancaster Center. Described in 1905 as a "happy combination of old

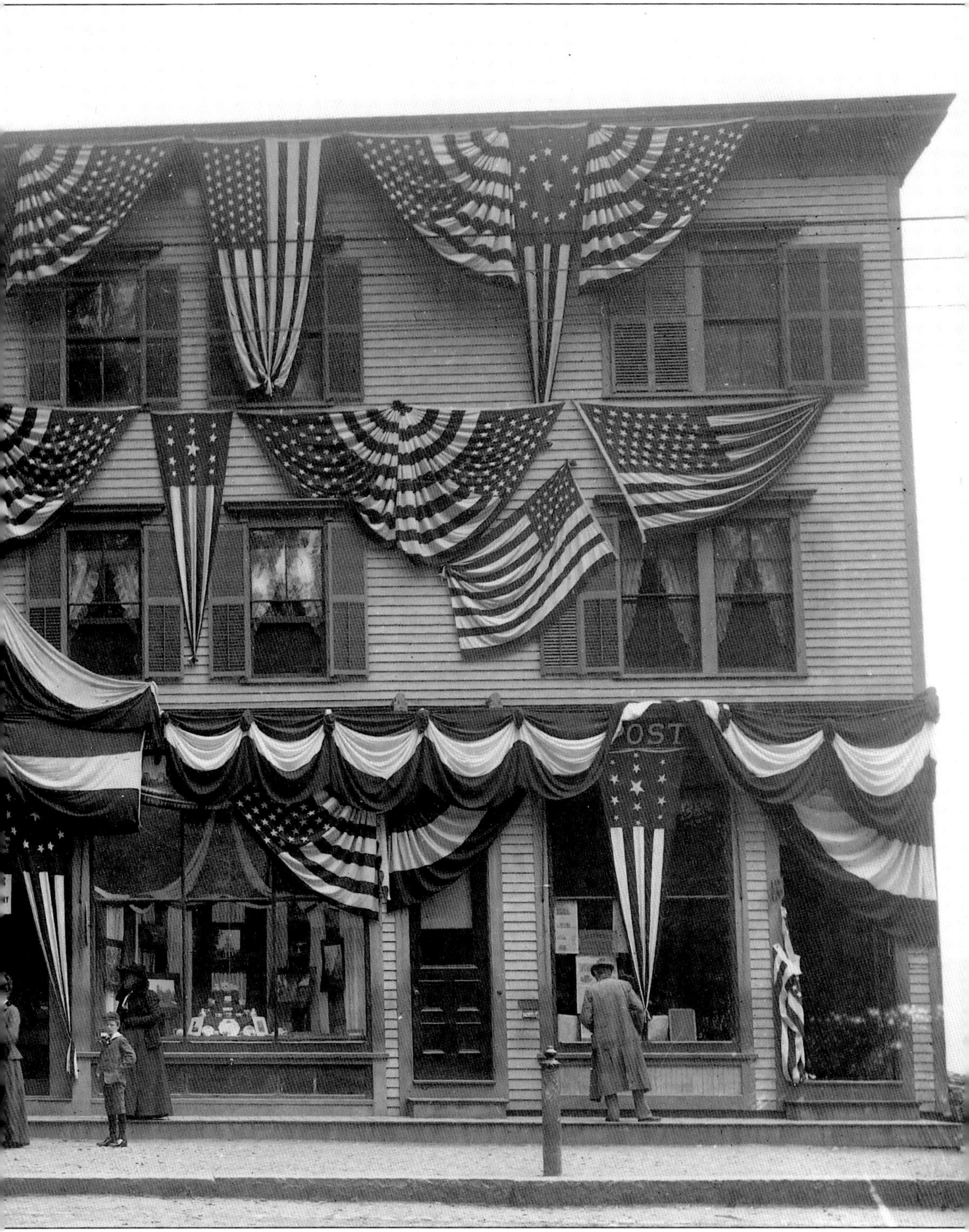

country variety and modern department store," proprietor Safford operated the establishment for more than 20 years in the late 19th and early 20th centuries.

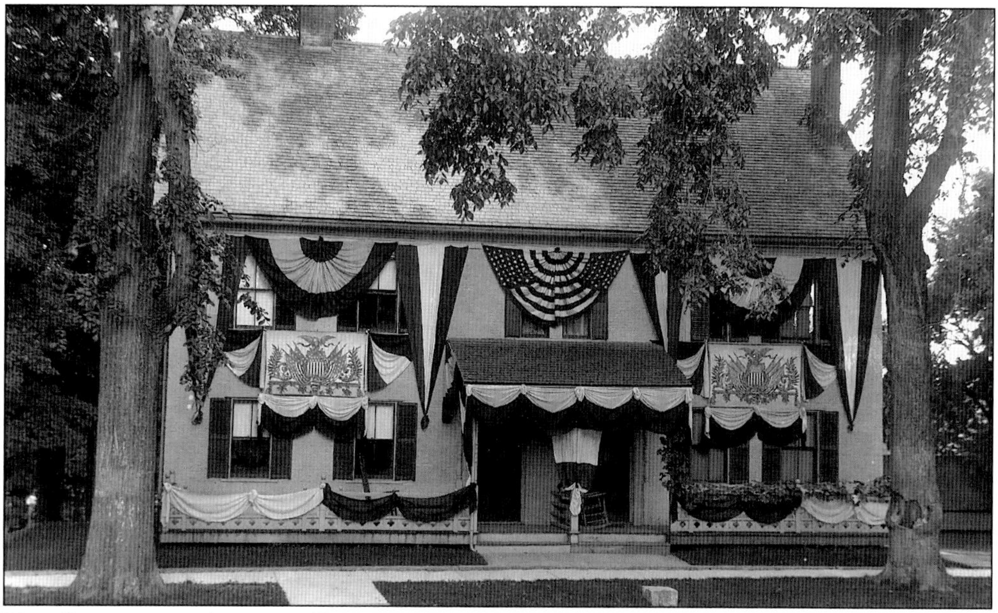

The Carter and Andrews Publishing Firm. Shown patriotically decorated for the town's 250th anniversary is the former Carter and Andrews publishing firm on the corner of Main Street and Barnes Court in Lancaster Center. In the early 19th century, the firm was among the leading in the country in the line of printing, engraving, illustrating, and binding. At one time, the company employed nearly 100 people. However, the business went to pieces in the Panic of 1837.

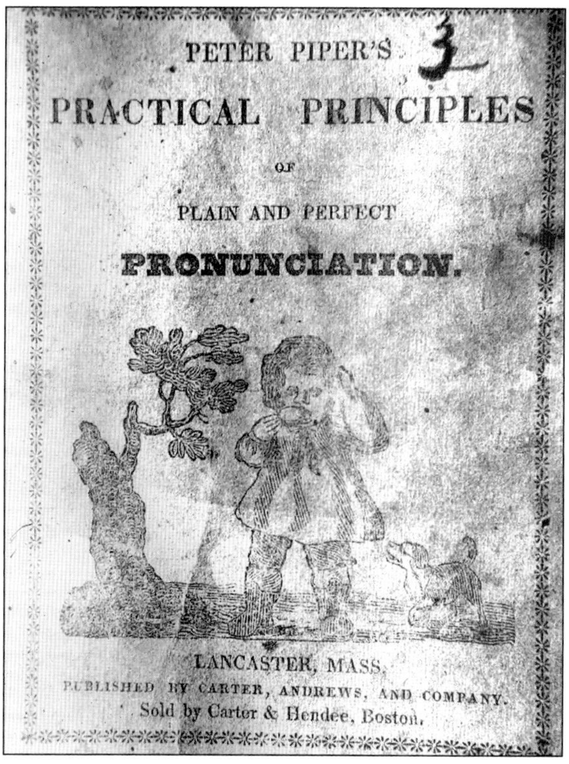

PETER PIPER'S

PRACTICAL PRINCIPLES

OF

PLAIN AND PERFECT

PRONUNCIATION.

LANCASTER, MASS.

PUBLISHED BY CARTER, ANDREWS, AND COMPANY.

Sold by Carter & Hendee, Boston.

A Title Page. The Lancaster firm of Carter and Andrews dealt in such things as book publishing, map printing and coloring, wood engraving, and lithography. At the height of the company's success, from 1827 to 1834, they produced up to 250,000 maps a year. Shown here is the title page from one of their publications for the instruction of children.

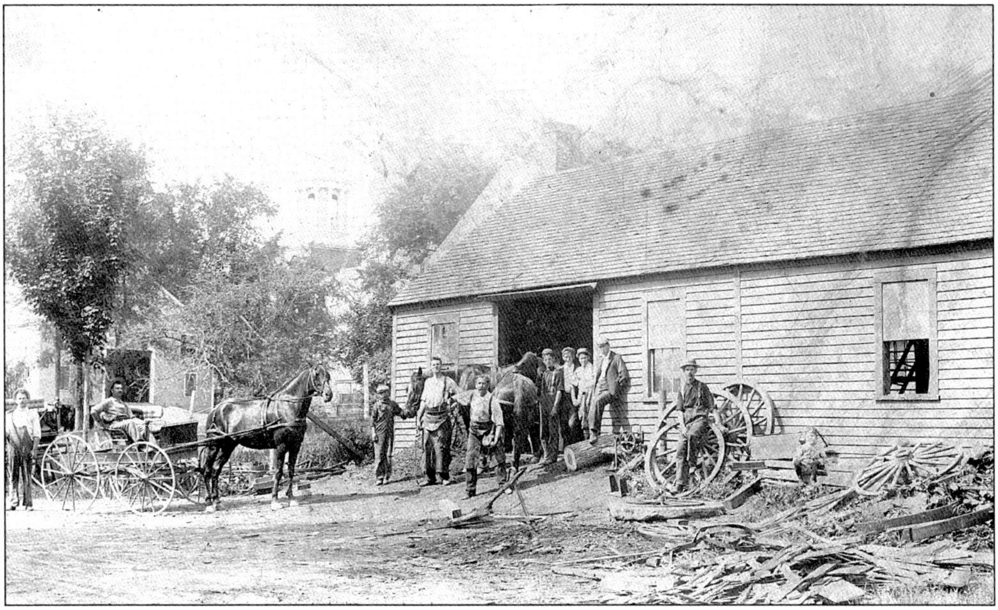

The Sanborn Blacksmith Shop. Pictured here in the 1890s is a group of men at the Lyman B. Sanborn Blacksmith Shop, which was located on the southwest corner of Packard Street and Harvard Road in Lancaster Center.

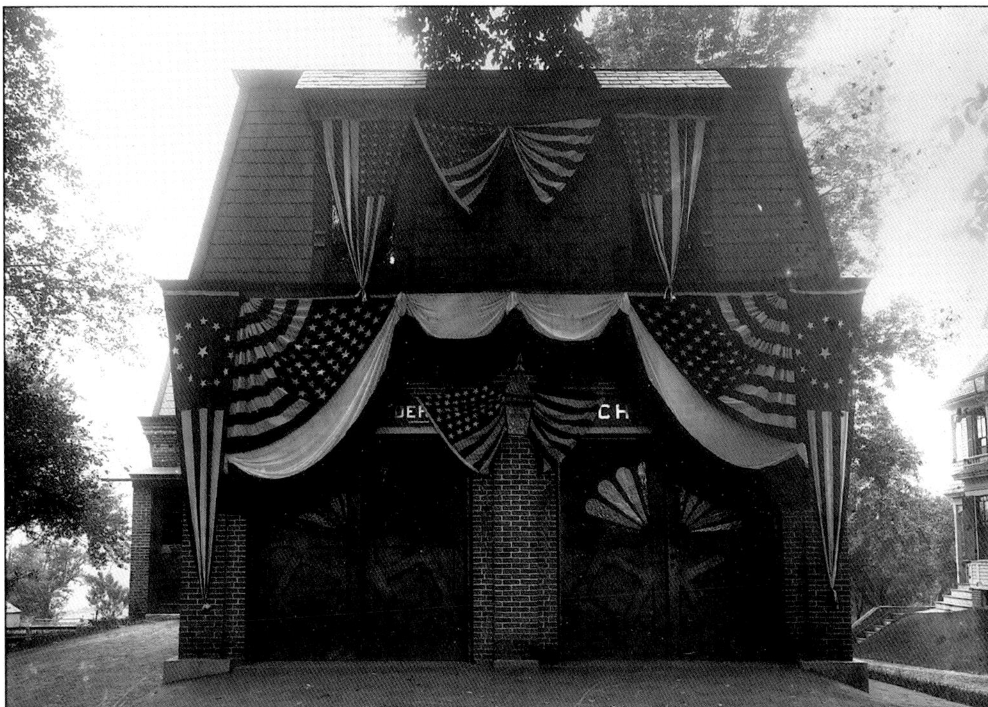

The Old Lancaster Bank. The Lancaster Bank was established in 1836 and, in 1864, became the Lancaster National Bank. In 1882, it was moved to Clinton. From 1883 to 1967, the building was used as the Lancaster Center Fire Station. Most recently, it has been used to house town ambulances and as a communications center.

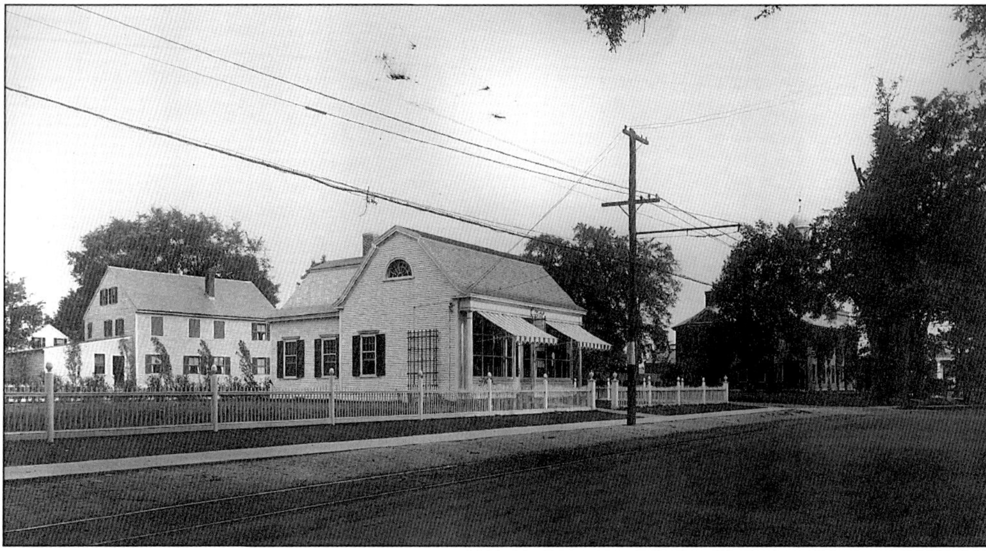

The Gould's Apothecary and Poplar Sweet Shoppe. Frank Gould's Apothecary Shop was located in Lancaster Center. Located on the site of the A.L. Safford Store and Post Office (which burned down in 1913), it was built by Col. John E. Thayer, who wanted to ensure an architecturally pleasing building. Equipped with a marble soda fountain, it later became the Poplar Sweet Shoppe, so named for the row of poplar trees just to the north of the building. The elaborate white fencing was subsequently moved to the late Herbert Hosmer's property on East George Hill Road in South Lancaster. Note the trolley tracks running along Main Street.

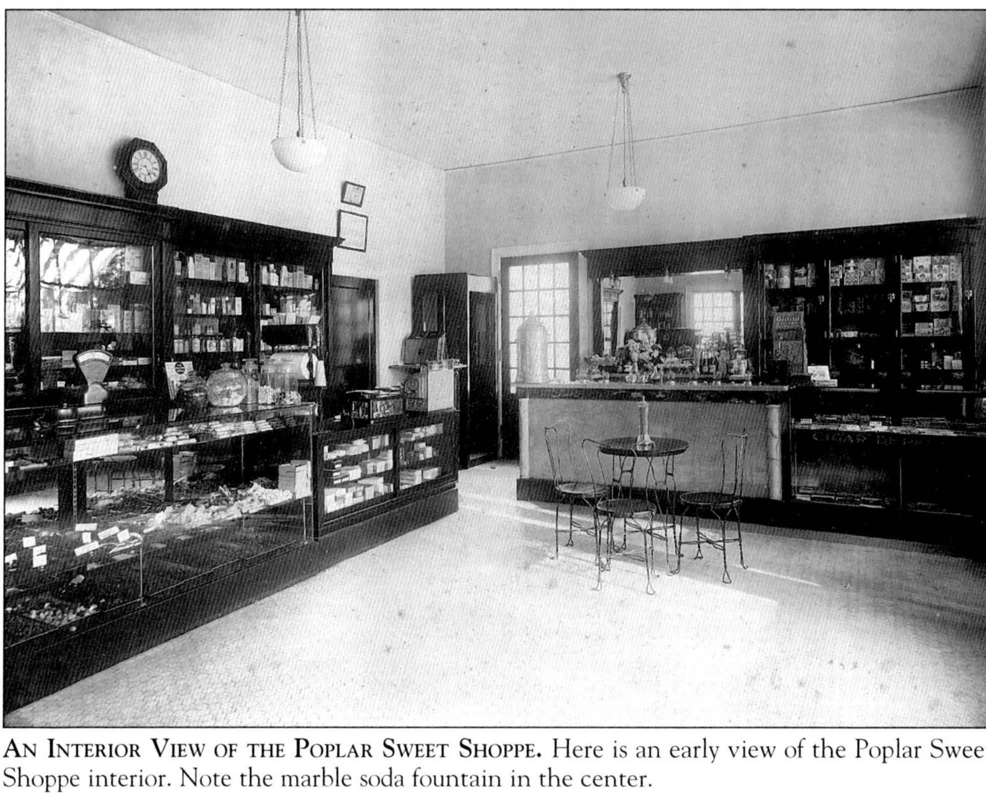

An Interior View of the Poplar Sweet Shoppe. Here is an early view of the Poplar Sweet Shoppe interior. Note the marble soda fountain in the center.

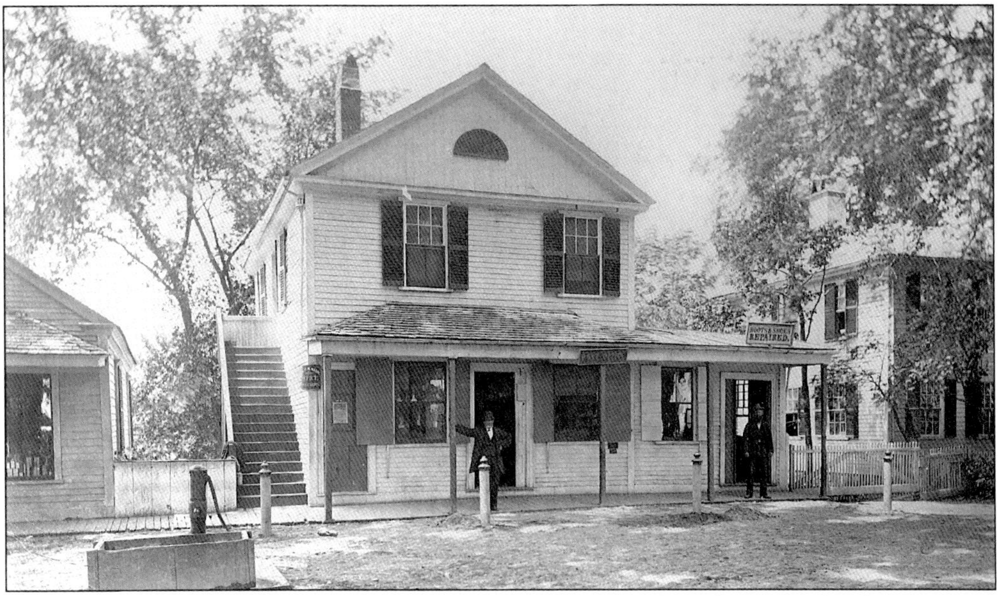

THE LANCASTER DRUG STORE. This building was once located on the west side of Main Street in Lancaster Center, just south of the Rand-Huntington-Dorr House. It was used for shops and, in the late 19th century, served as the Lancaster Drug Store. It was later moved to Clinton, and pieces of the structure were incorporated into a house.

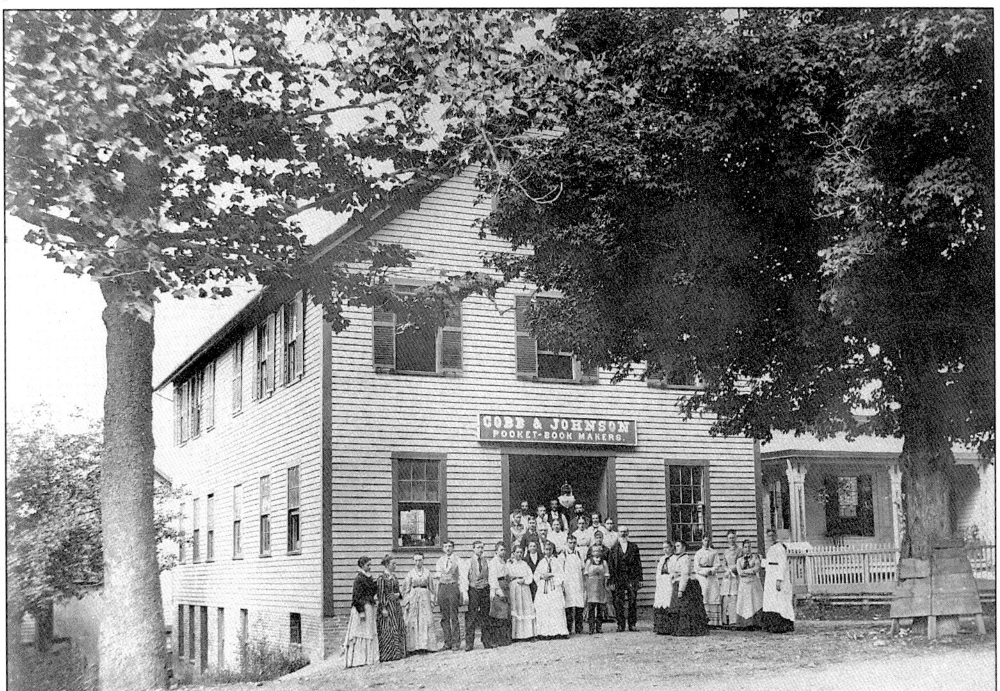

THE POCKETBOOK MAKING SHOP. This shop was founded by B.M. Cobb c. 1835 and was located on Main Street in Lancaster Center, opposite Carleton Place. In 1852, G.A. Johnson entered the business and became the sole proprietor from 1866 to 1875. The large building was later converted into a private dwelling.

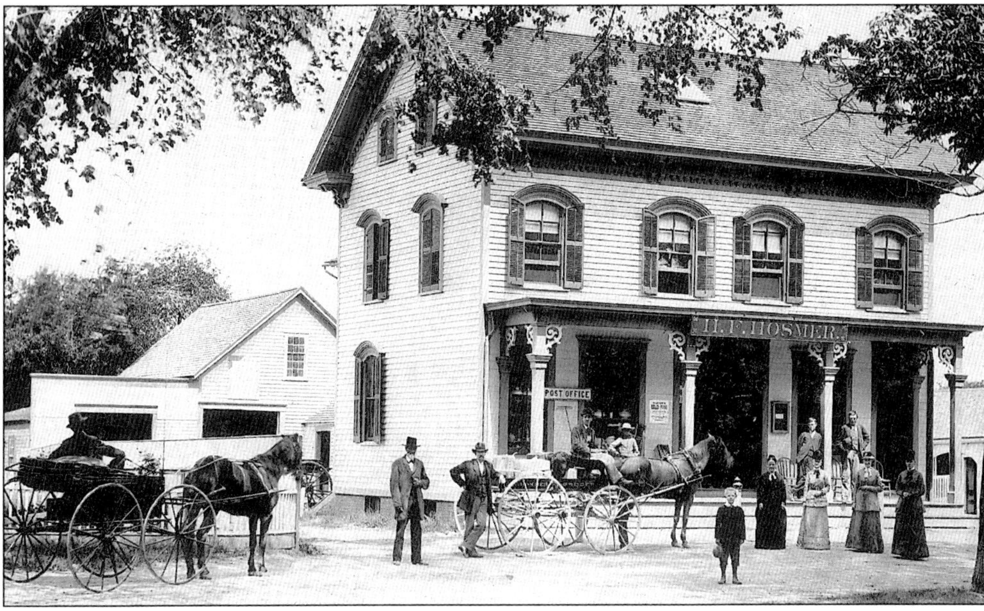

The H.F. Hosmer Store and Post Office. The H.F. Hosmer Store and Post Office was located on the Main Street in South Lancaster. Hosmer opened his store in 1879 and was appointed as South Lancaster postmaster in 1881.

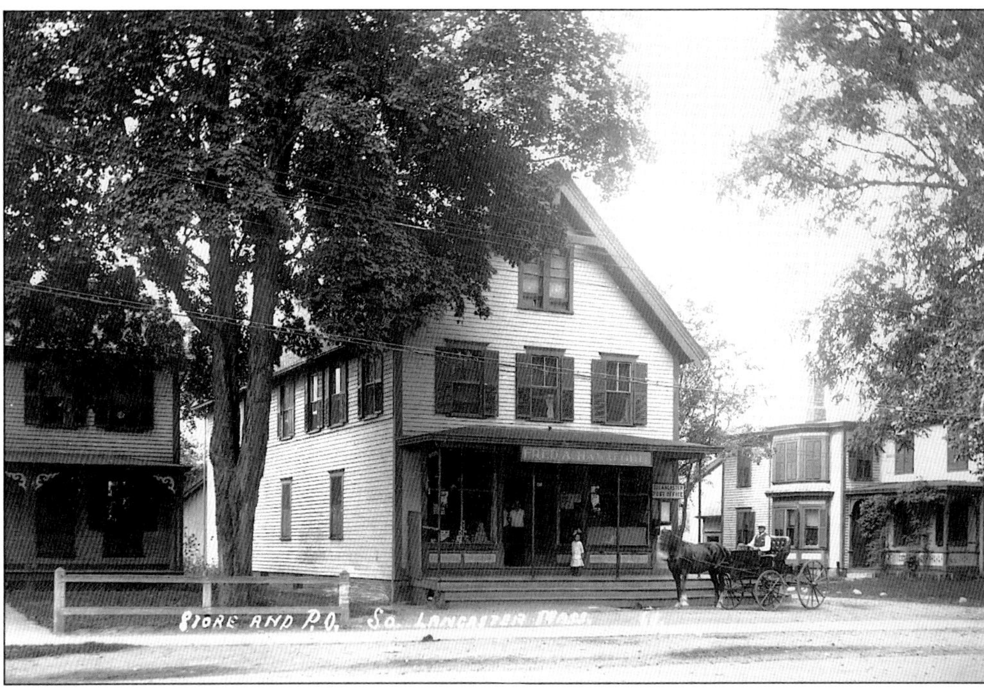

The Fred A. Hanaford Store and Post Office. Pictured is the Fred A. Hanaford Store and Post Office, which was located near Prescott and Main Streets in South Lancaster. In earlier times, the establishment had been run by Henry F. Hosmer. When Atlantic Union College expanded its program in the 1920s, the building was moved to the campus and was used as a woodworking shop. The structure burned on April 27, 1944.

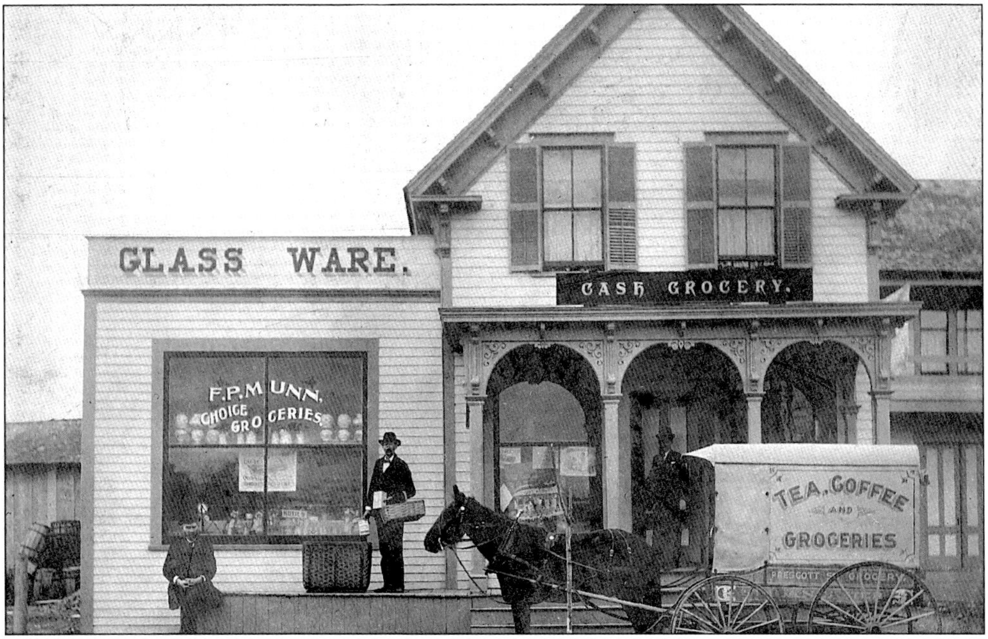

The F.P. Munn Grocery Store. F.P. Munn's store (no longer standing), which was on the south side of Prescott Street just west of the Trolley Stop in South Lancaster, was a favorite shopping place for South Lancaster Academy students in the early days. Munn, a native of Vermont, lived in town from 1900 until his death in 1918. In later times, the facility was used variously as a restaurant and a barbershop, among other things. (Schumacher-Hardy.)

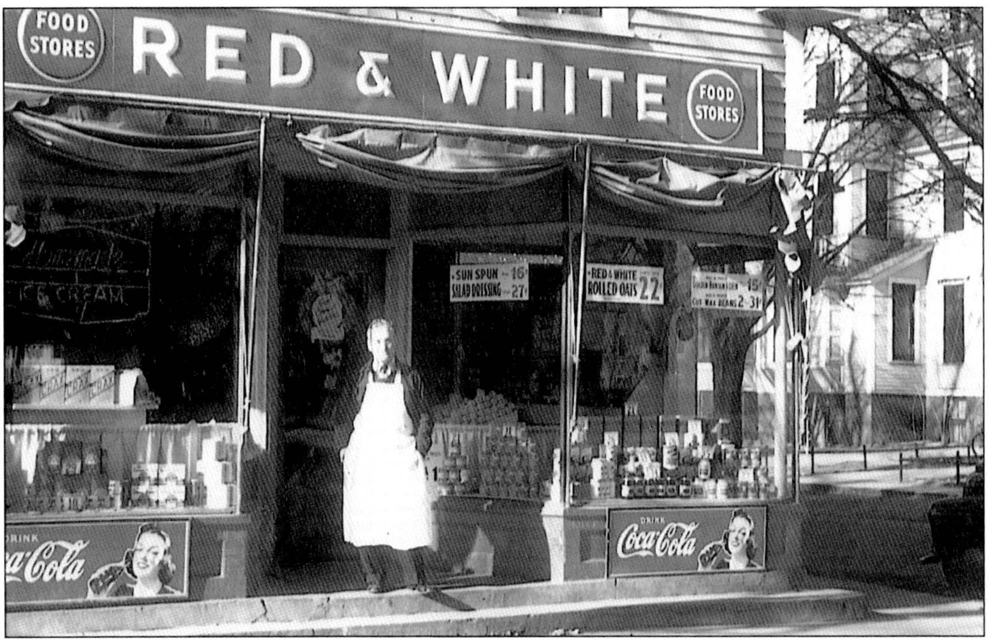

The Red & White Store. Proprietor Vic Hilbert is standing in front of the Red & White, formerly located on the west corner of Sawyer and Prescott Streets in South Lancaster. The store had many proprietors through the years and, in the 1940s, offered customers the convenience of grocery carts for self-service, a new concept at the time. (Taylor.)

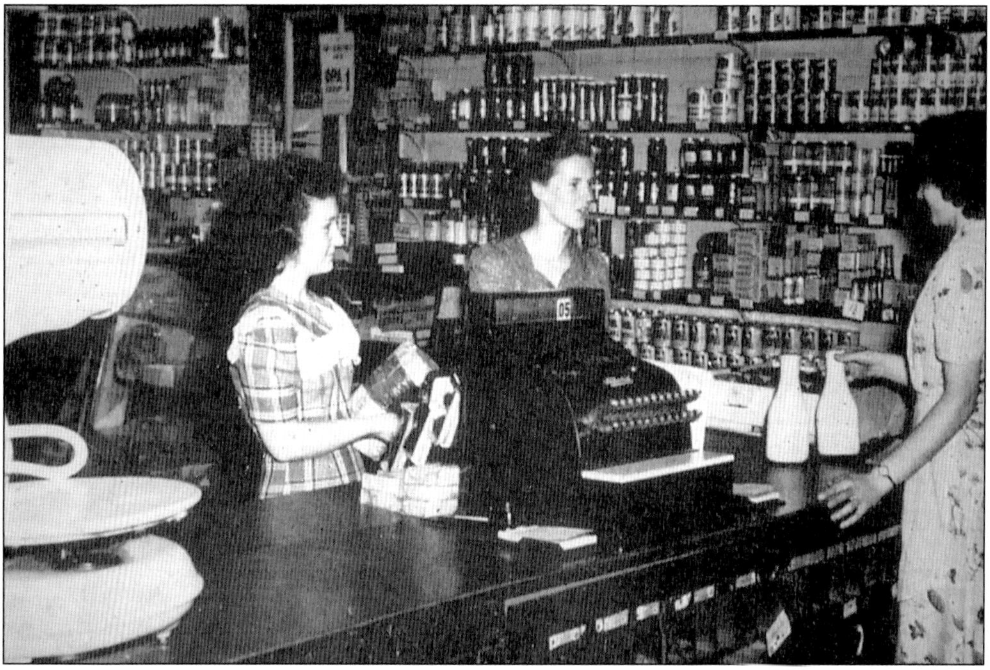

ROWELL'S MARKET. Longtime residents may remember shopping at Hubby (Hue-bee) Rowell's Grocery Store on the south side of Prescott Street in South Lancaster. This view shows the interior in the mid-1940s, shortly after the store began operating under Rowell's name. Rowell's was well known locally for its 5¢ ice-cream cones. The Trolley Stop, a pizzeria, is now located on the site. (AUC.)

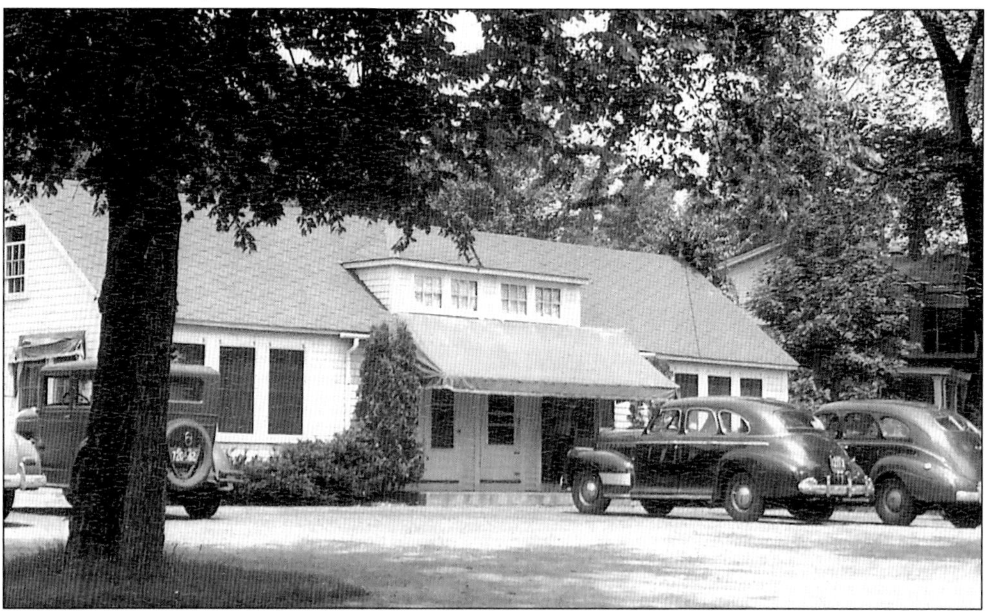

THE CREAM CROCK. Advertised as "South Lancaster's Cozy Little Nook," the Cream Crock (no longer standing), located at the intersection of Main Street and Sterling Road, was a popular spot for ice cream and sandwiches in the 1940s. Harmon Tymeson was the proprietor. (Schumacher-Hardy.)

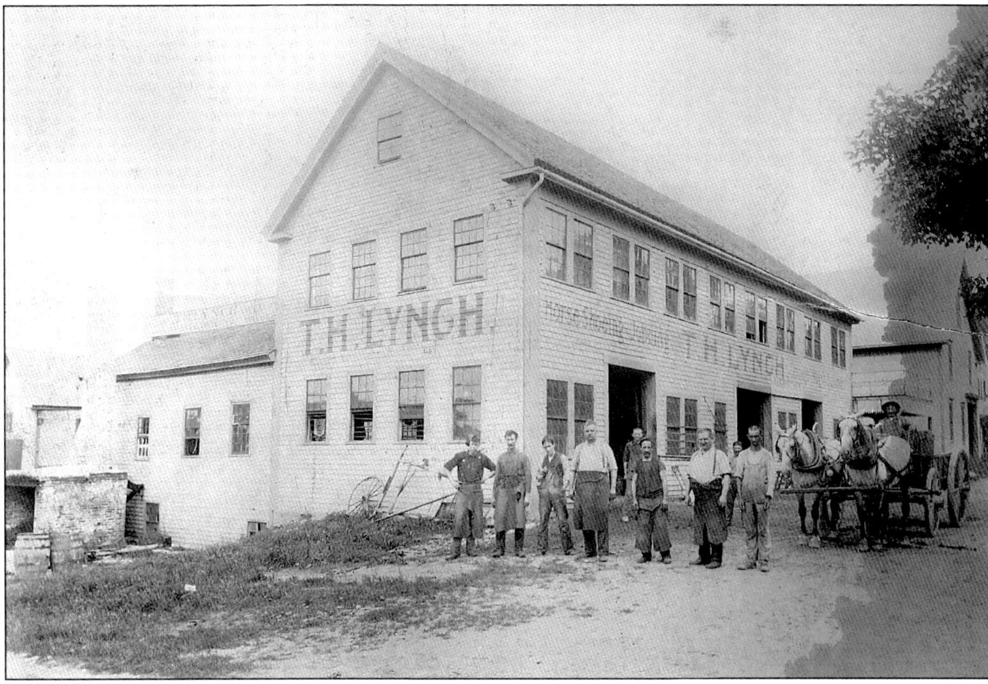

Lynch's Blacksmith Shop. Several leather-aproned blacksmiths pose here in front of the T.H. Lynch Blacksmith Shop (no longer standing), which was located on the north corner of Charlotte and Main Street in South Lancaster. Today, a Cumberland Farms store is located on the spot.

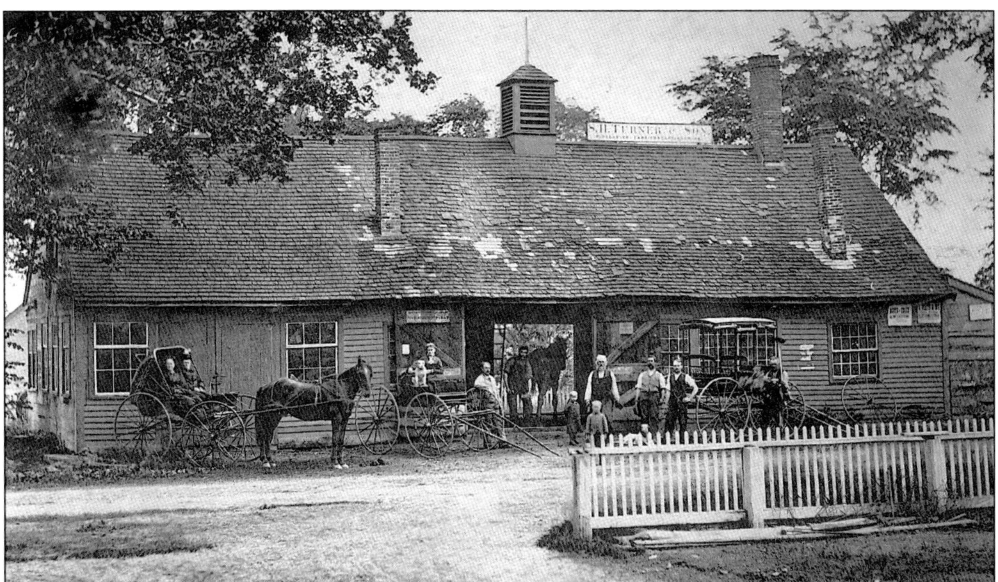

Turner's Blacksmith Shop. This is the blacksmith shop of S.H. Turner & Son, which was on a triangle of land between Mill Street and Sterling Road. After this building burned in 1909, a new shop (no longer standing) was built very near the same site.

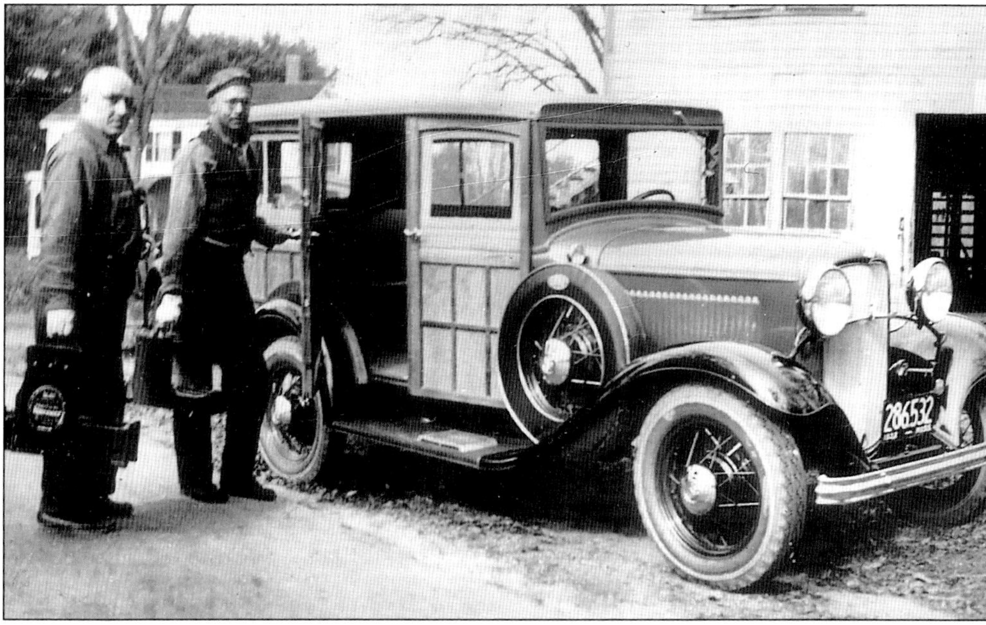

The Blacksmith Makes House Calls. Ernest S. "Steb" Turner and his employee Clarence Richardson prepare to visit a customer. With the coming of the automobile, the demand for the blacksmith's skill dwindled in the early decades of the 20th century. (Tefft.)

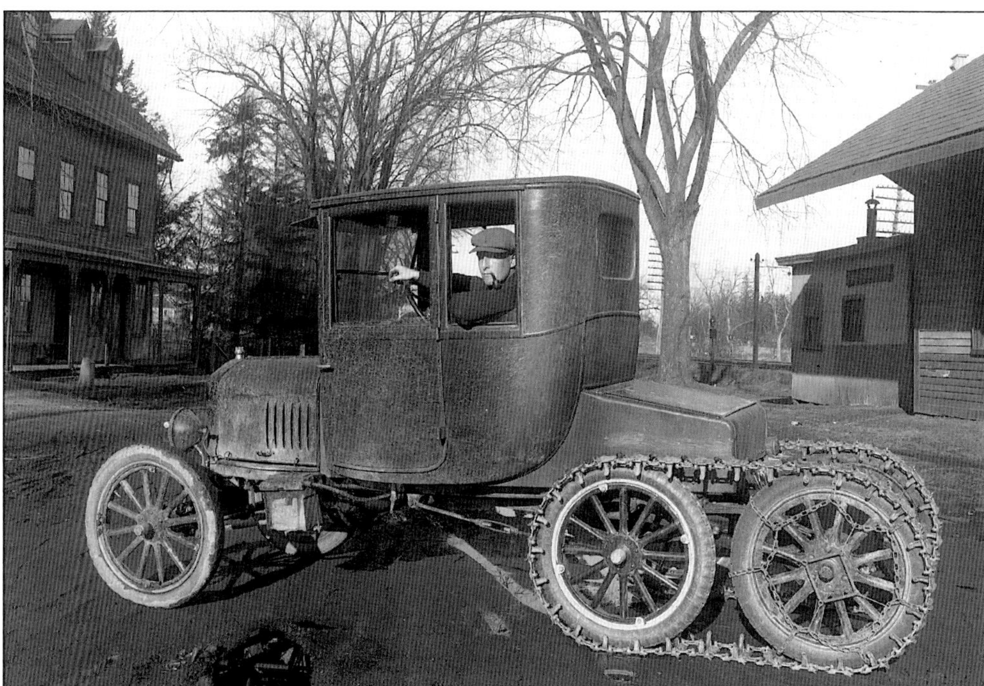

Mail Delivery via Snowmobile. Harold Follansbee is shown here with his snowmobile, which was used for mail delivery. During heavy snow conditions, the front wheels were removed and runners were attached. The railroad depot and a baggage house are on the right.

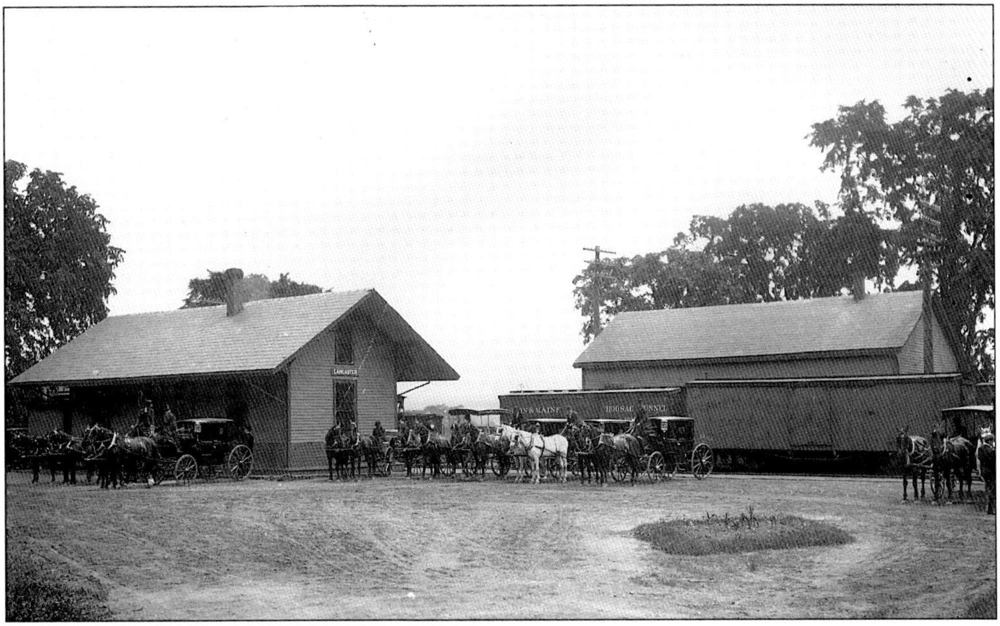

The Train Depots. The Lancaster and South Lancaster Depots were busy places in the early 20th century. The Worcester and Nashua Railroad first entered Lancaster in the mid-19th century, and the Boston and Maine Railroad had regular routes through town. For many years, the Thayer family, among others, made frequent commutes into Boston from Thayer Station, as the South Lancaster Depot was known. (Colley.)

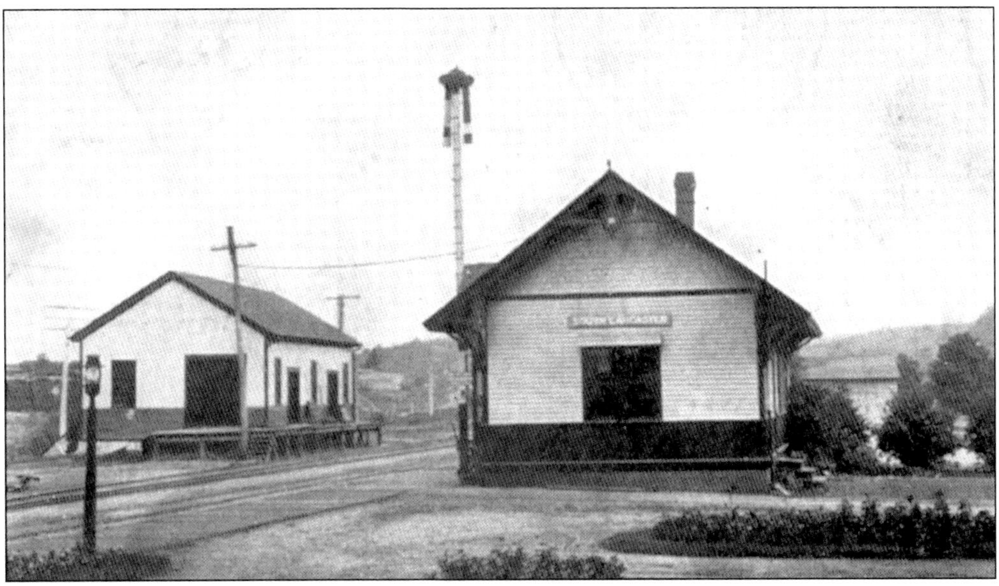

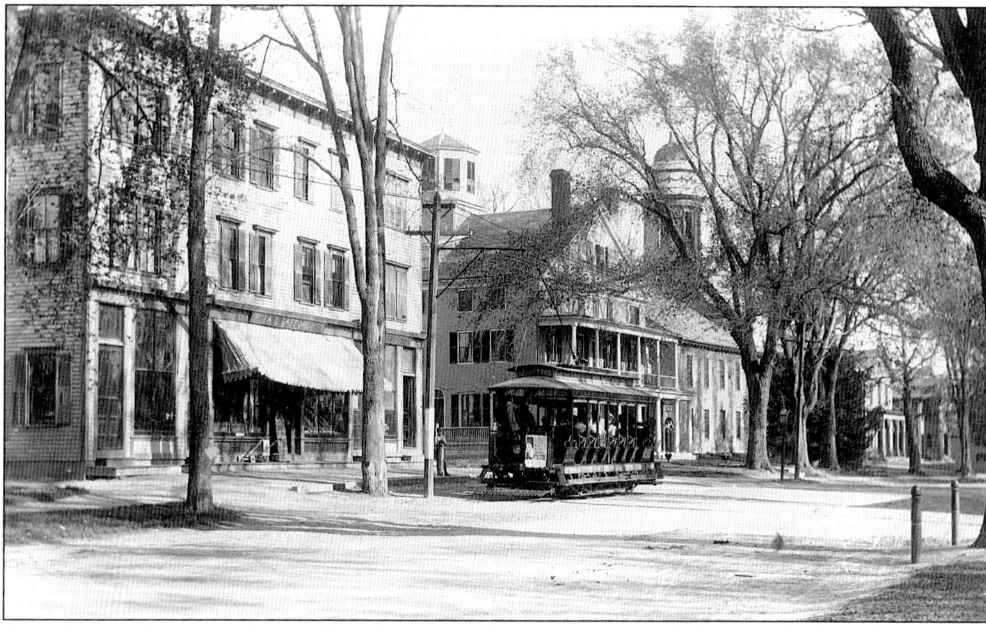

The Center Trolley Stop. The electric road was opened between Fitchburg and Worcester in 1894–1896. A trolley stopped in the center of town between the Lancaster Hotel and Safford Store. The open cars, called "breezers," made for cool traveling on hot summer days. When the Clinton-Lancaster Company merged with the Leominster-Clinton Company, larger, four-motor cars were purchased, increasing the top speed from 20 to 35 miles per hour.

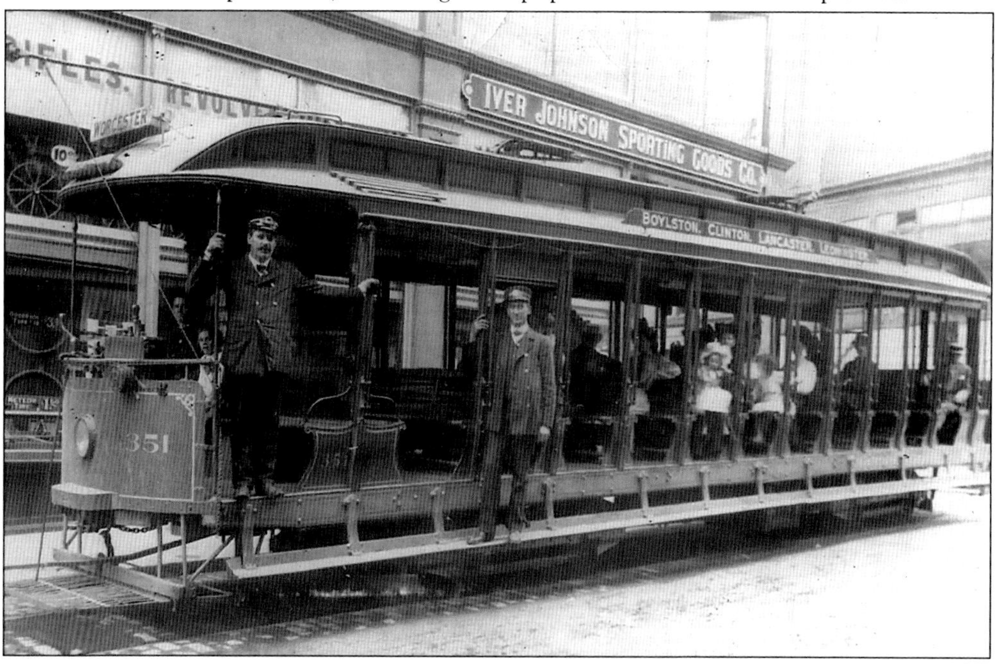

A Trolley Motorman and a Conductor. Motorman Thomas Burke (left) and conductor Charles Blood (right) worked on the trolley line that passed through Lancaster *c.* 1900. This view shows the trolley stopped in front of the Iver Johnson Sporting Goods Company in Fitchburg. The photograph was taken *c.* 1905. (Ponte.)

Five

Life on the Farm and at the Mill

Although located in the heart of the Nashua Valley, Lancaster (unlike some of her daughters) never developed into a predominantly mill town. The fertile land and number of intervales along the river made the place well suited for agriculture, and farming was a way of life for many. Lancaster, with its rolling hills and many vales, still has open farmland, providing many pastoral vistas.

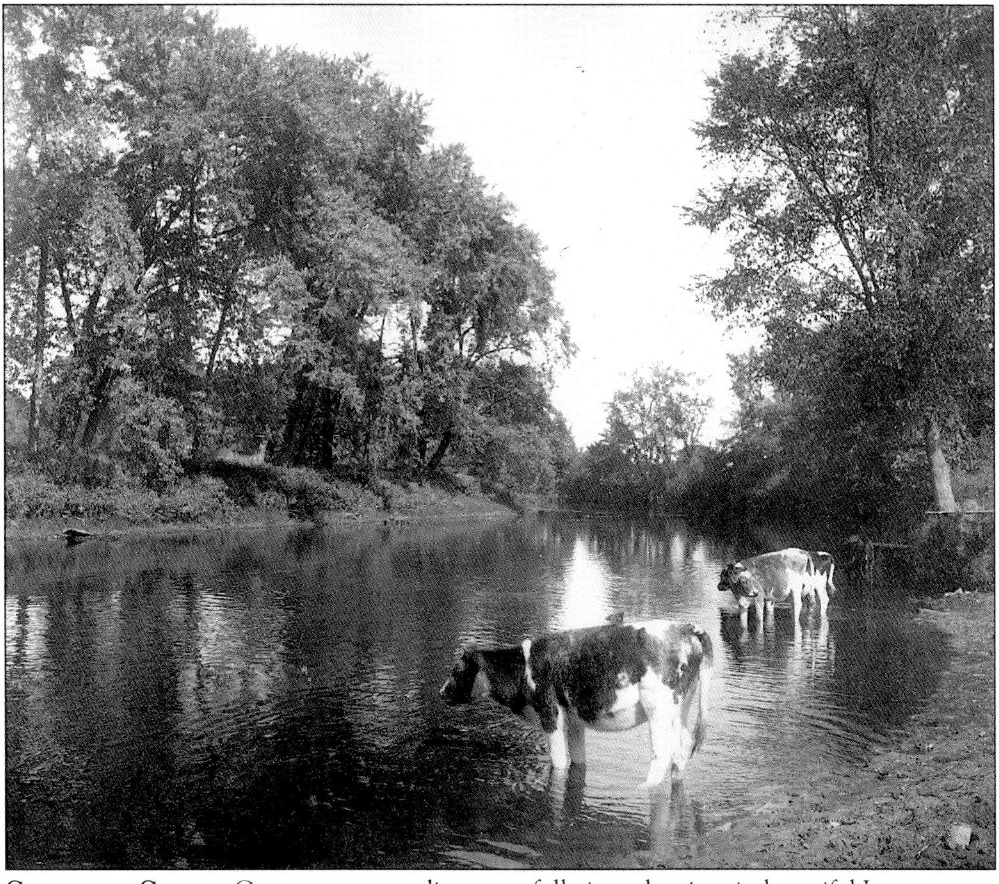

Contented Cattle. Cows are seen wading peacefully into the river in beautiful Lancaster.

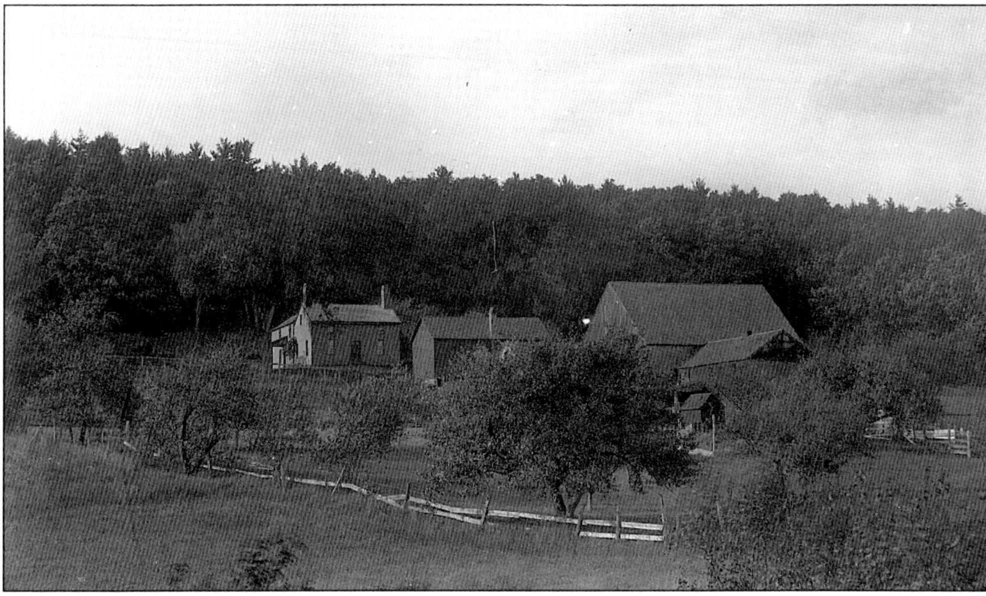

The Carr Farm. This view, taken from a pasture below, shows the Carr Farm, which was once located in the Harvard Road area. E.W. Carr was a native Lancastrian who served the town as a selectman for many years in the late 19th and early 20th centuries. The buildings were demolished when Fort Devens took over the area.

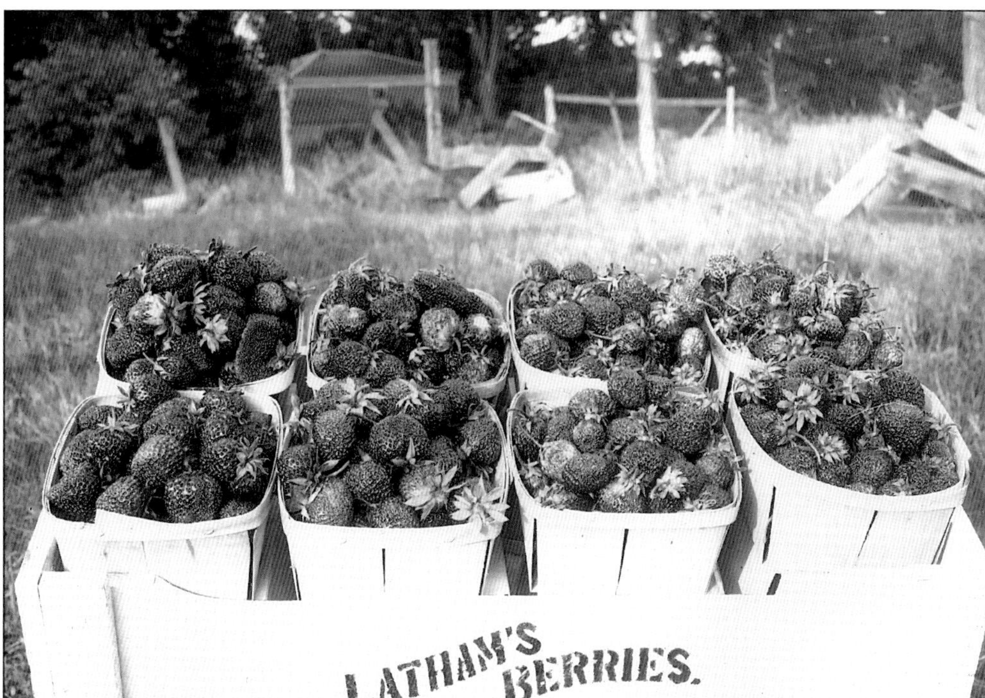

Fresh Strawberries. As a rural and agricultural community, Lancaster has had a number of prosperous farms with an abundance of fine produce, as shown here with this luscious-looking fruit. Charles H. Latham, who lived on the Neck Road in the early 20th century, also dealt in fancy birds as did his neighbor A.C. Hawkins.

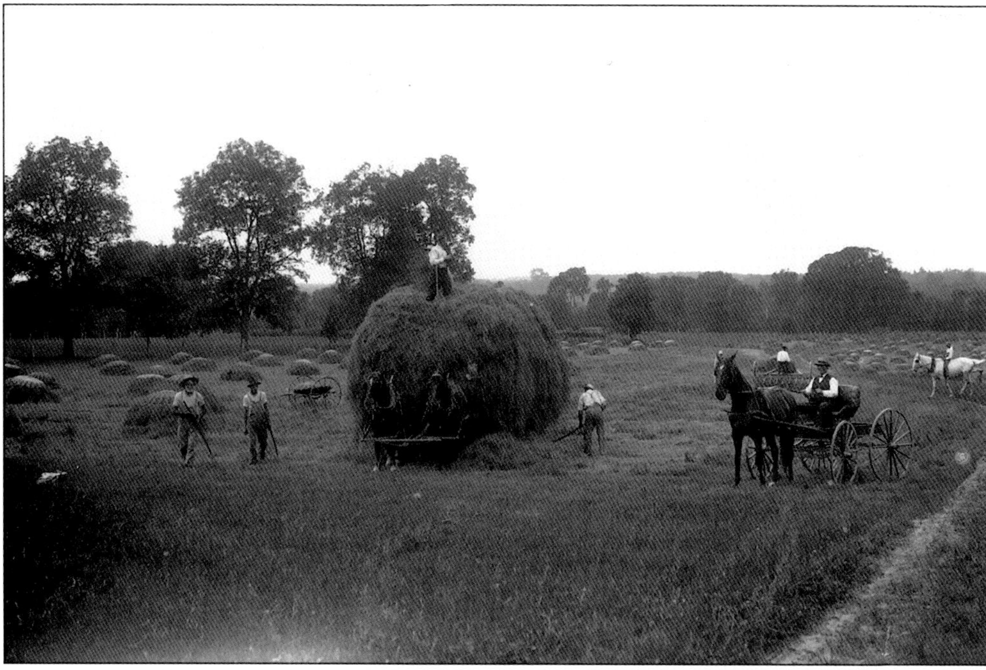

Making Hay. This pastoral scene from days gone by shows Lancaster men out haying in the fields. In the earliest times, the many vales (as the meadowlands along the river were called) attracted the English settlers.

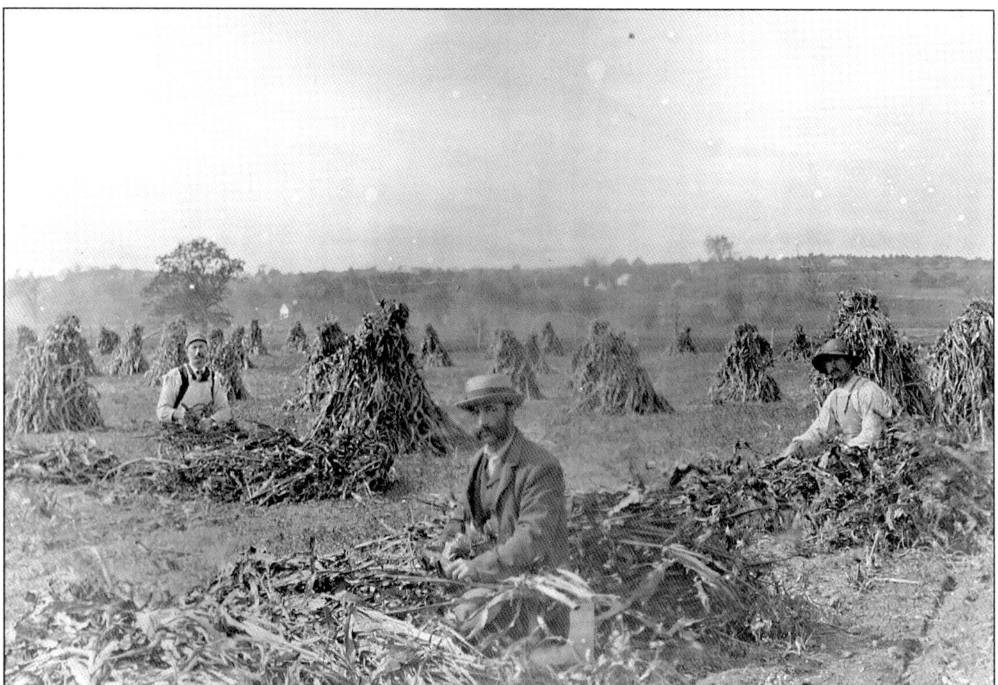

The End of the Harvest. The end-of-harvest task of clearing and gathering the stalks is shown here in one of the many cornfields planted on the fertile plains in the "neck" area of town.

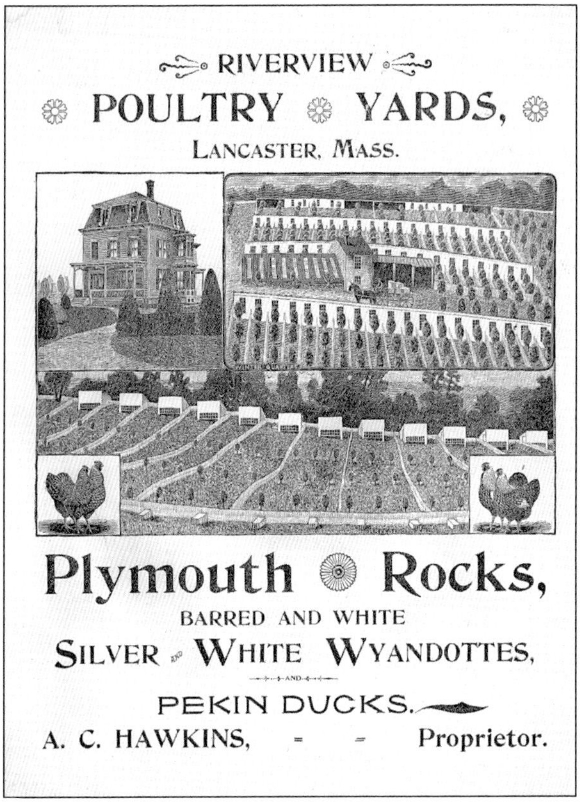

THE HAWKINS HEN YARDS. This brochure shows the former Hawkins Hen Yards, located on the Neck Road, as they looked in the late 19th century. In 1895, the Riverview Poultry Yards, run by Arthur C. Hawkins, was described as "the largest and most successful poultry establishment in the world." Hawkins, who specialized in raising silver and white Wyandottes, won many awards for his exceptional poultry. (Sczerzen.)

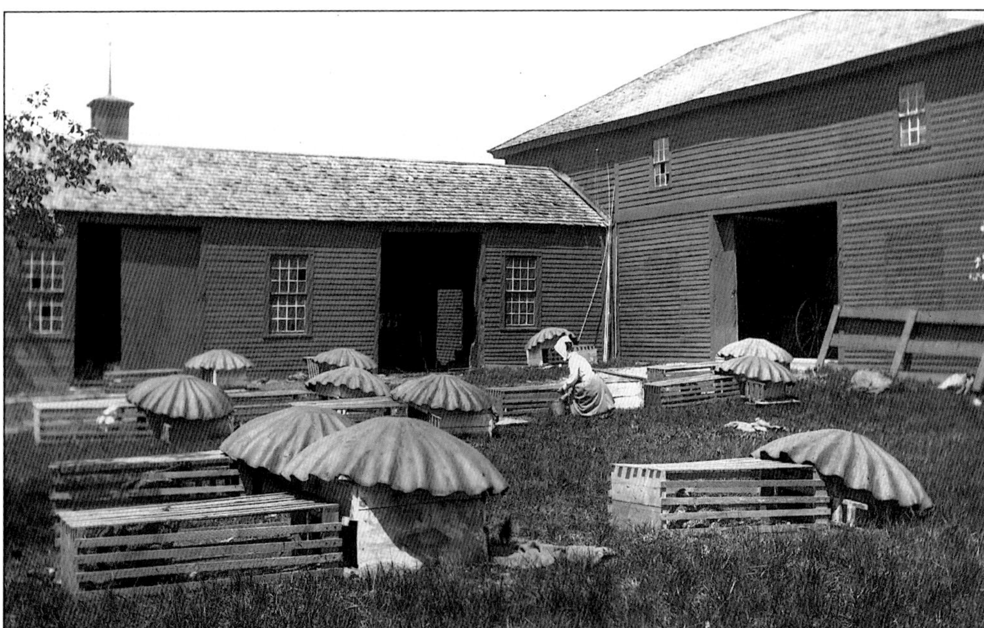

MARY'S CHICKEN YARD. In addition to shade from the sun, as shown here, one can imagine the chicks received excellent care under Mary's diligent hand.

RAISING TURKEYS. Pictured here is Lancaster resident Archie MacMackin, who lived on the west side of Harvard Road. In addition to raising turkeys on his farm, he also served as a superintendent at the town farm in 1928 and as a local school bus driver in the 1930s.

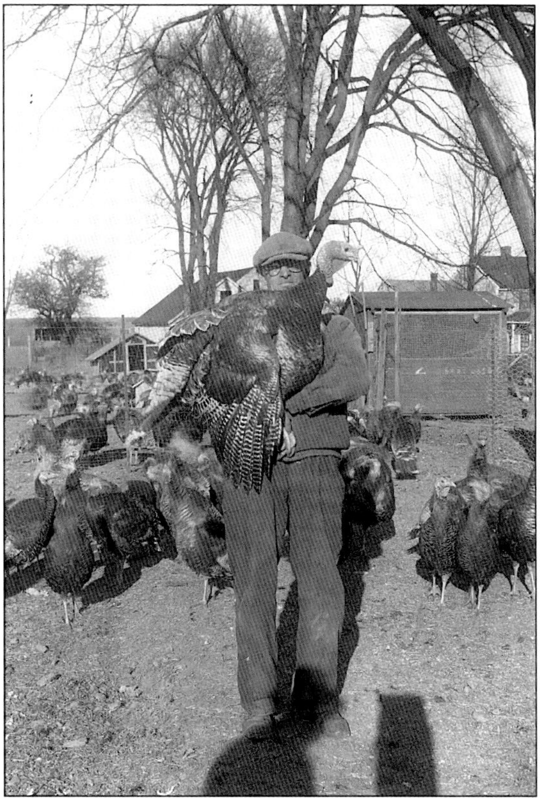

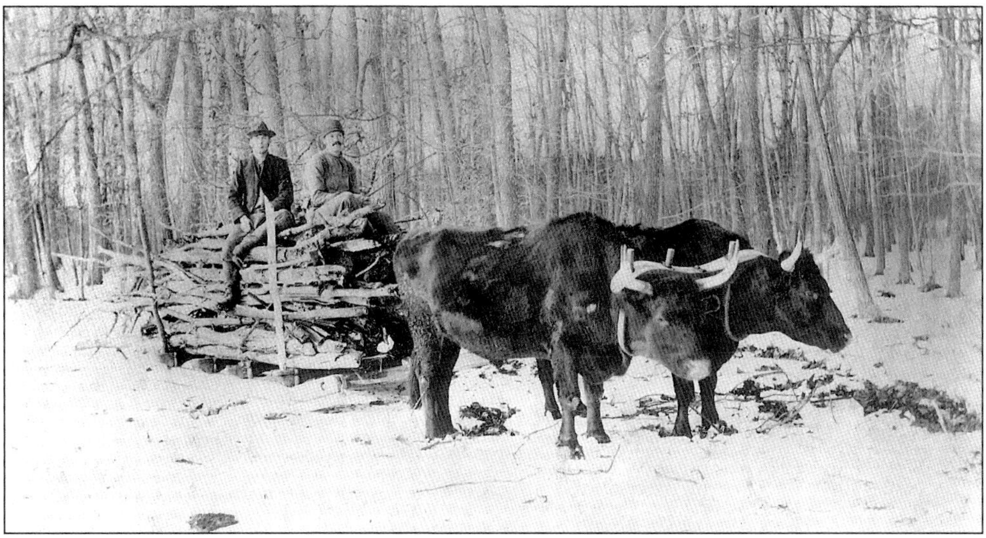

OXEN IN THE SNOW. Men and beasts pause as they make their way home from the woodlot on a snowy day. This photograph was taken near the former Cunningham farm on Back (Langen) Road.

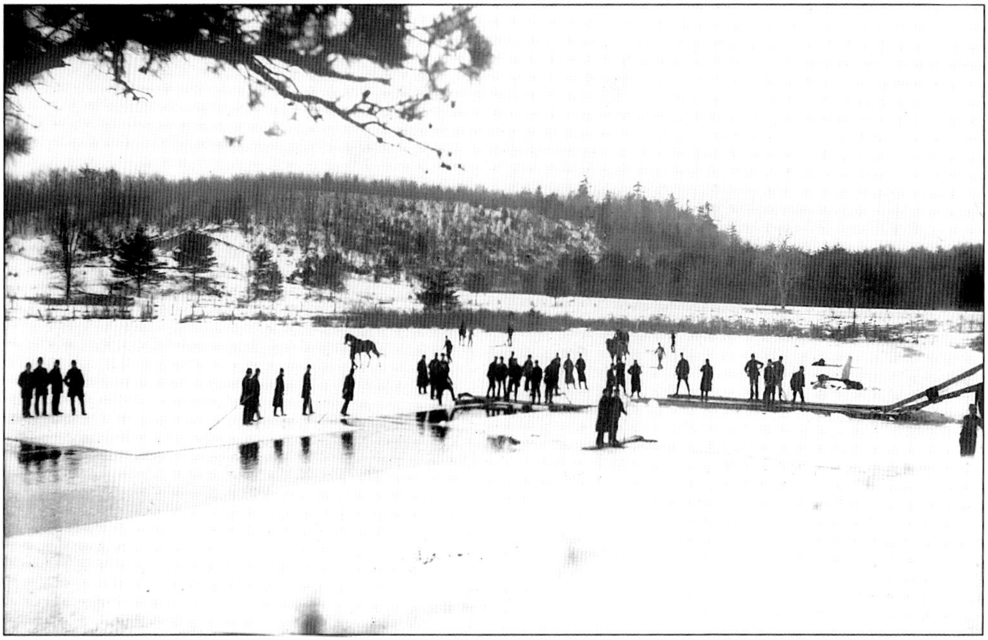

Ice Cutting. Men are shown here tending to the task of ice cutting on Fuller Pond. Farmers would often supplement their incomes during the unproductive winter months by cutting blocks of ice, storing them in well-insulated icehouses, and selling them for use in iceboxes during the hot summer months.

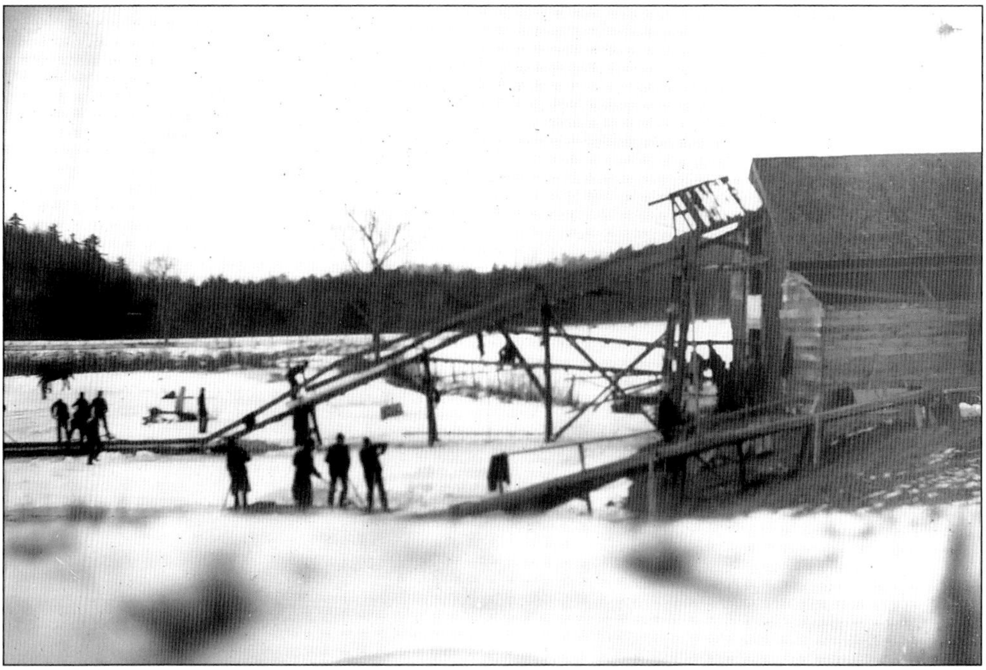

An Icehouse on Fuller Pond. Men are cutting the ice in blocks to be stored away in the icehouse on Fuller Pond. Longtime residents may remember putting cards in the windows of their homes to specify the size of the ice blocks they wished to purchase from the iceman as he made his rounds.

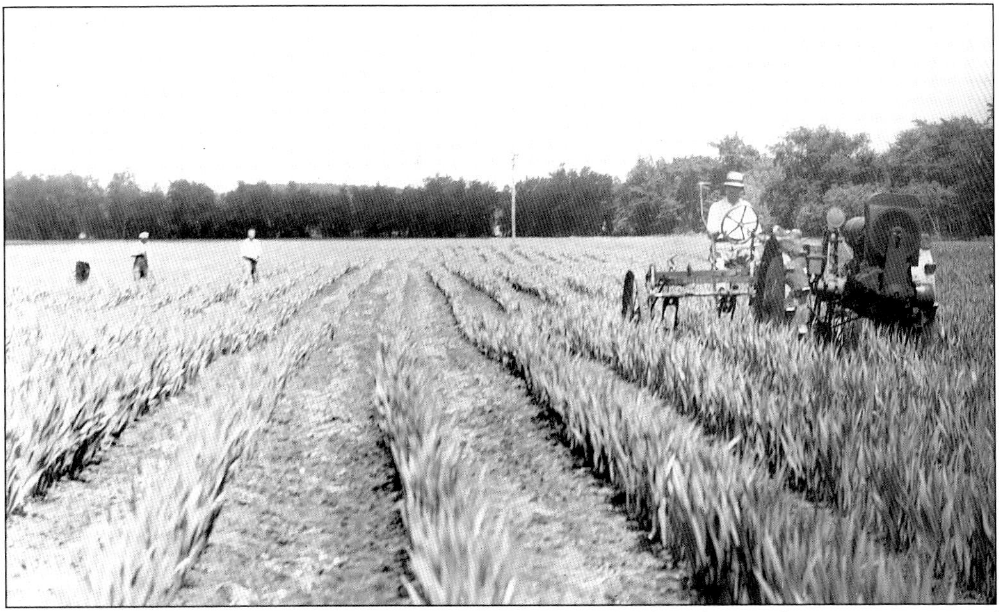

A Field of Sword Lilies. Shown is a 20-acre gladiolus field in the northeasternmost part of Lancaster on an intervale bounded on three sides by the Nashua River. The field was cultivated by John E. Farnsworth and his son Custer in the 1920s. In season, two shipments of 200 to 300 dozen gladioluses per day went out to Boston and New York from the Lancaster railroad station. Previously, prisoners of war from World War I had been held at this site.

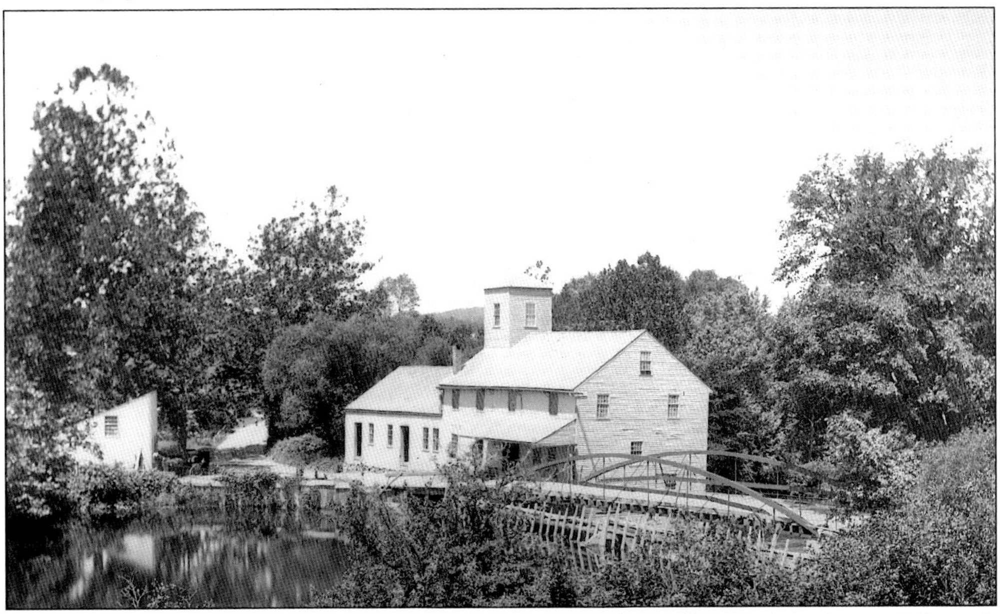

South Lancaster Mill Site. On this site (near present-day Mill Street) on the south branch of the Nashua River, Sawyer and Wilder, *c.* 1805, first built a dam, a sawmill, and a gristmill. Later, Samuel Carter operated a fulling mill for the processing of wool for clothing nearby. Through the years, ownerships and functions changed several times. Pictured here is the Sawyer-Carter Grist Mill as it appeared *c.* 1900. On the site for 50 years, the building burned in a spectacular blaze on the night of June 21, 1906.

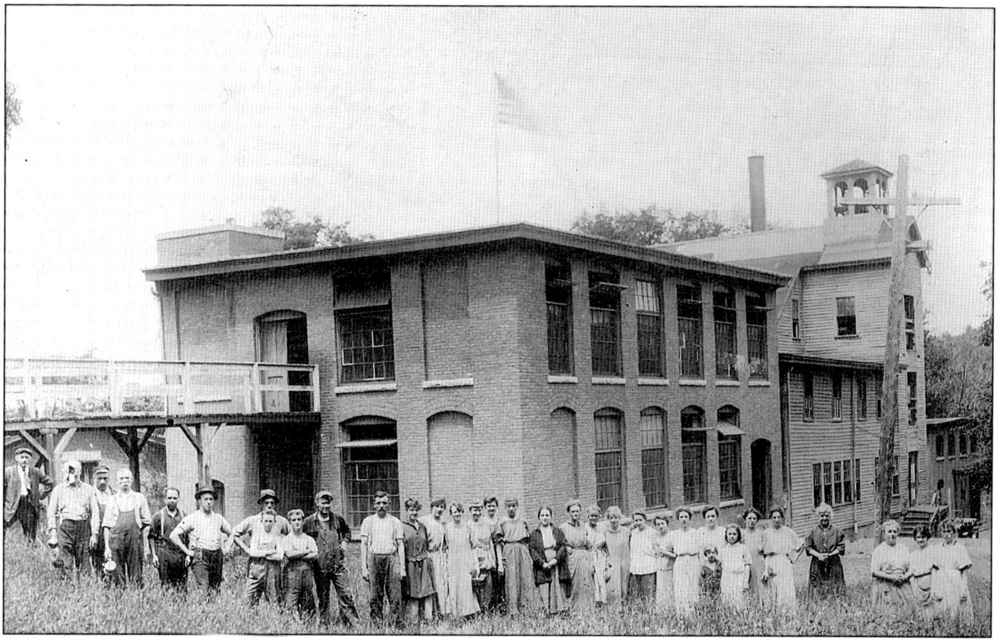

The Ponakin Mill. Workers from the Ponakin Mill in North Lancaster take time out for an early photograph. The privilege had been used first for sawmills and gristmills and later for ironworks and nail making. After 1861, the site was used for a textile factory and after World War II it became a plastics factory until destroyed by fire in 1963.

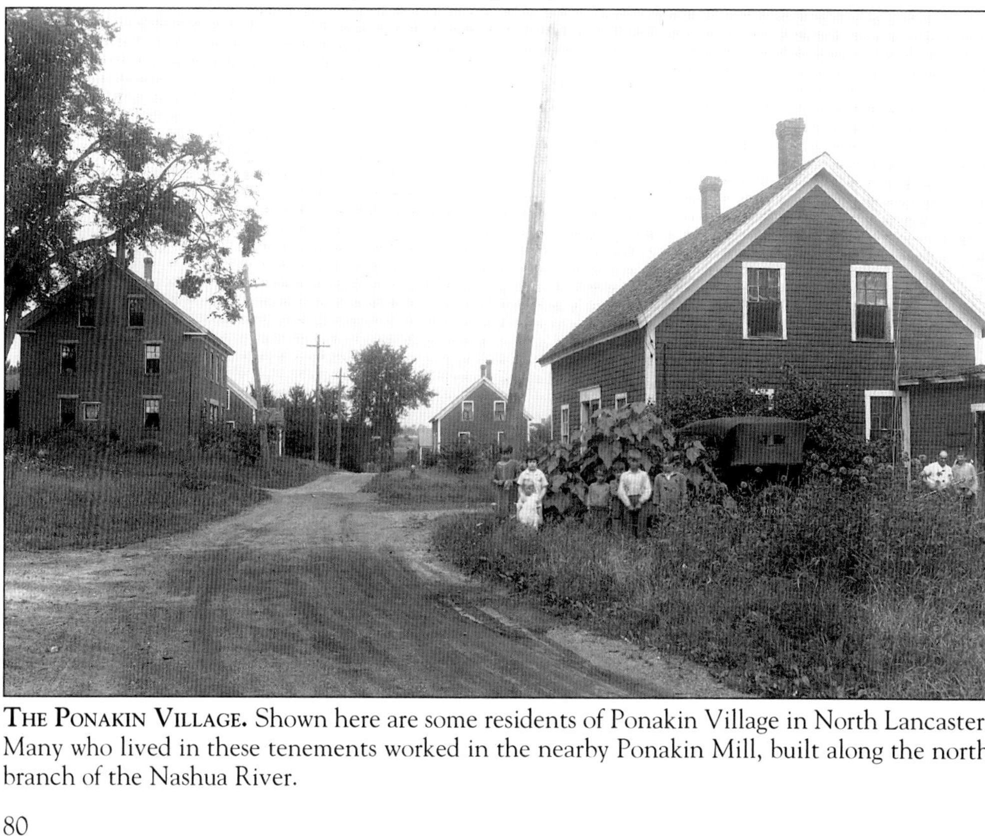

The Ponakin Village. Shown here are some residents of Ponakin Village in North Lancaster. Many who lived in these tenements worked in the nearby Ponakin Mill, built along the north branch of the Nashua River.

Six

THE PEOPLE AND EVENTS

The Lancaster Town Green has been the center of town life and the setting for many special and significant events. In 1824, General Lafayette spoke from the steps of the church. During times of war, the green has been a gathering place for rallies, fundraising events, and memorial services. Events of all kinds—patriotic, musical, historical, theatrical, and sporting—are represented in this chapter. Disastrous events, fortunately, have been few.

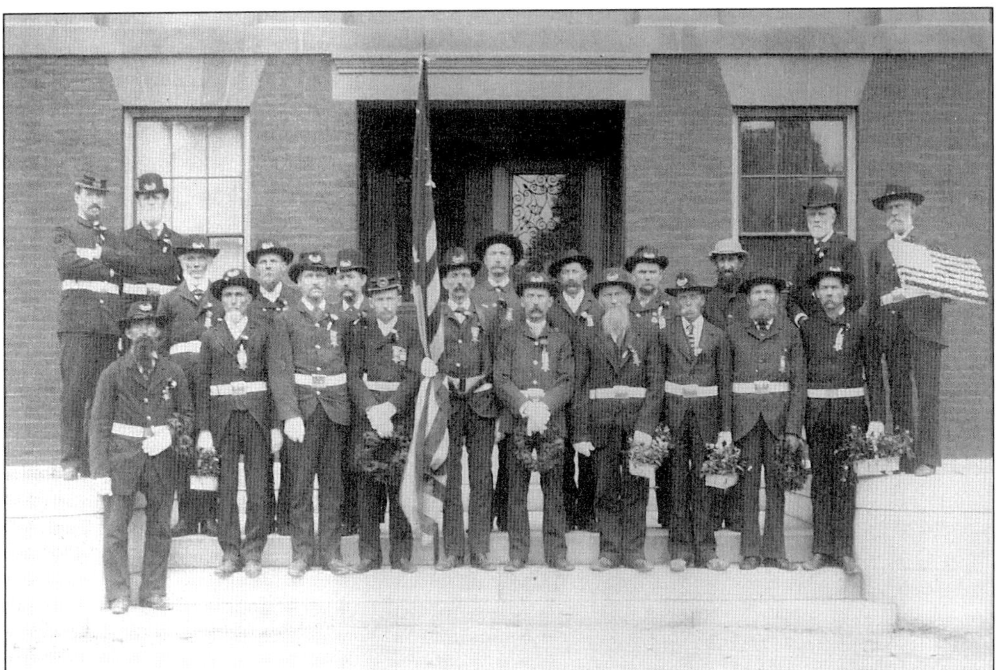

CIVIL WAR VETERANS ON MEMORIAL DAY. A dignified group of veterans poses on the steps of Memorial Hall. They are, from left to right, as follows: (front row) Linenkemper, Sargent, Farnsworth, Nash, McNamara, Lyman, Brockelman, Bliss, Blood, and Preston; (middle row) Jackson, Sartelle, unidentified, Hardy, Fay, Hosley, and Lawrence; (back row) Mann, Wyman, Nourse, and Wilder. No less than 181 Lancaster men served in the Civil War.

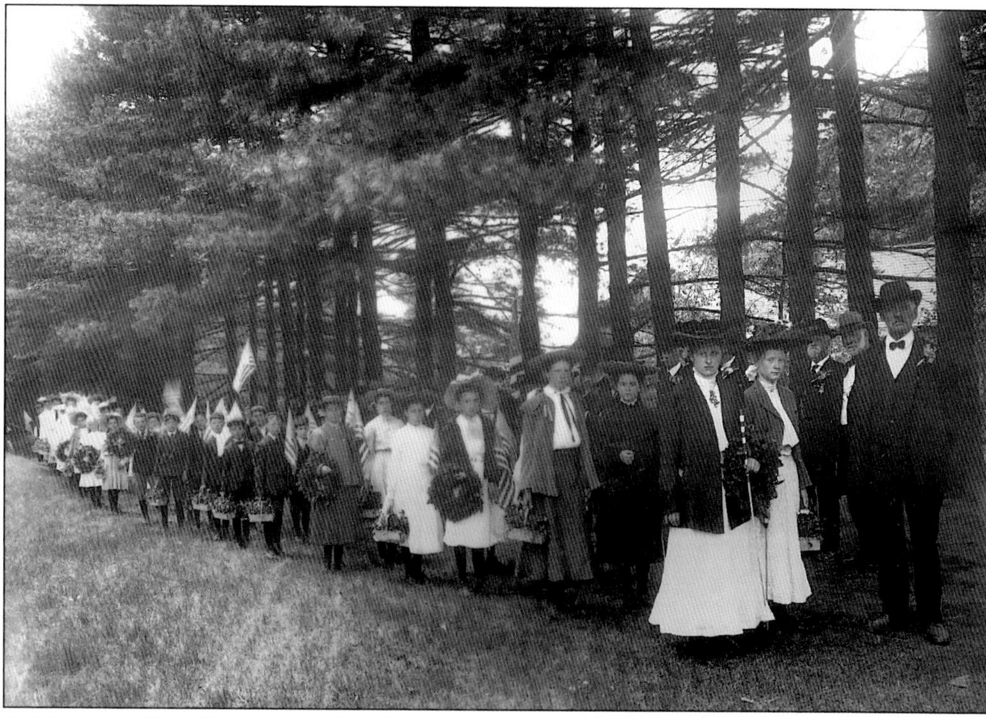

A Memorial Day Procession. Residents in a traditional Memorial Day procession make their way, with wreaths and flowers, to honor Lancaster's war veterans.

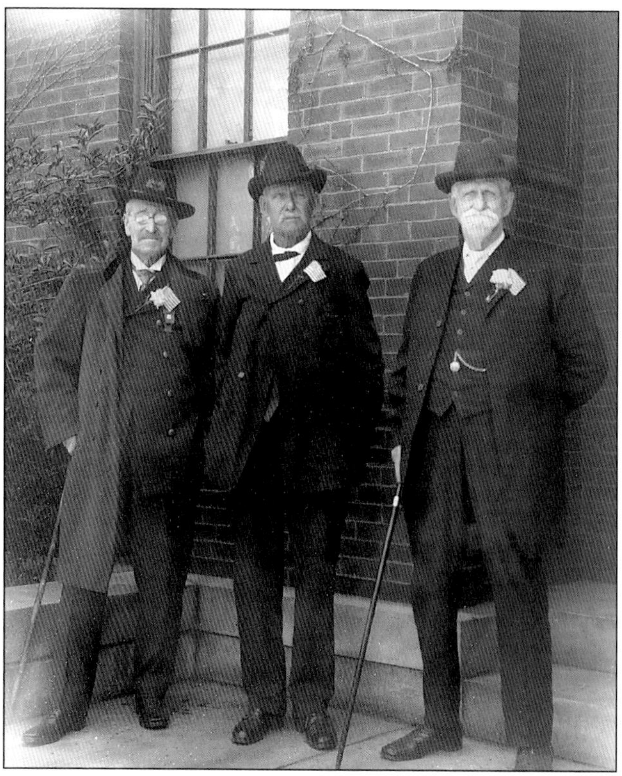

The Last Remaining Civil War Veterans. Pictured here are Lancaster's three last Civil War veterans. Eben Mann and John E. Farnsworth lived on Harvard Road. Benjamin Wyman resided on Neck Road. Farnsworth, who was born in 1843 and died in 1929, was the very last to survive.

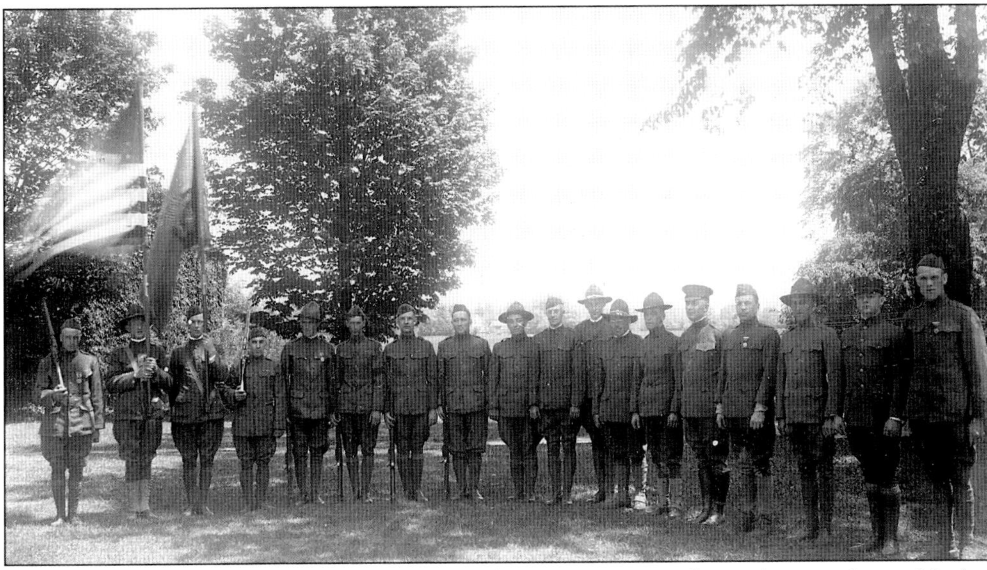

World War I Veterans. Veterans of World War I pose proudly in their uniforms. No less than 119 men from Lancaster served their country during the war.

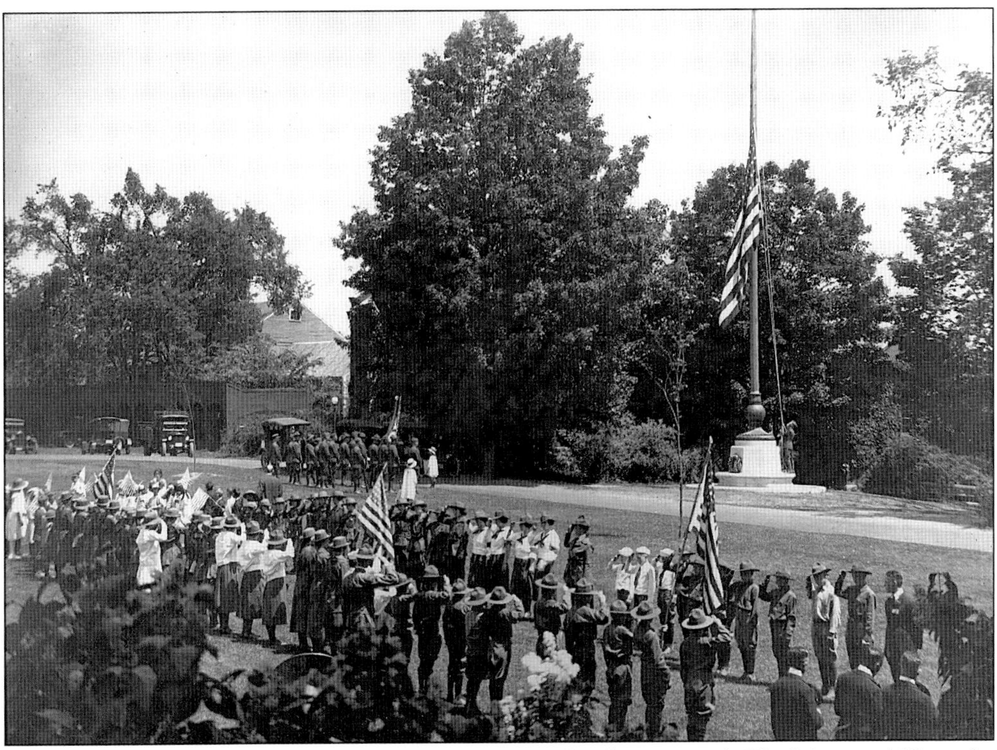

The Memorial Flagpole. All stand at attention as the flag is raised. The Memorial Flagpole, on the Lancaster Town Green, was erected by the citizens of Lancaster in 1922 as a tribute to those who served their country during World War I. It bears an inscription composed by Henry Holton Fuller.

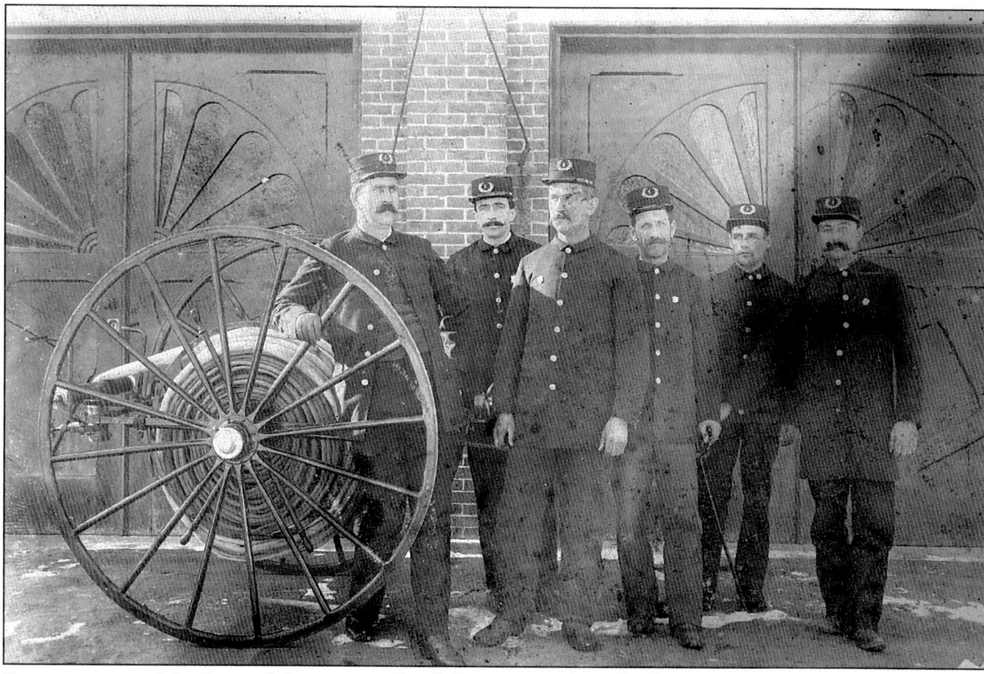

Firefighters. Uniformed Lancaster firefighters stand with their equipment in front of the Center Hose House. All members of the Lancaster Fire Department were required to march in the parade on Memorial Day. The penalty for not marching was a 25¢ docking of their pay.

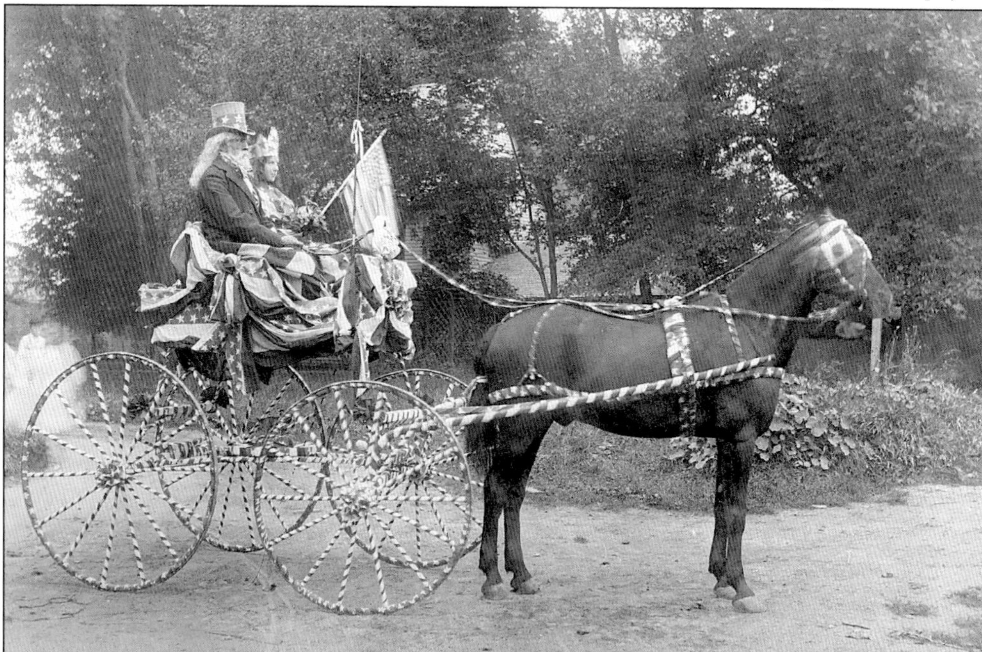

Uncle Sam and Lady Liberty. Sanford B. Wilder and his granddaughter Marion Burrage, dressed as Uncle Sam and Lady Liberty, are ready for a Fourth of July festivity as they head out in the vehicle Wilder used on his rounds as lamplighter on the streets of Lancaster in the 1890s. Lancaster did not use electricity for streetlights until *c.* 1905.

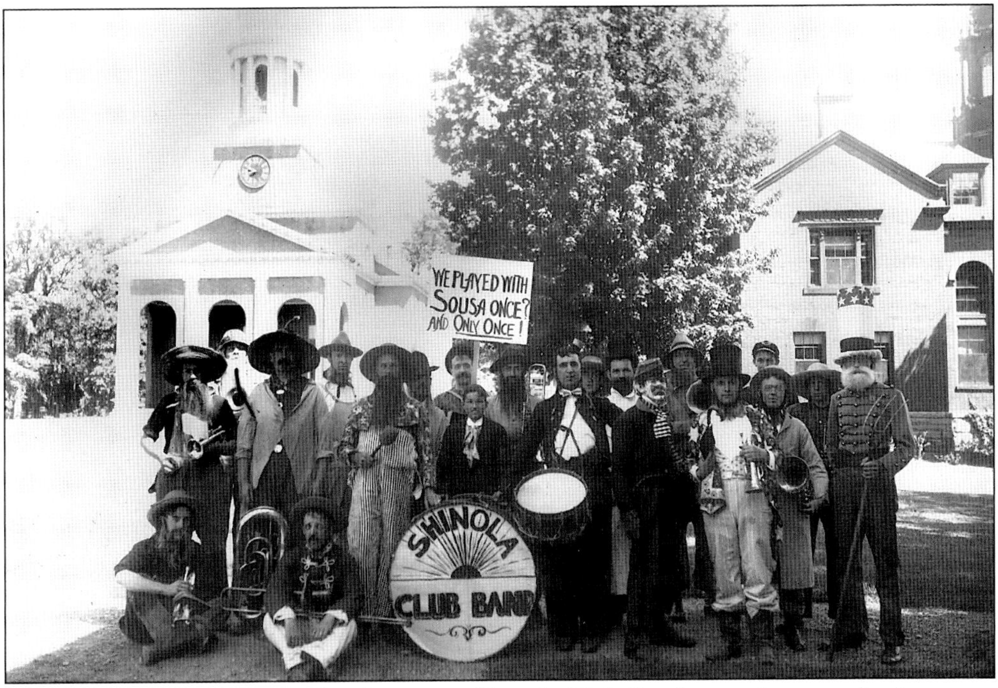

The Shinola Club Band. The Lancaster Shinola Club Band poses here on the Lancaster Town Green on the Fourth of July c. 1900. As was their custom, band members would all dress in ridiculous clothing on that day. Standing third from the right, in the front, is photographer James McDonald with his trumpet.

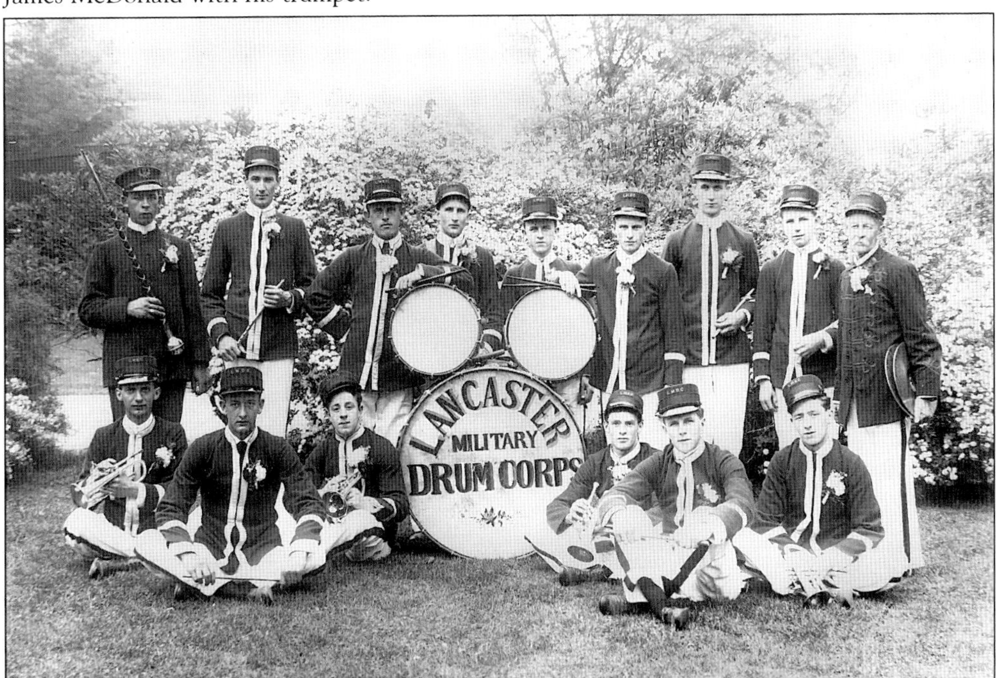

The Lancaster Military Drum Corps. Smartly uniformed and ready to perform, the members of the Lancaster Military Drum Corps pose near the Lancaster Town Green.

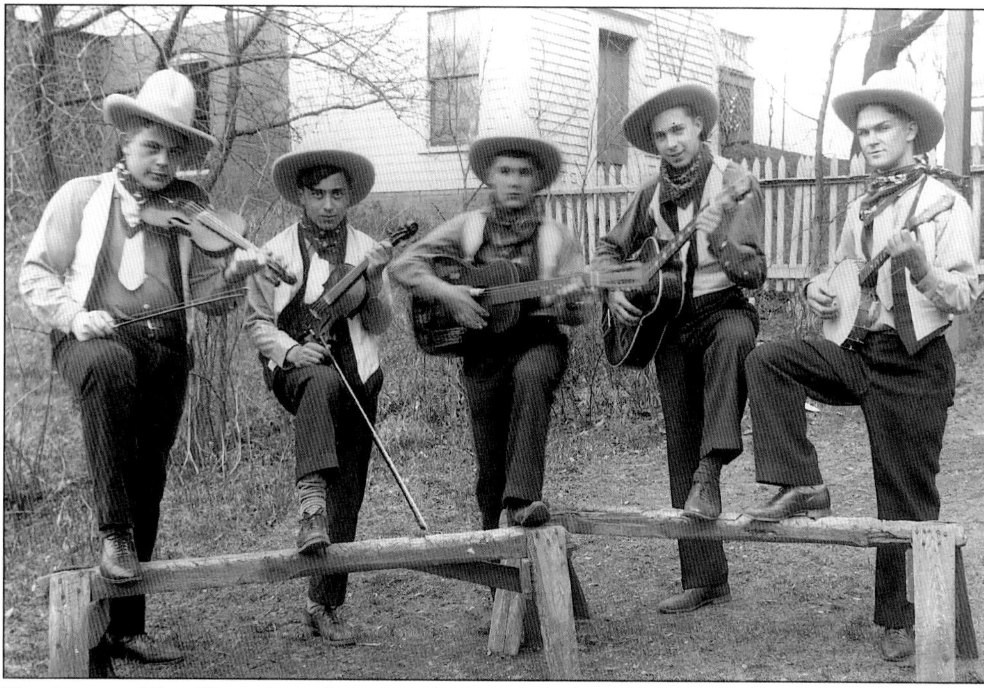

The Yonder Hill Boys. In earlier times, Lancaster had a variety of minstrel shows, which were held as early as the 1880s. Posing here with fiddles, guitars, and banjo are the Yonder Hill Boys. They are, from left to right, Leon Valley, John Rouleau, Duncan McDonald, Wilbert Locke, and John Gosselin. The group performed country-western music in the mid-1930s. Minstrel shows were discontinued in the early 1950s.

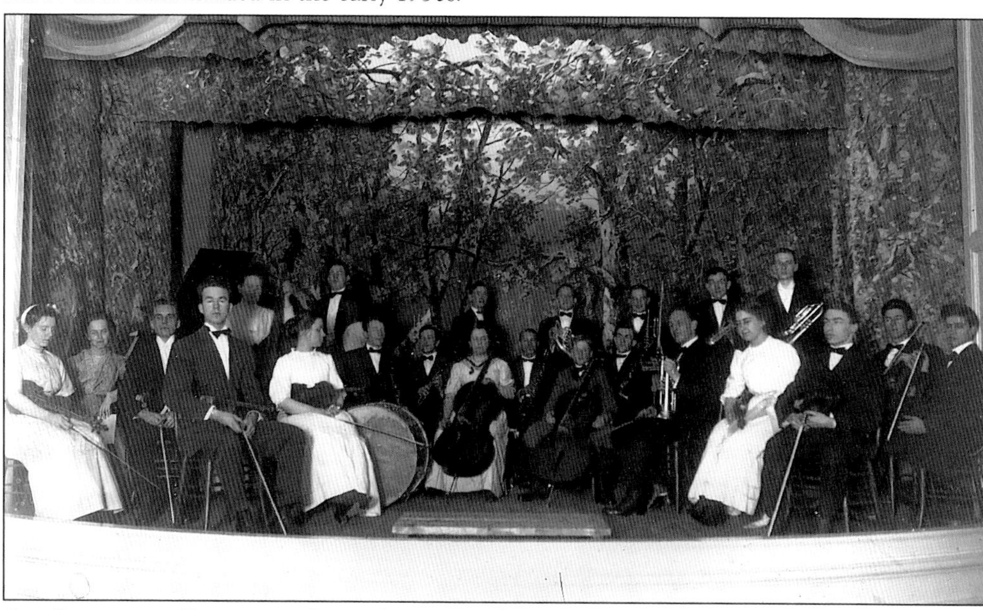

An Orchestra Performs. An orchestra, ready to perform, is shown here on the stage in the Lancaster Town Hall. The Lancaster Town Hall has been the scene of many orchestral concerts through the years. The first was performed by the Boston Symphony Orchestra when the building was dedicated on September 11, 1908.

A Pageant Program. On July 4, 1912, an elaborate historical pageant was held on the Lancaster Town Green. The day's events are listed on the front cover of the program shown here.

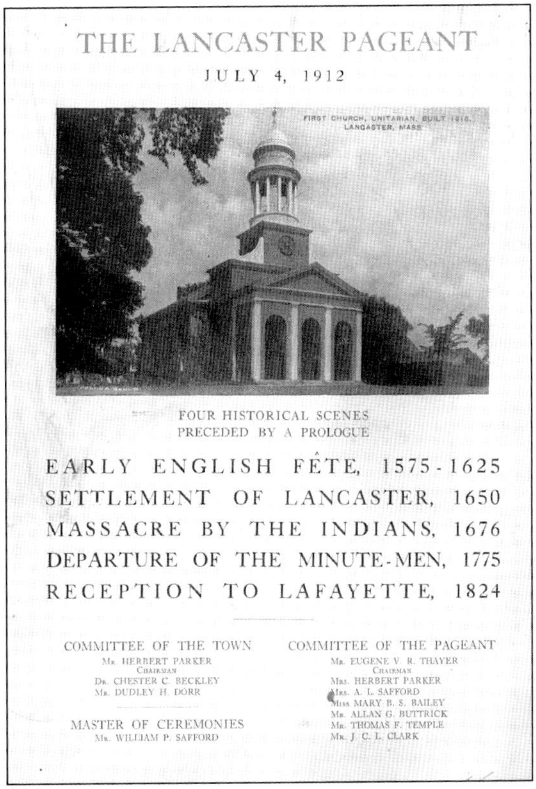

THE LANCASTER PAGEANT

JULY 4, 1912

FOUR HISTORICAL SCENES
PRECEDED BY A PROLOGUE

EARLY ENGLISH FÊTE, 1575-1625
SETTLEMENT OF LANCASTER, 1650
MASSACRE BY THE INDIANS, 1676
DEPARTURE OF THE MINUTE-MEN, 1775
RECEPTION TO LAFAYETTE, 1824

COMMITTEE OF THE TOWN
Mr. HERBERT PARKER
Chairman
Dr. CHESTER C. BECKLEY
Mr. DUDLEY H. DORR

MASTER OF CEREMONIES
Mr. WILLIAM P. SAFFORD

COMMITTEE OF THE PAGEANT
Mr. EUGENE V. R. THAYER
Chairman
Mrs. HERBERT PARKER
Mrs. A. L. SAFFORD
Miss MARY B. S. BAILEY
Mr. ALLAN G. BUTTRICK
Mr. THOMAS F. TEMPLE
Mr. J. C. L. CLARK

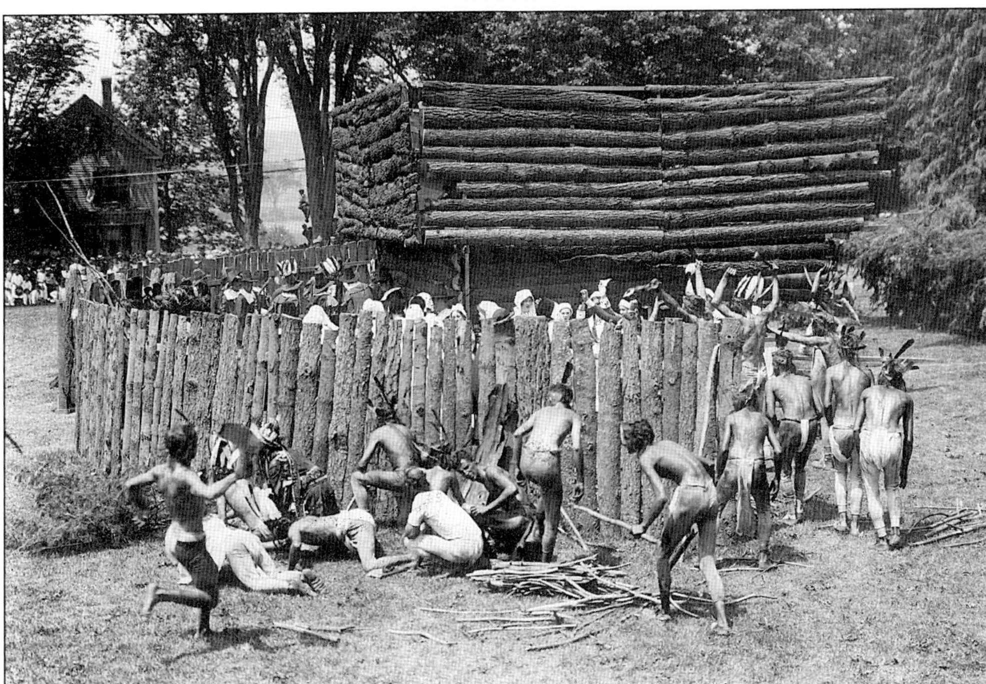

Ready to Attack. A fierce group of warriors launches an attack on the garrison house of Rev. Joseph Rowlandson at the 1912 pageant on the Lancaster Town Green.

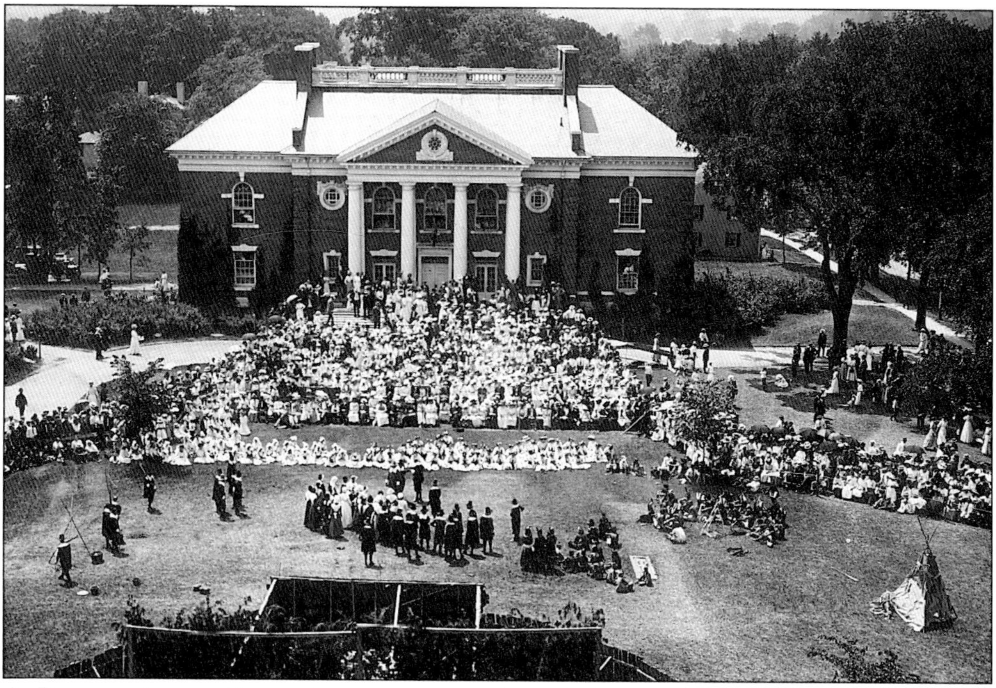

A Perfect Stage. Shown here are scenes from *Settlement of Lancaster* and *Reception of Lafayette*. Architect Robert H. Mutrux notes of the green in *Great New England Churches*, "In its layout and in the orientation and the quality of the buildings that face it on three sides, it resembles a self-conscious stage set." It was estimated that about 4,000 people witnessed the pageant.

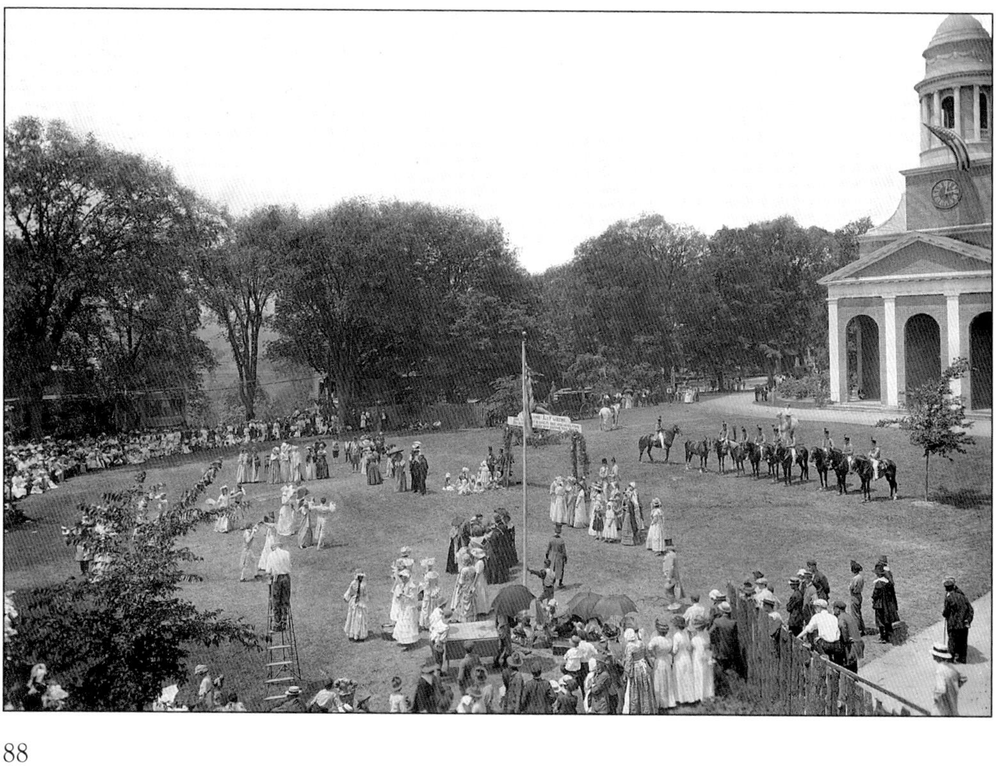

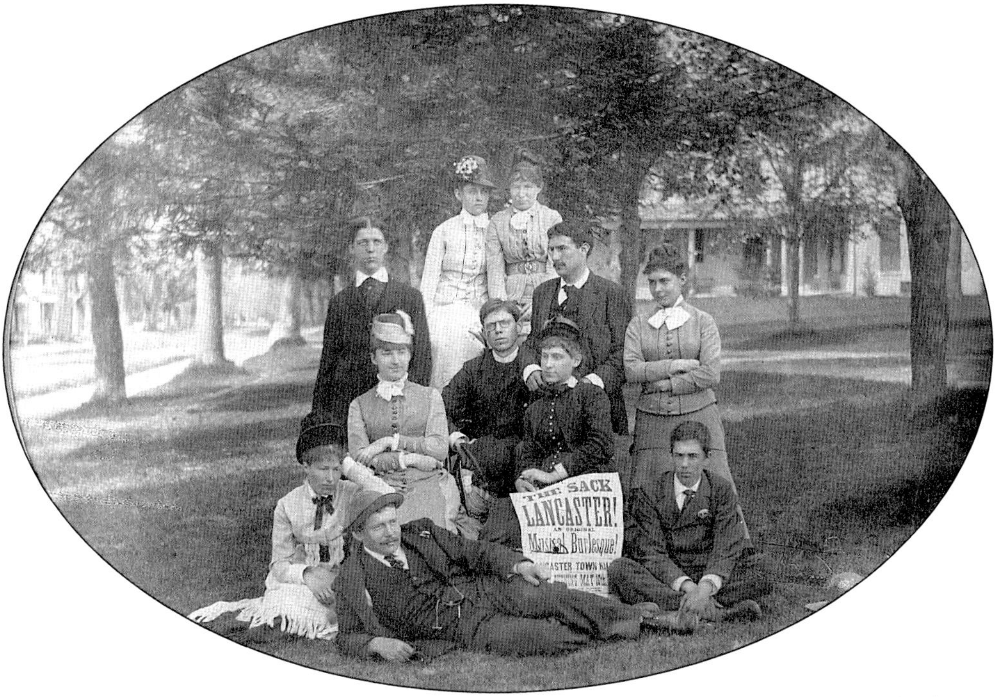

A MUSICAL BURLESQUE. Shown here is the cast of *The Sack of Lancaster*, a musical burlesque presented by the Theatre Lancaster Social Union on Friday evening, May 16, 1879, at the Lancaster Town Hall. These live burlesques, in which the serious was treated lightly and the frivolous seriously, were a popular form of entertainment in the days before film and television.

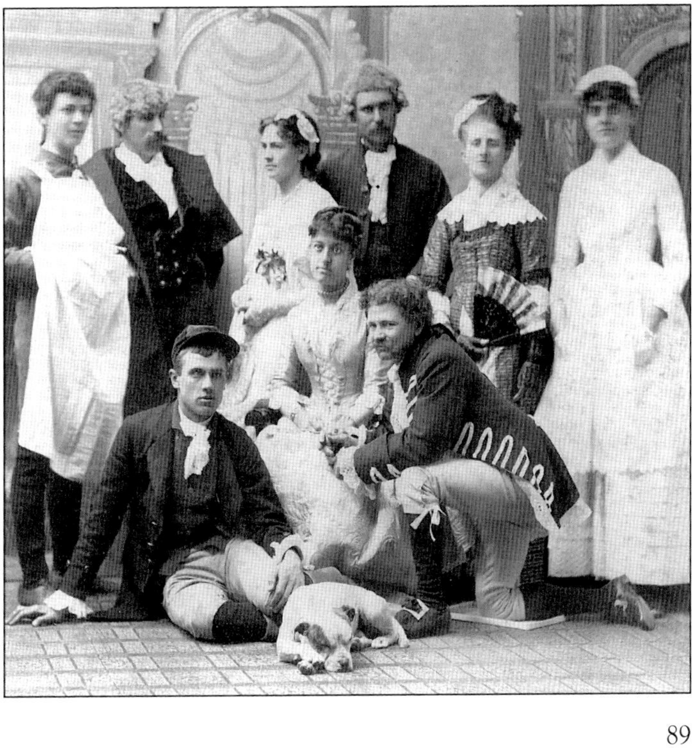

***SHE STOOPS TO CONQUER*.** The Theatre Lancaster Social Union presented a revival of the English drama *She Stoops to Conquer* on May 6, 1885. Members of the cast are, from left to right, as follows: (front row) Charles Vickery, Mary Dix, and John Cunningham; (back row) Will Cunningham, Herbert Parker, Nannie Cunningham, Chester Damon, Fanny Chandler, and Marion Green. The dog, belonging to Charles Vickery, was named Max.

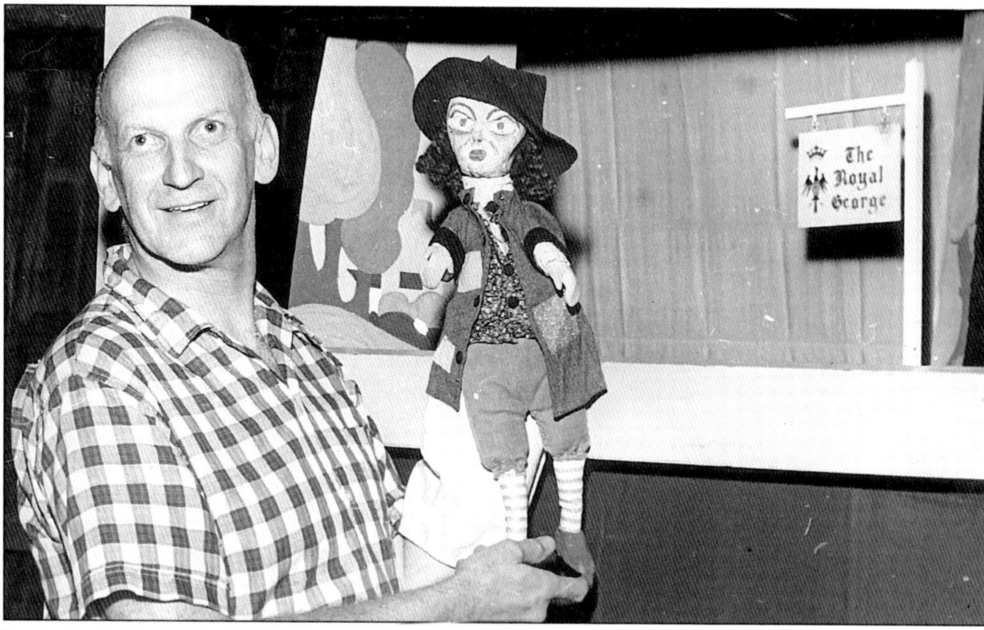

PUPPETEER HERBERT HOSMER. Herbert Hosmer of the Toy Cupboard Theater displays one of his many puppets. Hosmer initially started puppet shows in 1941 to draw customers into a toy store he had opened on his property on the north corner of Main Street and George Hill Road in South Lancaster. Those puppet shows have become happy childhood memories for many Lancaster residents. (L'Ecuyer.)

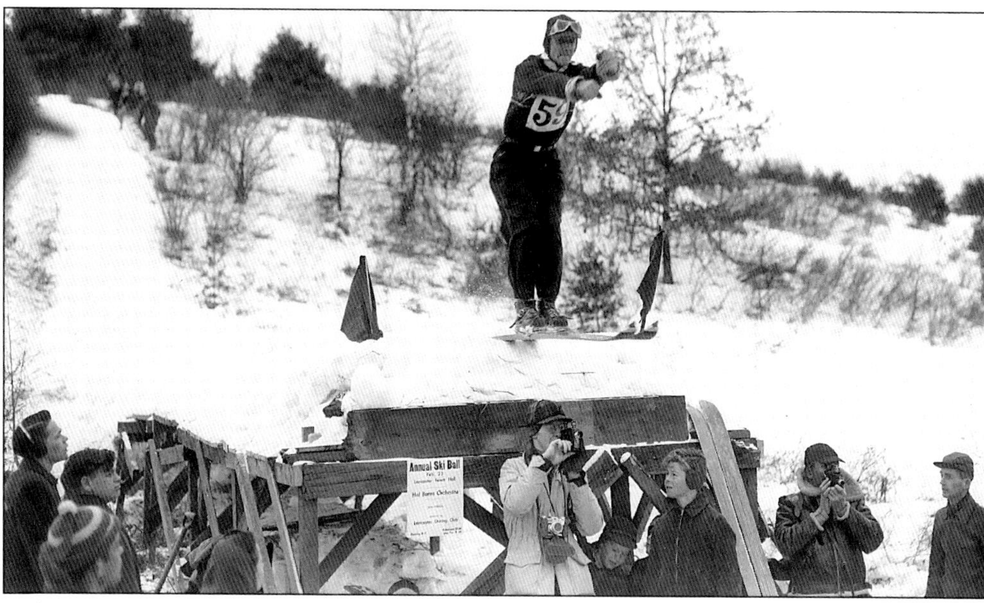

A SKI JUMP CHAMPIONSHIP. One of Lancaster's most eagerly awaited winter sporting events was the Massachusetts State Ski Jump Championship. The event, which began in 1928, was sponsored by the Lancaster Outing Club and was held each February 22 on George Hill. Related events included a five-mile cross-country skiing trek and the crowning of a ski queen at the Lancaster Town Hall Annual Ski Ball. With the threat of World War II, interest in the event declined and the last event meet was held *c.* 1943. (TML.)

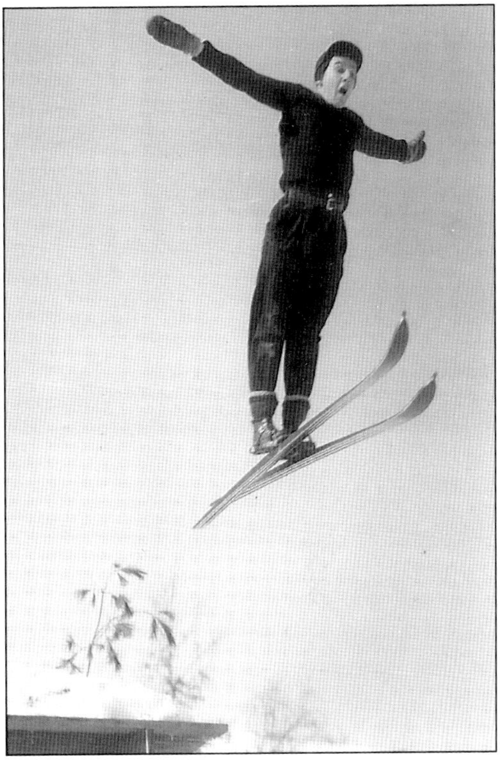

Flying High. A 15-year-old Robert S. Follansbee Sr. is shown flying high in the sky at the Massachusetts State Ski Jump Championship. This photograph was taken in 1937. (Follansbee.)

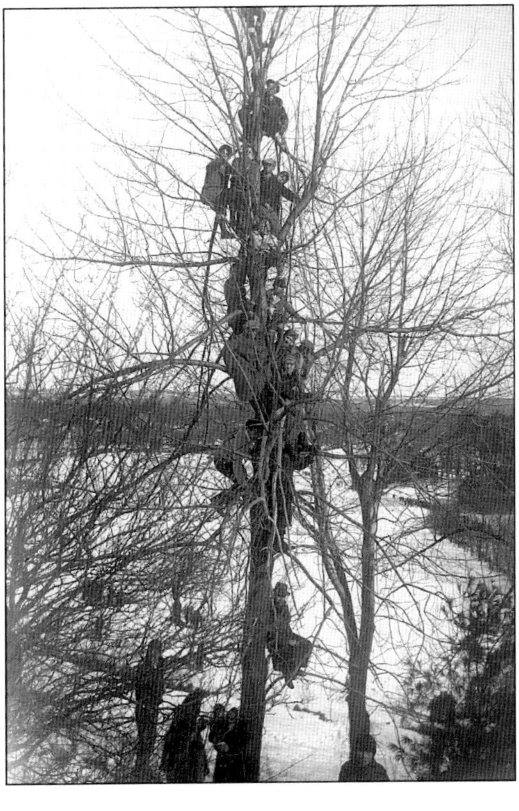

A Bird's-Eye View. Spectators eagerly scale the trees for a bird's-eye view of the proceedings at the Massachusetts State Ski Jump Championship on George Hill. The 50¢ to $1 entrance fee was more than some kids could afford.

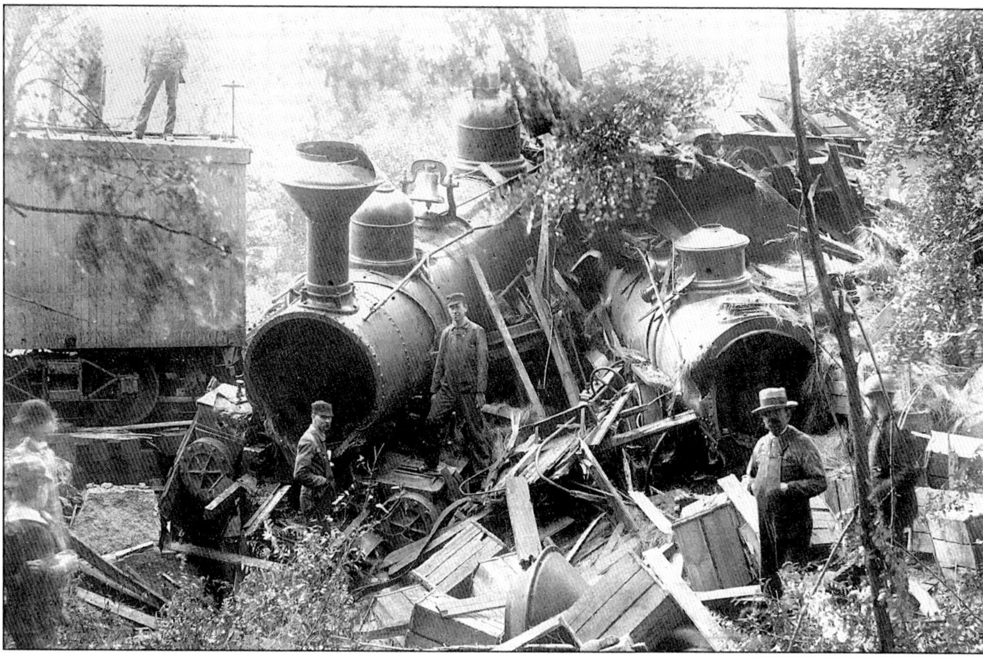

The Train Wreck of 1893. Two Worcester & Nashua freight trains collided head-on about 3:35 a.m. on September 21, 1893. The crash, which occurred in back of the Middle Cemetery, killed a fireman, injured an engineer, wrecked the engines "Boscawen" and "Hollis," and damaged 13 freight cars. It was rumored that a mistake in the Ayer telegraph office led to the accident. The dramatic event drew a curious crowd of 2,000–3,000 to the scene the next day.

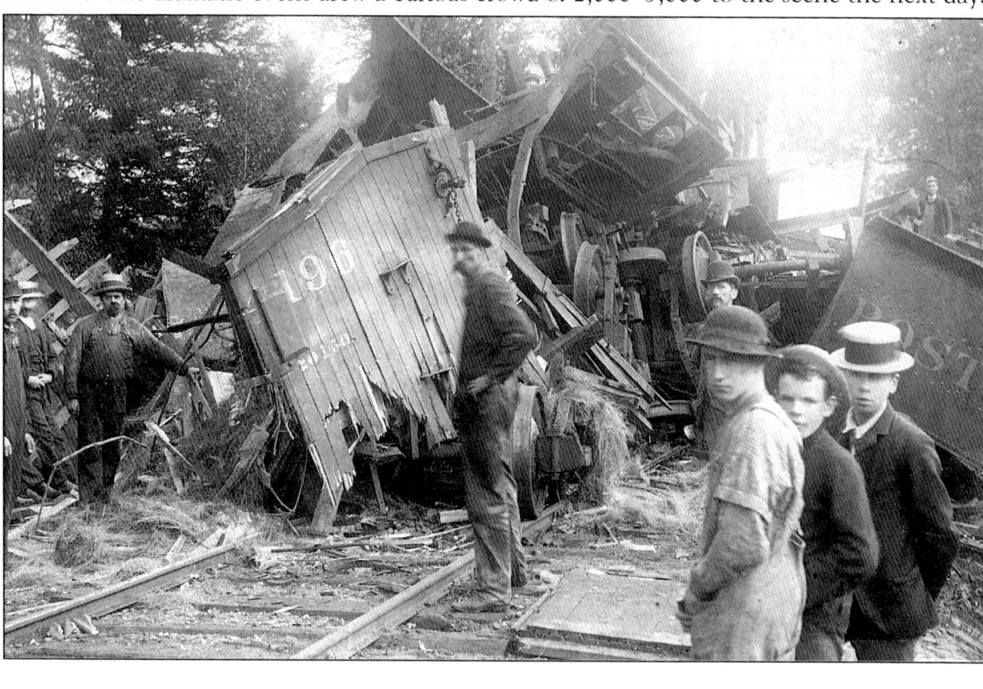

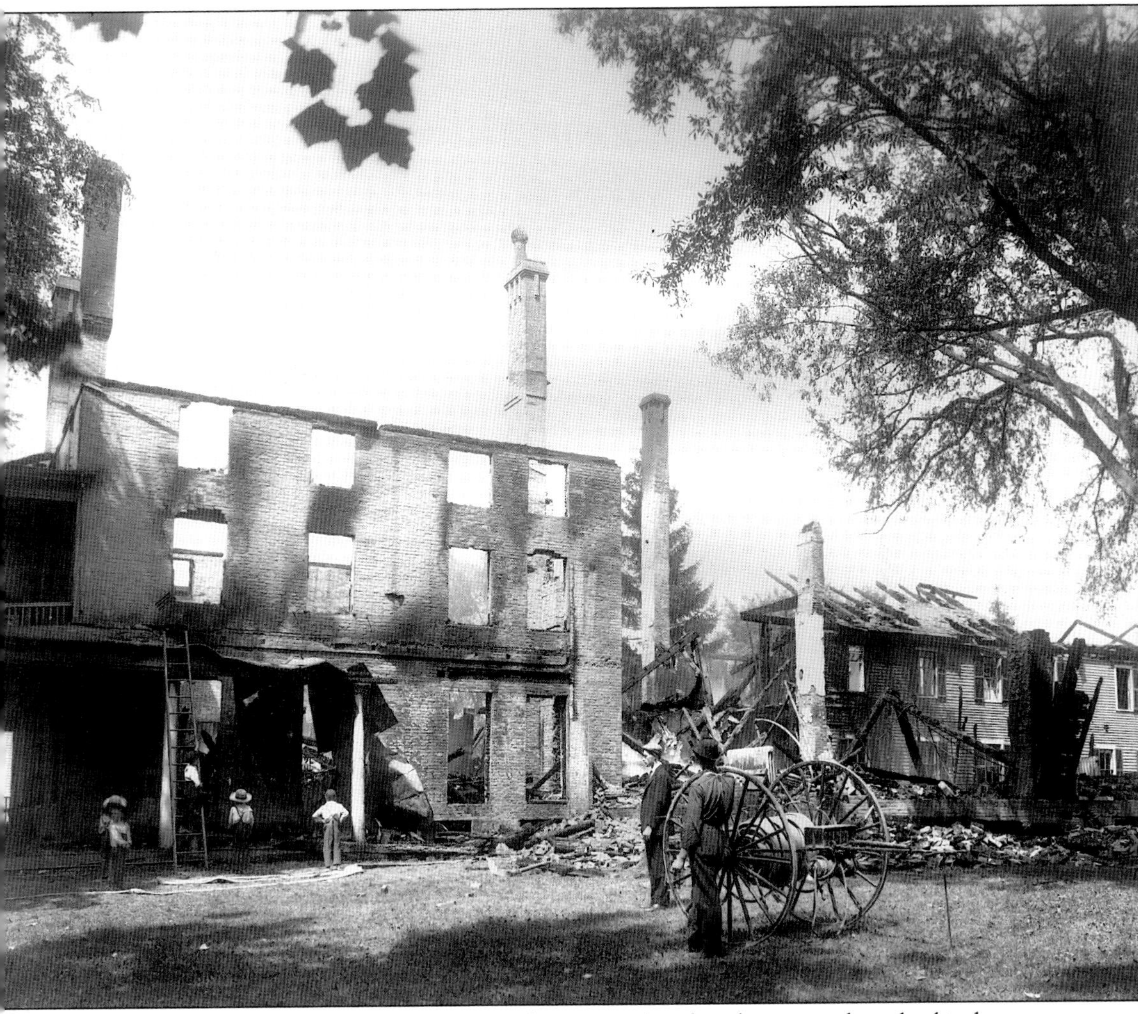

A Hotel Fire. Late on the evening of July 18, 1906, a fire that started in the kitchen area spread throughout the Lancaster Hotel. Although there was no loss of life, about 30 guests were routed from their beds in their nightclothes. The combined efforts of the Lancaster and Clinton Fire Companies could not contain the blaze, and the building was a total loss.

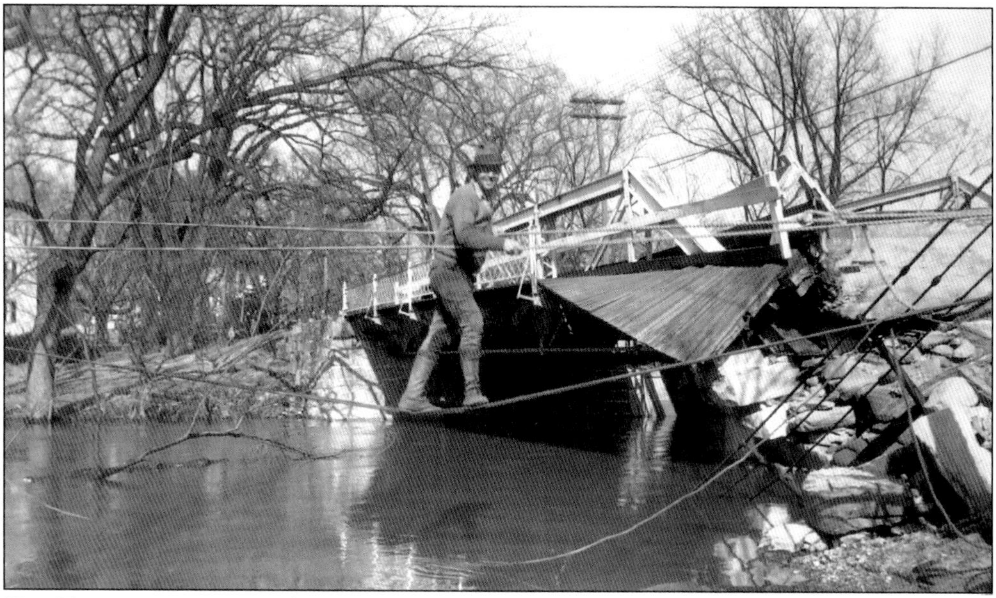

The Flood of 1936. With Lancaster's proximity to the Nashua River, flooding along the banks is not uncommon. However, the Flood of 1936 was more severe. That year, many bridges in town were destroyed, isolating Lancaster Center for several days. Here, an unidentified resident walks the ropes across the river at the washed-out Vose Bridge.

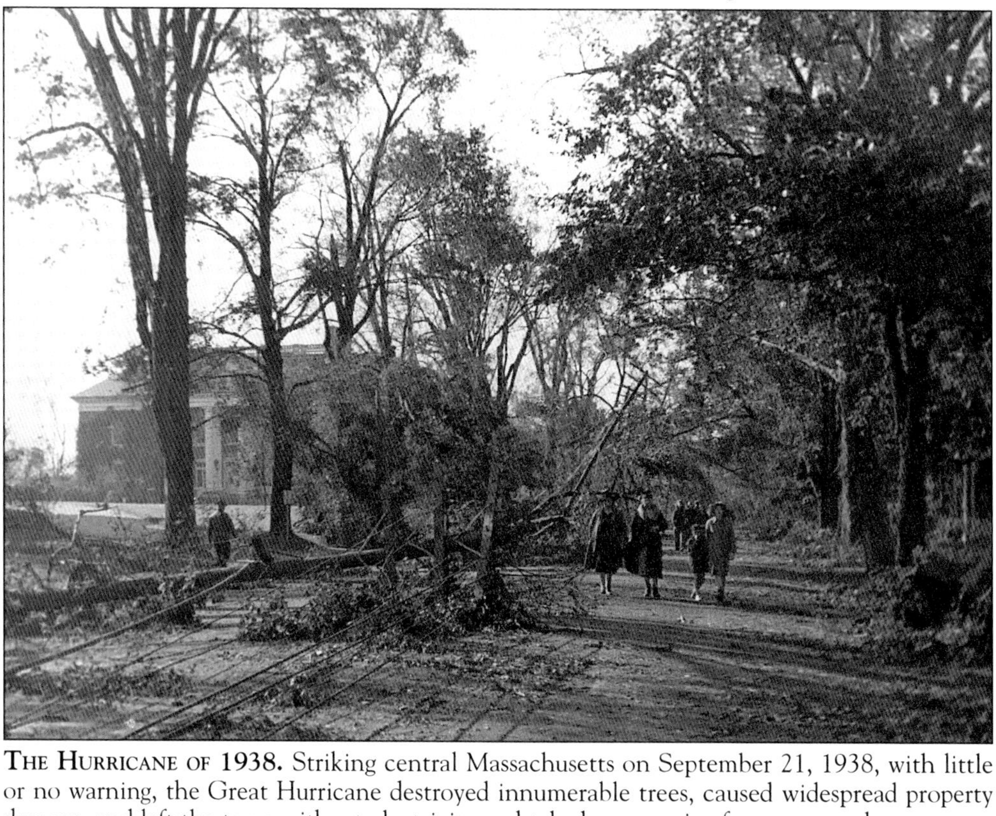

The Hurricane of 1938. Striking central Massachusetts on September 21, 1938, with little or no warning, the Great Hurricane destroyed innumerable trees, caused widespread property damage, and left the town without electricity and telephone service for many weeks.

Seven

The Thayer Legacy to Lancaster

Speaking of Lancaster in a 1905 feature article in *New England Magazine*, Grace Agnes Thompson wrote, "There is a wondrous charm about the old town, a bewitching air of restfulness and inspiration, an exquisite mingling of hill and valley, of lake and woodland stream, of fertile fields and meadows, of quaint farmhouses and modern mansions that the camera can but imperfectly picture, and that the pen can only too inadequately describe." The Thayer family (living in Lancaster during this time) left the town an enduring legacy in the form of beautiful estates and public buildings, lingering reminders of a bygone era.

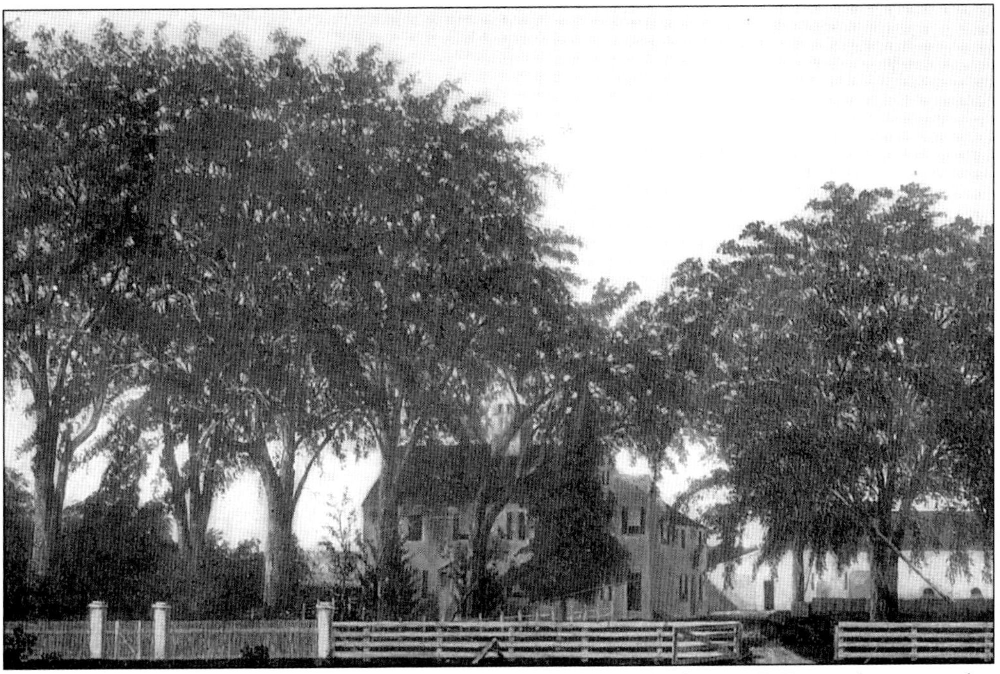

The Thayer Parsonage. The parsonage of Rev. Nathaniel Thayer, D.D., is shown in this painting. Thayer, a lineal descendant of John Cotton, had a 47-year pastorate in Lancaster. After he and his wife died in the mid-19th century, Nathaniel Thayer II (the banker) had the house razed and had his Victorian villa built farther back from the road. One of the features from the property that he was careful to retain was the well sweep shown on the right. (Kilbourn.)

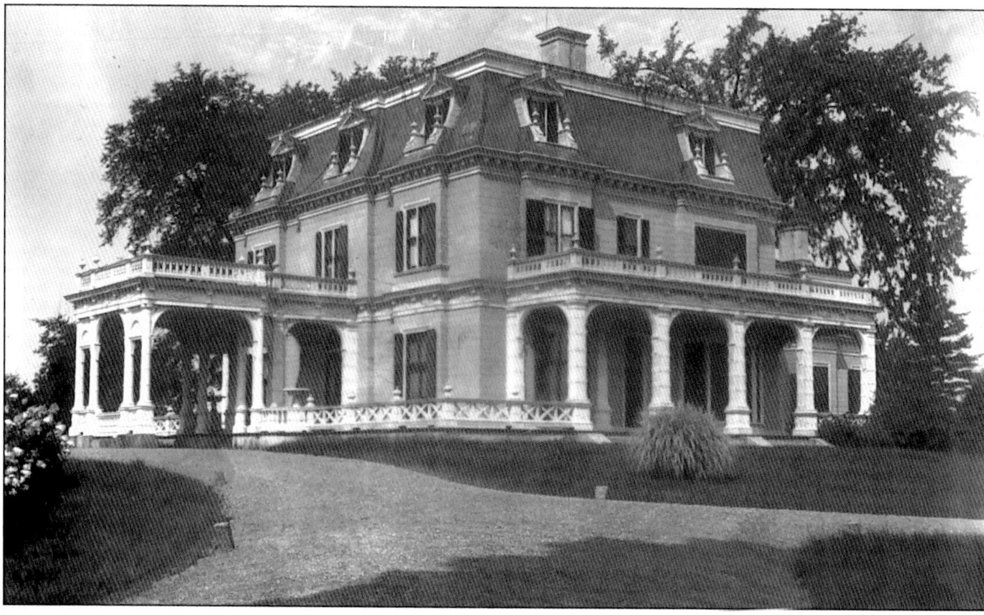

The Victorian Villa. This is an early view of the Victorian villa that Nathaniel Thayer II (the banker) built on the site of his father's parsonage, probably very shortly after his mother's death in 1857. Sentimentally called the Homestead, the dwelling was later greatly enlarged by his son Nathaniel Thayer III after the death of his mother, Cornelia van Rensselaer Thayer, in 1897.

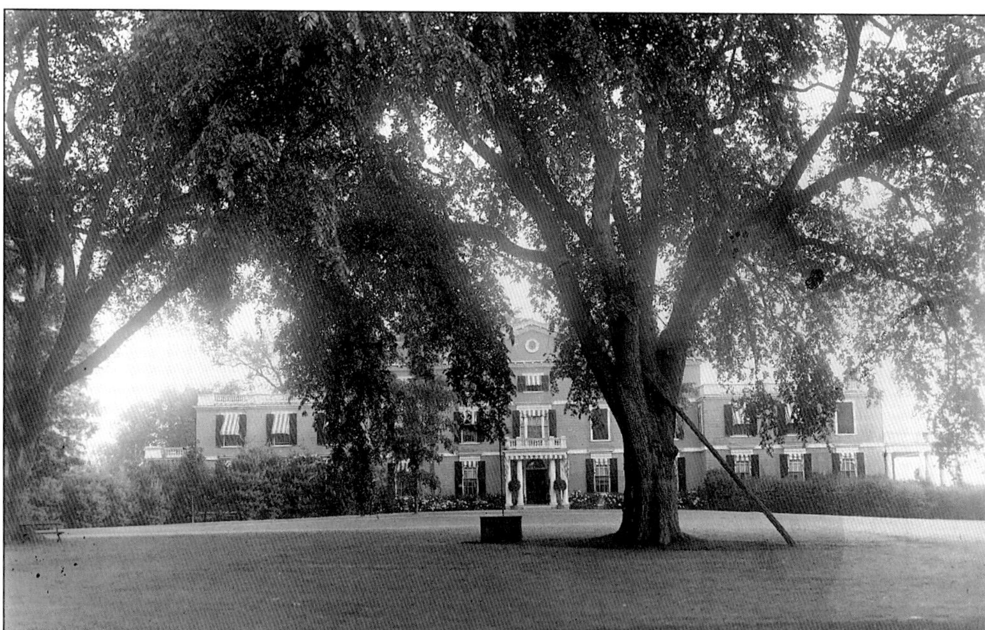

Remodeled and Enlarged Homestead. In 1902, Nathaniel Thayer III commissioned the prominent architect/interior designer Ogden Codman to remodel and enlarge the Homestead in the Colonial Revival style. Today, the building, with its long north and south wings, houses a music conservatory on the campus of Atlantic Union College. It has been listed on the National Register of Historic Places since 1976.

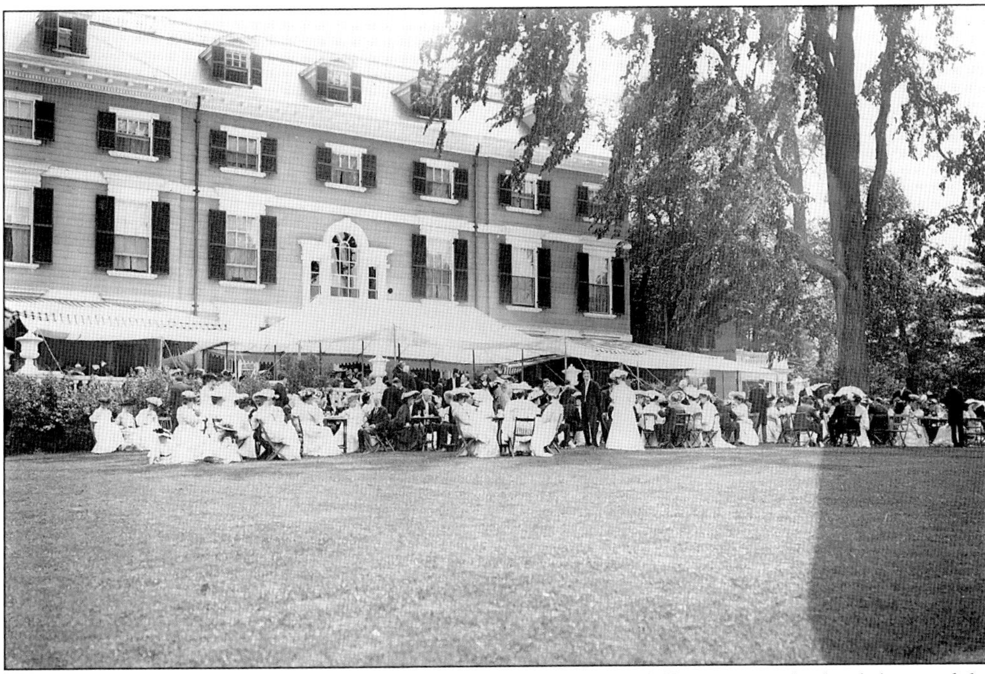

A Lawn Party. A turn-of-the-century afternoon party is in full swing on the back lawn of the Nathaniel Thayer estate, the Homestead, in South Lancaster.

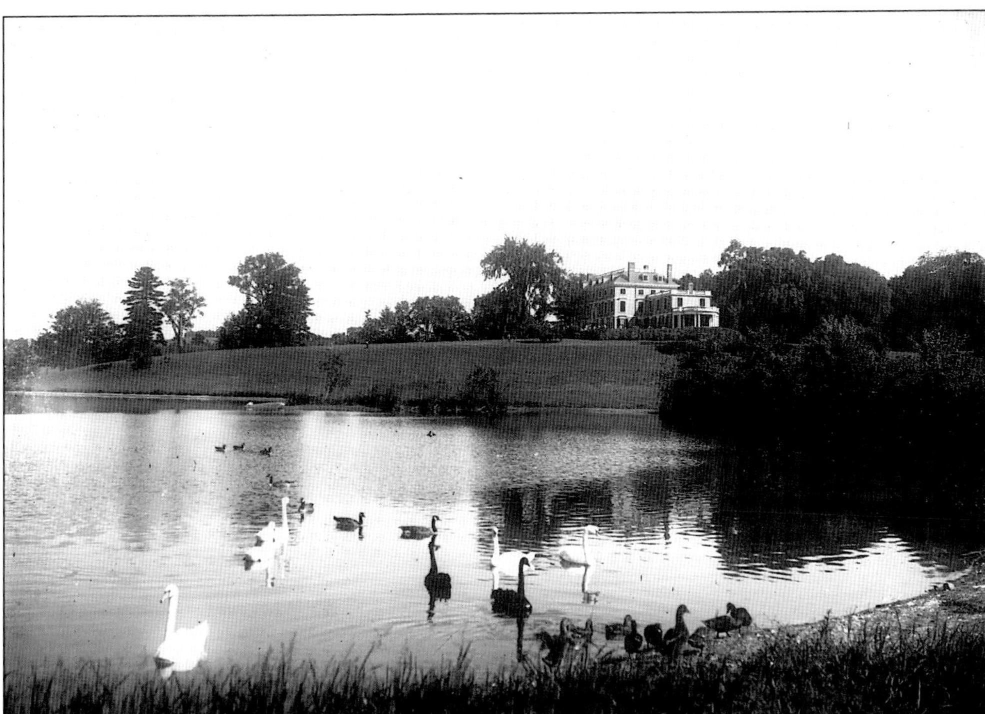

Swans on Thayer Pond. Graceful swans glide through the waters of Thayer Pond near the Homestead. To protect them during the winter season, they were housed in the Boston area.

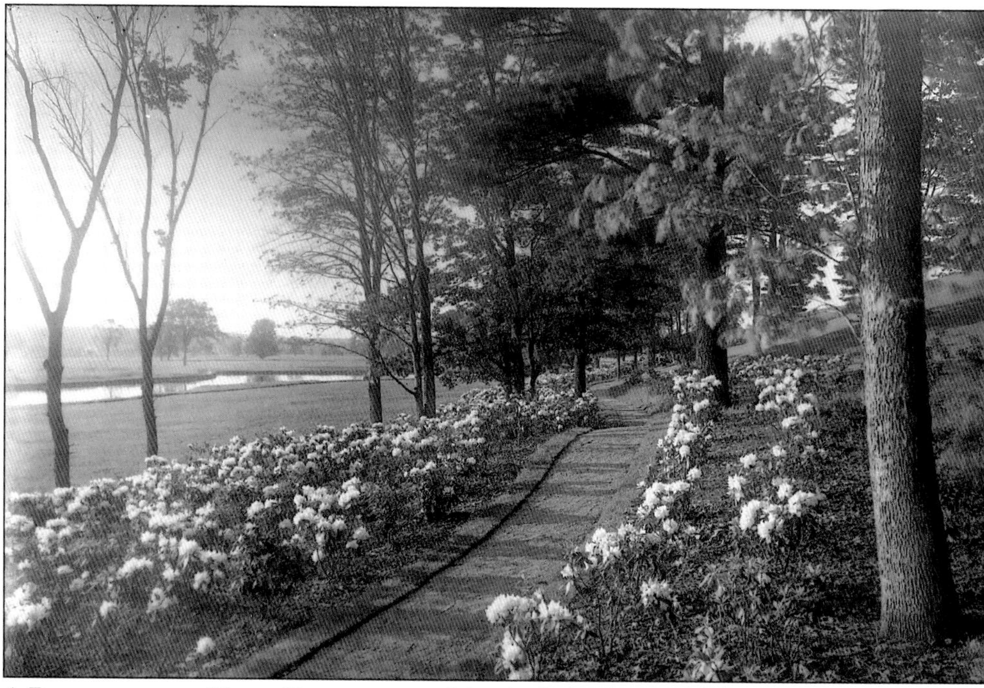

A Rhododendron Walk. Here is a view of the rhododendron in full bloom lining the walkway around Thayer Pond in back of the Homestead. The Hurricane of 1938 did extensive damage to the gardens and, today, nature has all but taken them back.

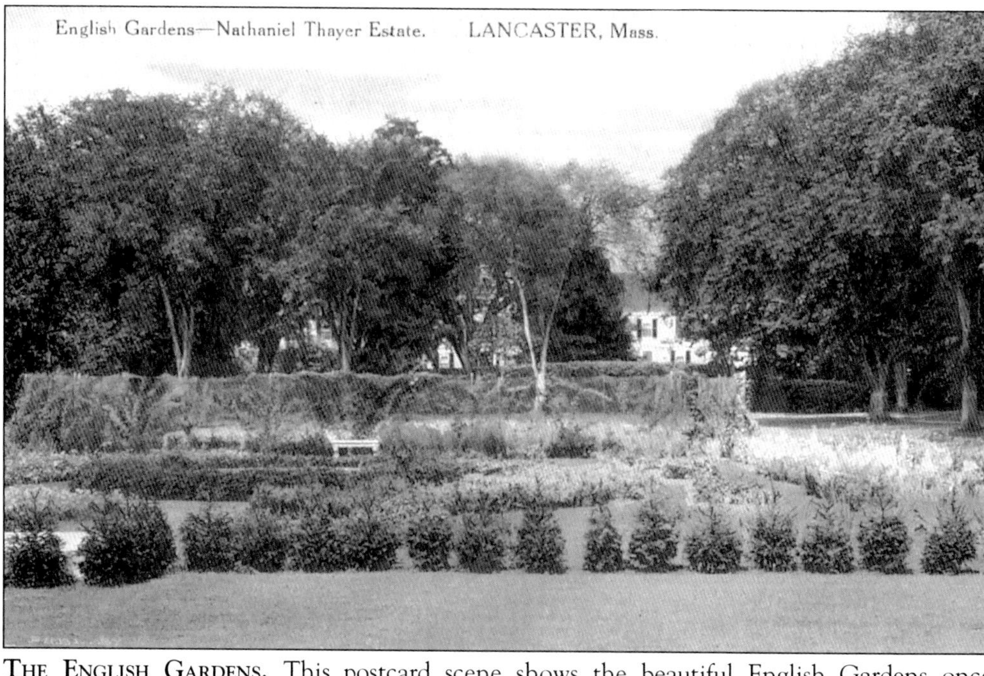

The English Gardens. This postcard scene shows the beautiful English Gardens once situated across the street from Nathaniel Thayer's Homestead in South Lancaster. Bigelow Gardens now occupies the site of this Garden of Eden, as local residents then called it. (Schumacher-Hardy.)

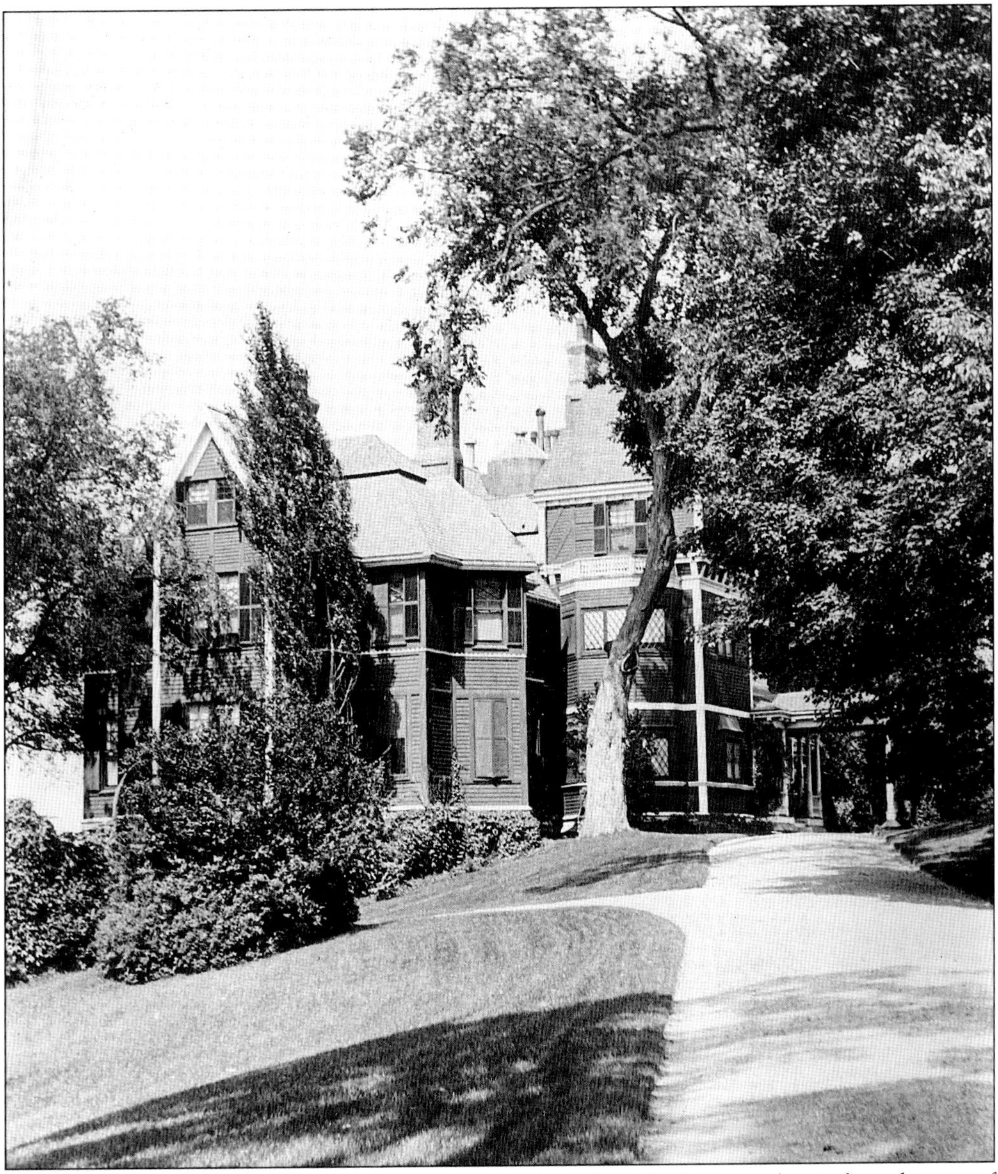

THE RED HOUSE. This is the only known photograph of the Red House, located on the site of the present Atlantic Union Conference Building in South Lancaster. The house, situated on an elevation, was built for Nathaniel Thayer III, probably between 1870 and 1880. Although the exact identity of the architect is unknown, the castlelike style of the house, with its towers and turrets, is characteristic of Boston's John Hubbard Sturgis. The Thayers, as a family, were known to be among the most consistent and frequent of his clients. After Nathaniel Thayer III inherited the Homestead, the house became a residence of Thayer's daughters Anna Thayer Patten Davies and Cornelia, the Countess von Moltke who spent only limited amounts of time in Lancaster.

In the mid-1930s, it was taken down. Longtime residents may remember a charming stone-walled terrace at the north end, which offered a commanding view of the intervale meadows below for many years after the house was gone. A small pet cemetery in back of the house site also remained for many years.

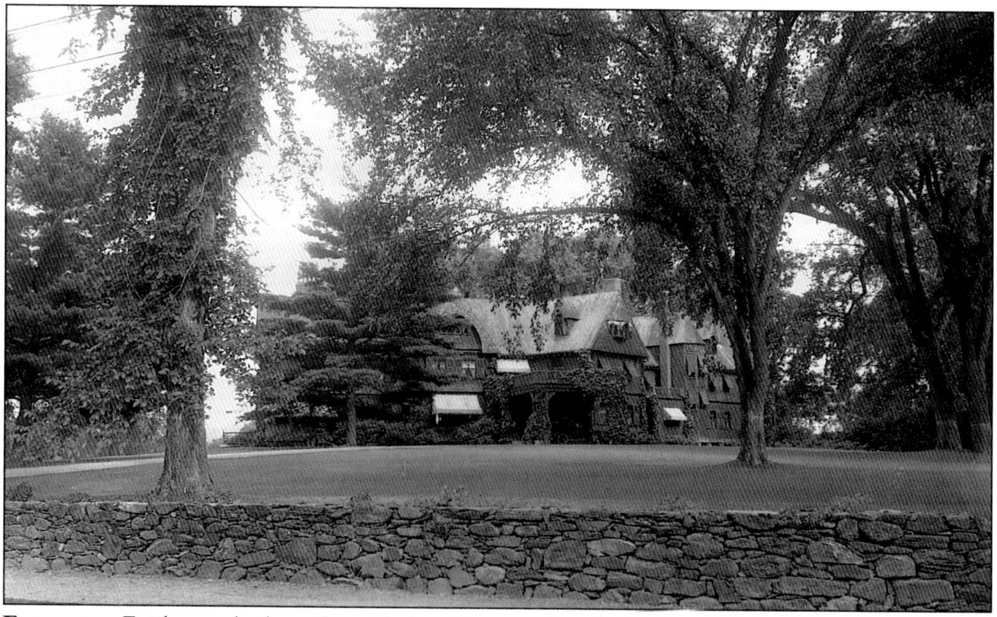

FAIRLAWN. Fairlawn, the heavily gabled and brown-shingled estate of Eugene V.R. Thayer, was built *c.* 1880 on South Main Street. The architect was most likely John Hubbard Sturgis, who was often commissioned by the family. In the early 1920s, architect Henry Forbes Bigelow (who had married Thayer's daughter Susan) greatly altered the building by removing many arches and covered entrances and painting it white. A servants' wing was removed and placed closer to the main street. The "White House" now houses the English department of Atlantic Union College. The servants' wing is used as apartments.

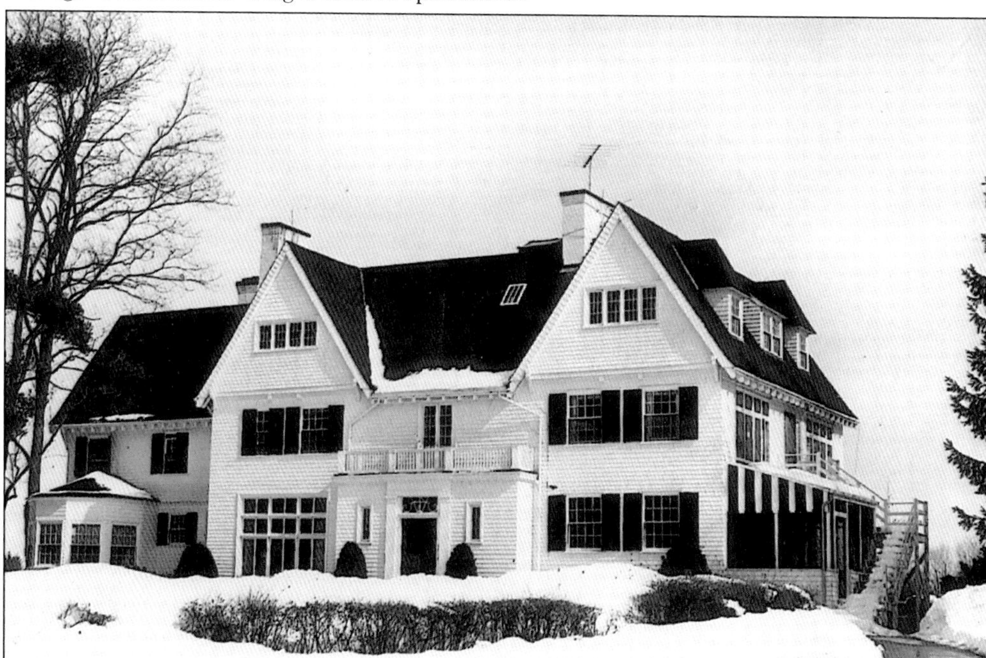

THE REMODELED FAIRLAWN. This view shows Fairlawn as it looked after remodeling in the 1920s. (AUC.)

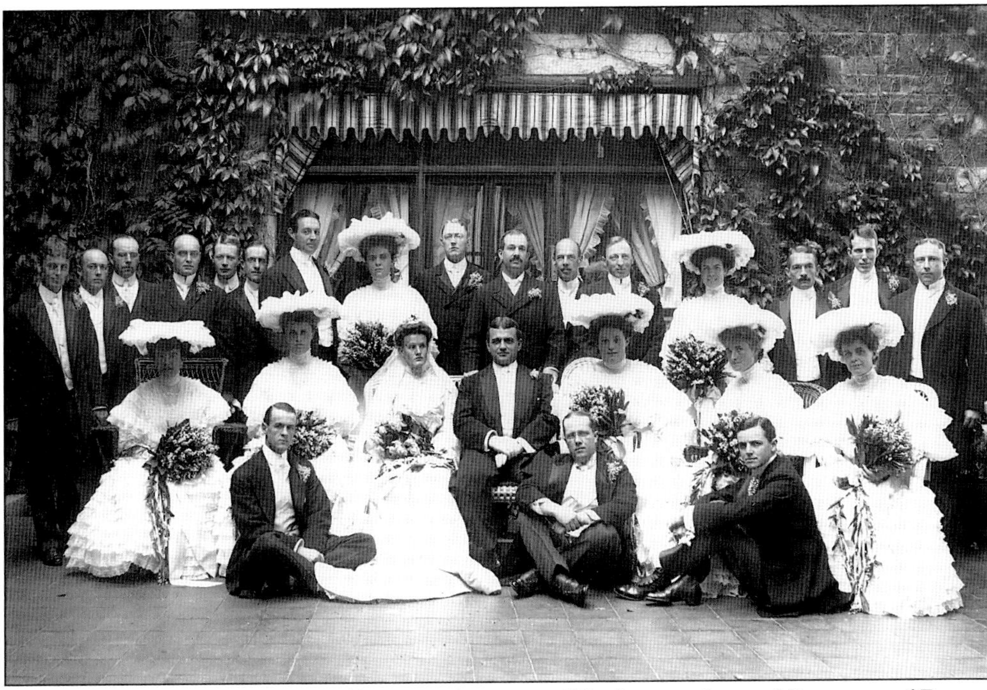

A **FAIRLAWN WEDDING.** Pictured here on the patio of Fairlawn is the wedding party of Eugene V.R. Thayer's eldest daughter, Katherine, who married Howland Russell on June 1, 1904. Lancaster was the setting for no less than six Thayer weddings between 1903 and 1913.

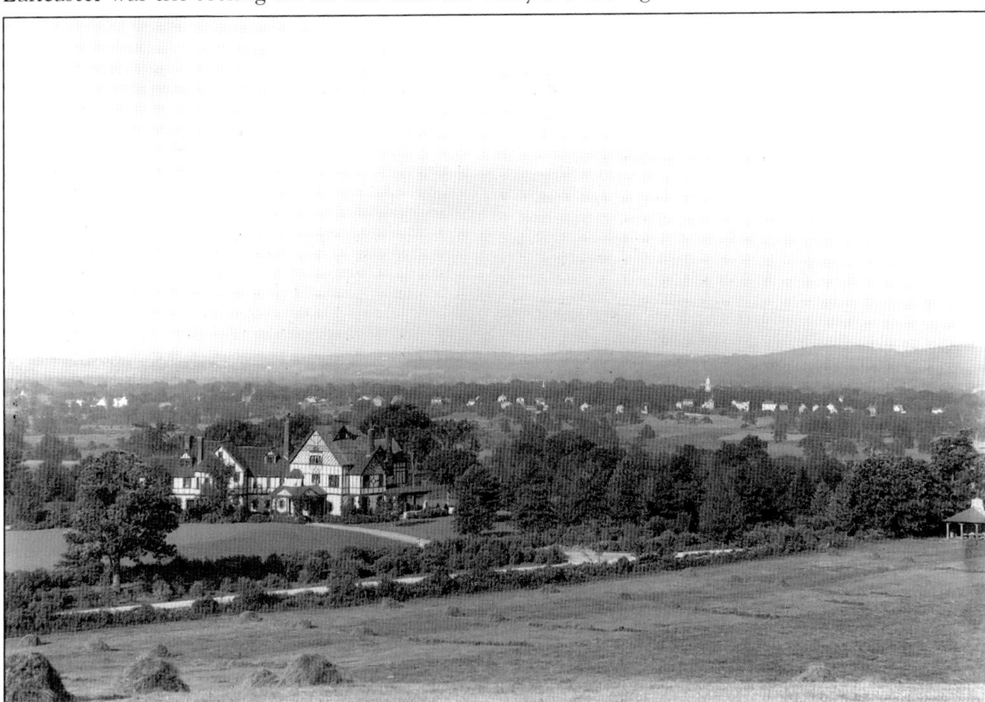

A GEORGE HILL PANORAMA. This panoramic view looking northeastward from George Hill shows the Col. John E. Thayer estate with buildings along the town's Main Street in the distance.

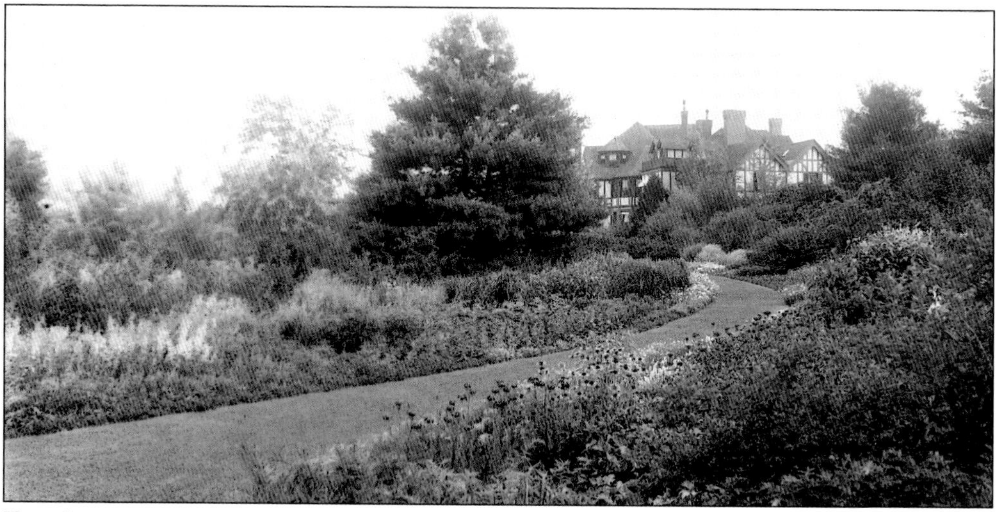

THE COL. JOHN E. THAYER ESTATE. This view shows the beautifully landscaped Col. John E. Thayer estate on George Hill. The architects for the mansion, which was built in 1886, were Boston's John Hubbard Sturgis and one of his nephews, R. Clipston Sturgis. After the Thayers passed away, their youngest son Duncan had 14 rooms removed from the house. It stayed in family hands for several years and is still a private residence today.

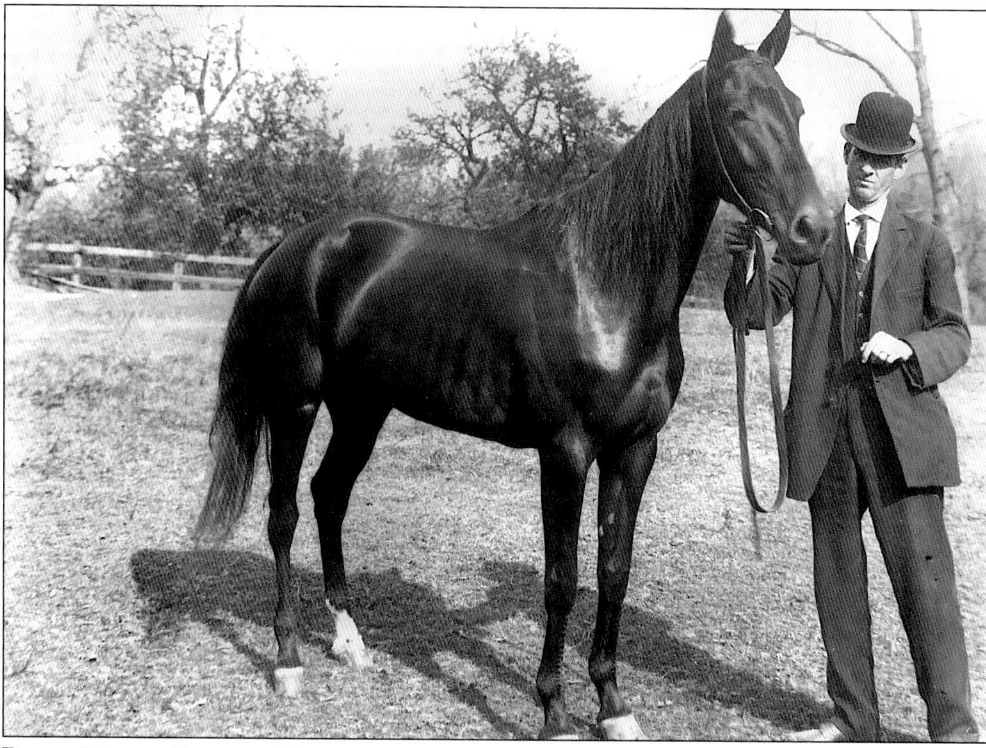

BARON WILKES. Shown with his groom is Col. John E. Thayer's famous Baron Wilkes. Thayer had a great interest in breeding fine harness horses at his Maplehurst Stock Farm, which was located at the end of a long drive on Goss Lane at the west end of Prescott Street in South Lancaster. To increase interest in fine harness horses, he organized and incorporated the Clinton-Lancaster Driving Park Association, which was located in the Greeley Hill area of Clinton.

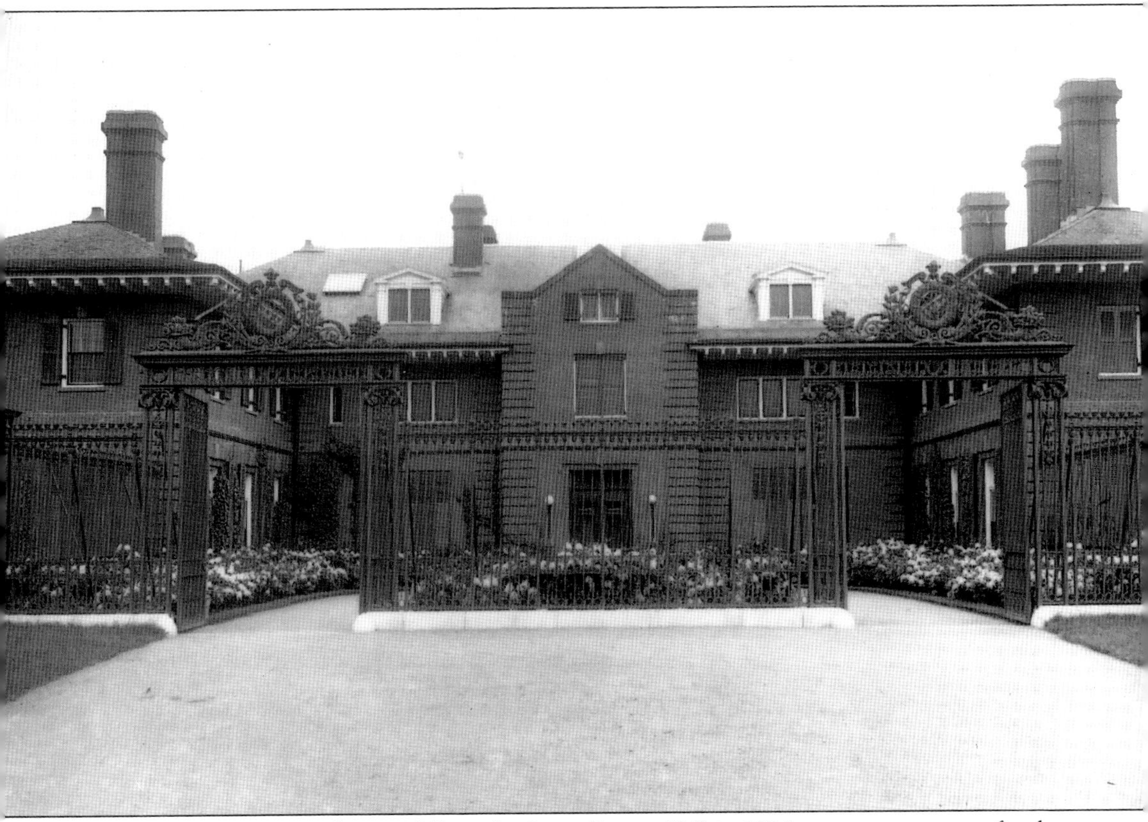

HAWTHORNE HILL. Hawthorne Hill was built on George Hill in 1904 as a country estate for the Bayard Thayer family. This ambitious undertaking combined some of the finest Boston talent of the day. Architect Guy Lowell worked with landscape architect and brother-in-law Robson Sargent on the placement of the house and gardens. (Robson's father was renowned Charles S. Sargent of the Arnold Arboretum.) Later, landscape architects Arthur Little and Herbert Browne did alterations on the gardens, and Ogden Codman (a nephew of John Hubbard Sturgis) did the estate's interior design. Since then, the property has had several owners. In 1953, the estate was a Catholic retreat house known locally as the Cenacle. Most recently, it was the Maharishi Ayurveda Health Center, which was established in 1986 by Dr. Deepak Chopra.

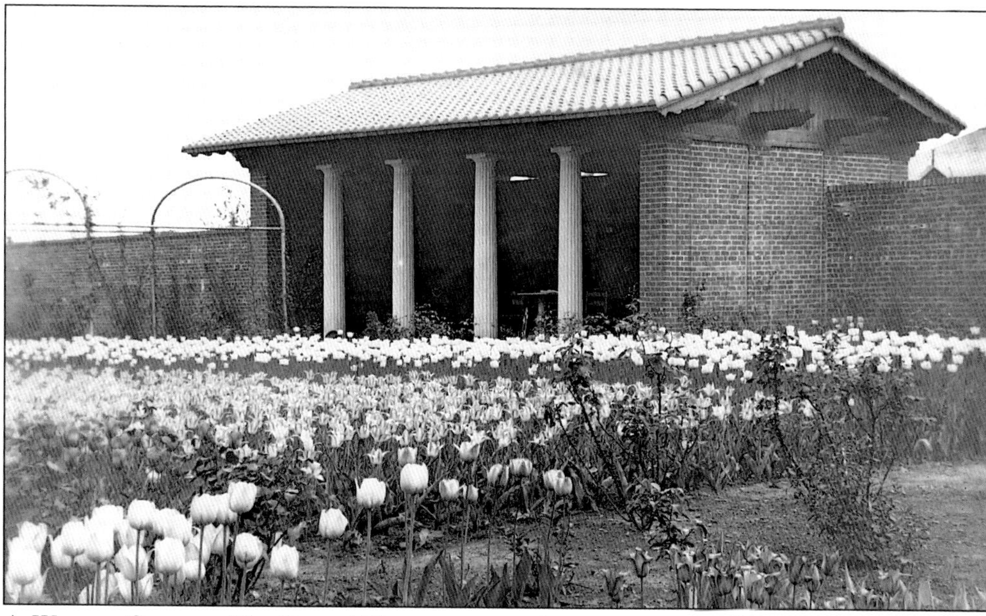

A Walled Garden. The Bayard Thayer estate in Lancaster was well-known for its beautiful gardens. Shown here is the one-acre, English walled garden, which was started in 1908. Spring flowers were confined to this space. Each year, no less than 75,000 bulbs would be planted, including narcissi, daffodils, lilies, and (as shown here) tulips, truly creating a display that was "gorgeous in the extreme."

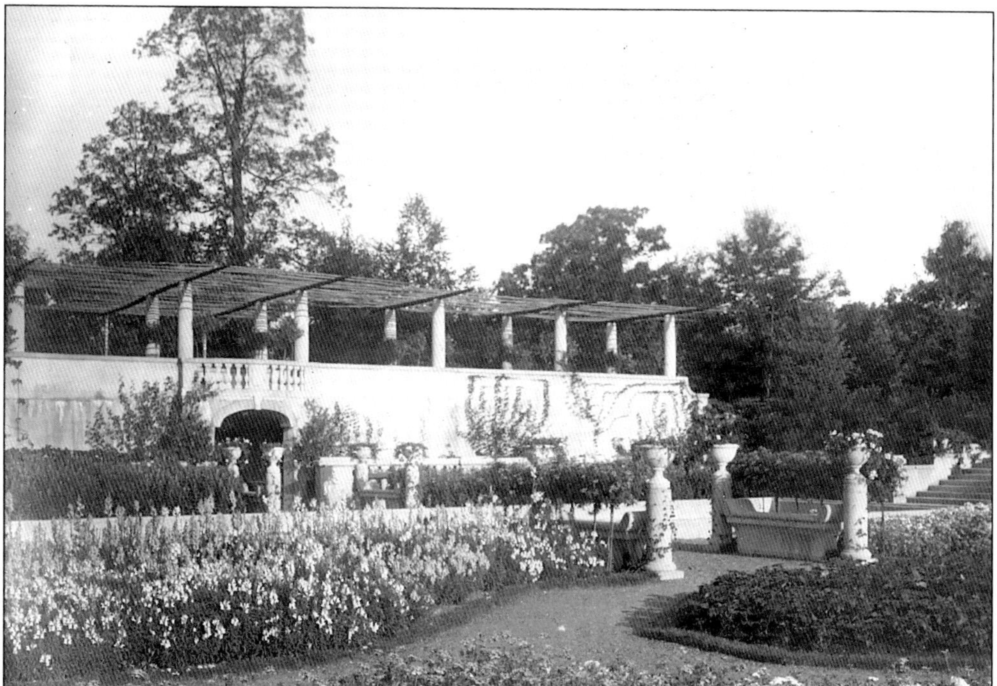

The Italian Garden. This views show some of the profuse plantings in the Italian Garden area at Hawthorne Hill. For many years, at appointed times, the estate gardens would be opened so the townspeople could enjoy their beauty.

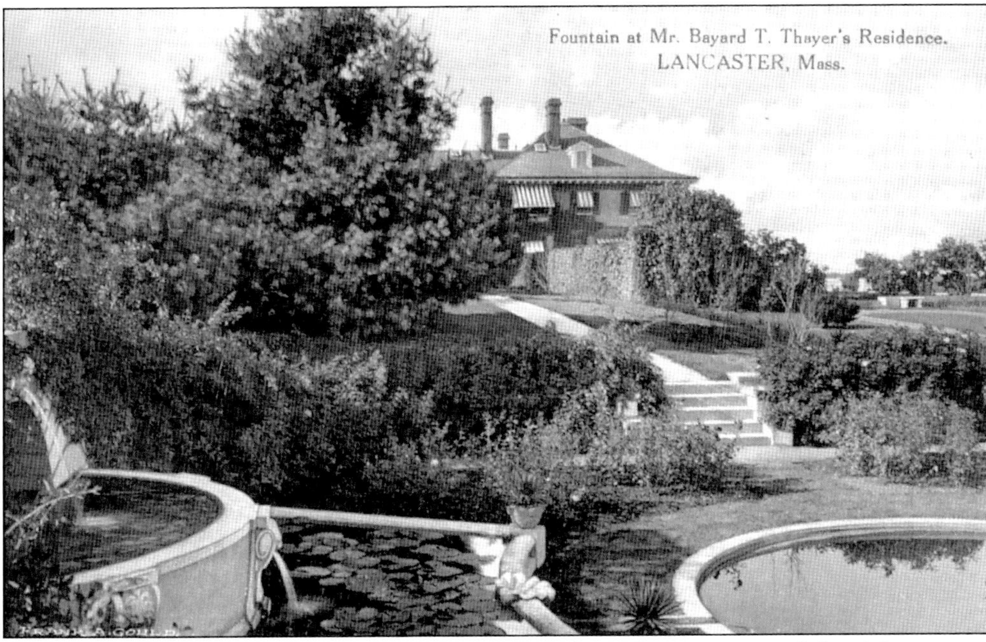

A Postcard View of Hawthorne Hill Gardens. Shown here is a view of the elaborate rose garden, fountain, and lotus pool.

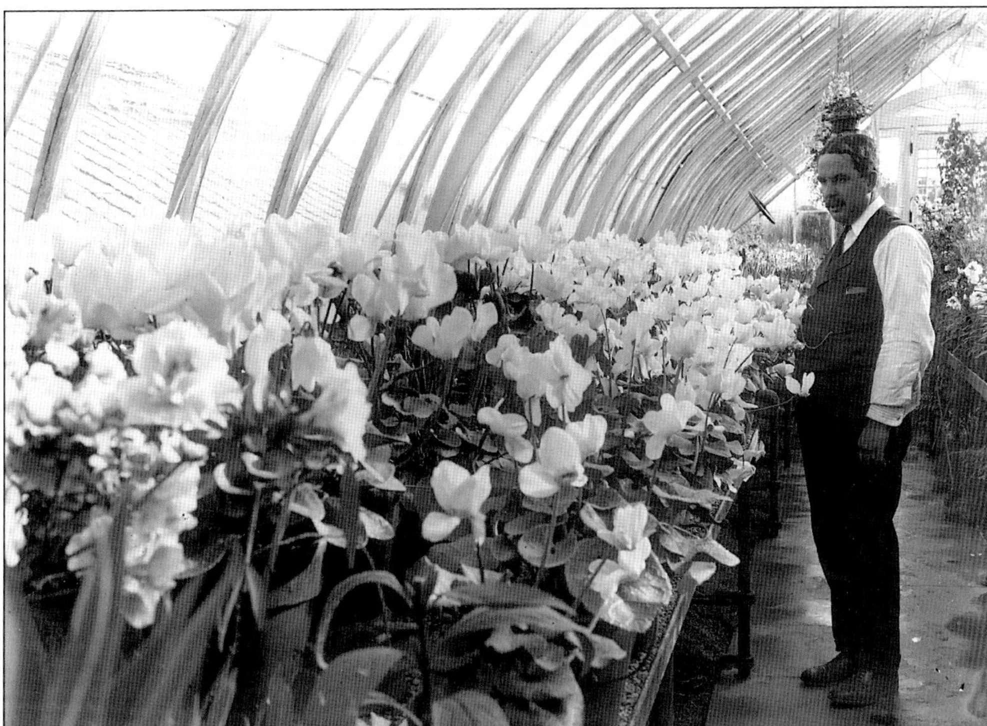

Hothouse Blooms. In one of the hothouses on the Bayard Thayer estate, an unidentified gardener looks over some of his beautiful blooms. In the early 20th century, groups of horticulturalists were often invited to the estate for field days.

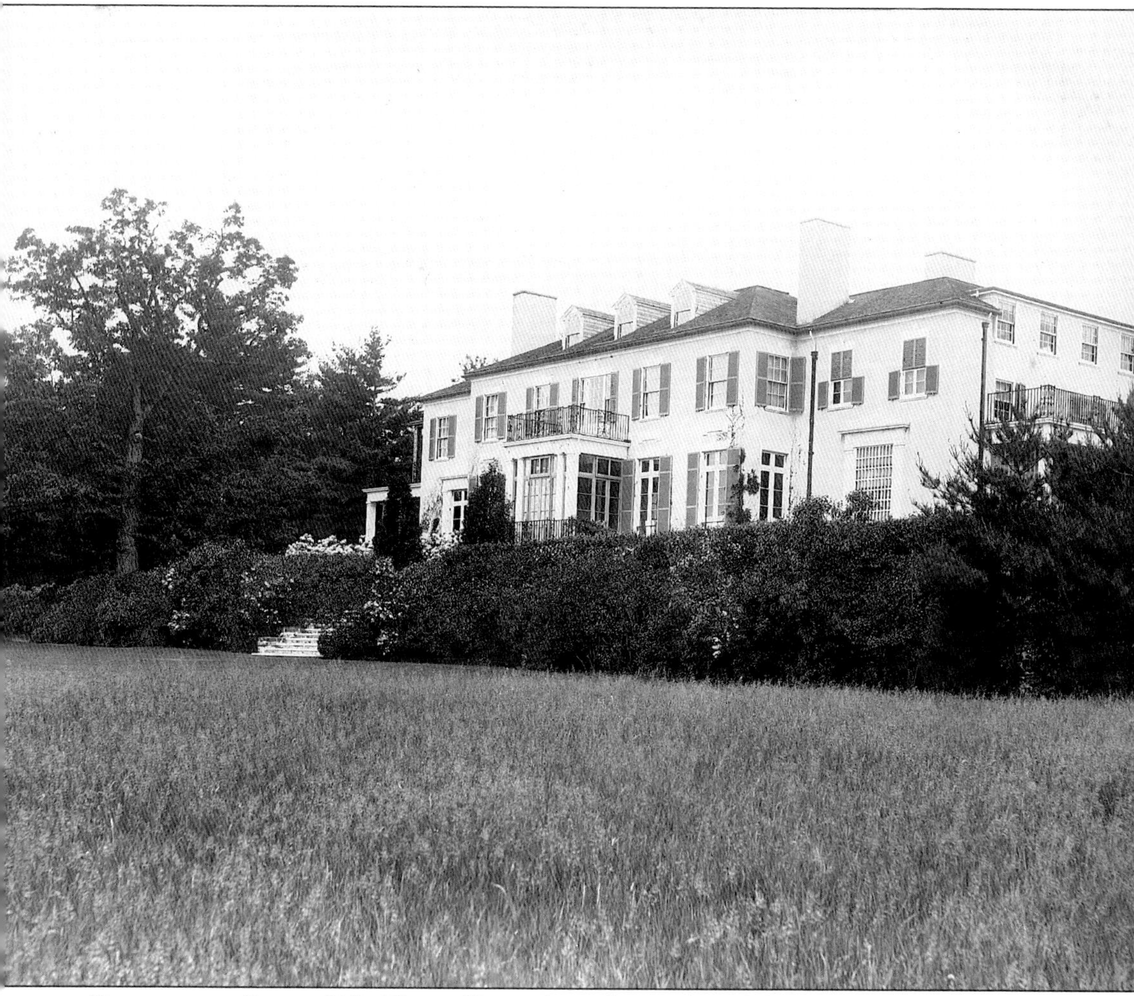

Crownledge. Eugene V.R. Thayer II was the only member of the fourth generation to build an estate in Lancaster. Plans for Crownledge, as the estate was known, were drawn up by the architectural firm of Wadsworth and Bigelow in 1908. (Henry Forbes Bigelow, grand-nephew of carpet loom inventor Erastus Bigelow, was well known to the family and, in fact, soon married Thayer's sister Susan.) Interior design for the $200,000 house was most likely done by Ogden Codman, who was frequently commissioned by the Thayer family to work on its homes in Boston, Lancaster, and Newport. Today, the mansion, located on Langen Road, is a private preparatory school called the Trivium. (Kilbourn.)

Eight

"That New England School"

"Lancaster . . . has been for many years a favorite for those who, in the heat of summer, seek rest and retirement from the city. . . . Its streets are lined with venerable elms, whose massive trunks and wide-spreading tops seem to give promise of security, comfort and abundance of refreshing shade. Many of the residences are backed with orchards and wide-rolling meadows. . . . Nothing is cramped or crowded, but everything is open and generous without being lavish." So observed new Lancaster resident Goodloe Harper Bell, first principal of South Lancaster Academy, in an 1882 edition of the *Review and Herald*. It was in this country setting that Advent pioneers chose to establish their work. As a people of strong conviction, Seventh-Day Adventists flourished in the South Village, and their small New England school became what is today Atlantic Union College.

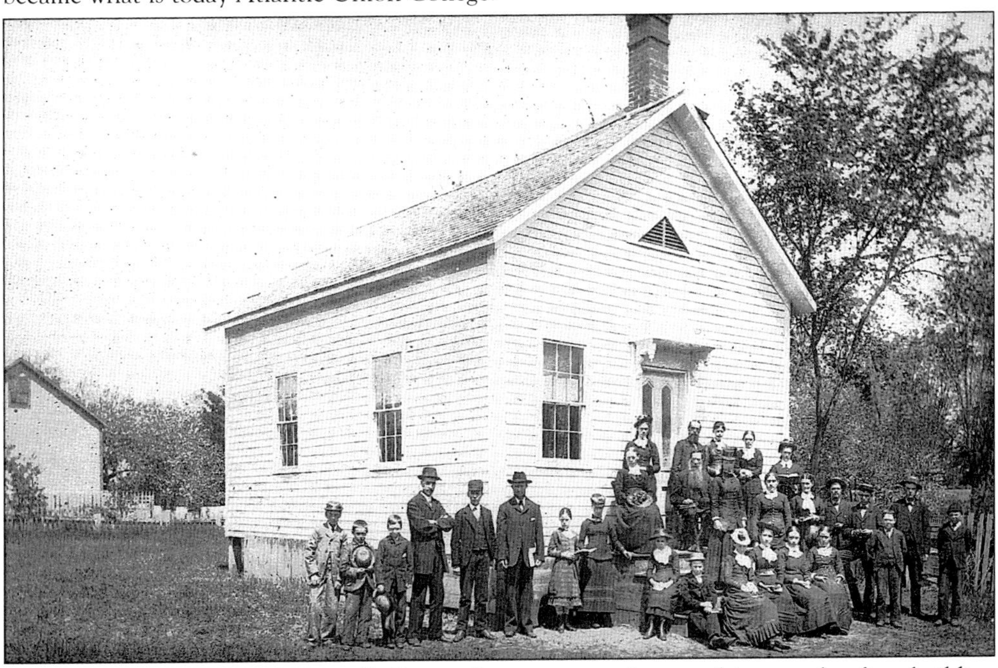

"That New England School." Originally a carriage house, this was the first building designated a school by Seventh-Day Adventists in South Lancaster. The first term opened on April 19, 1882. At first, it was referred to simply as "that New England school" by church leaders. On December 12, 1883, it was incorporated as South Lancaster Academy. The building (no longer standing) was located off Main Street near the Village Church. (AUC.)

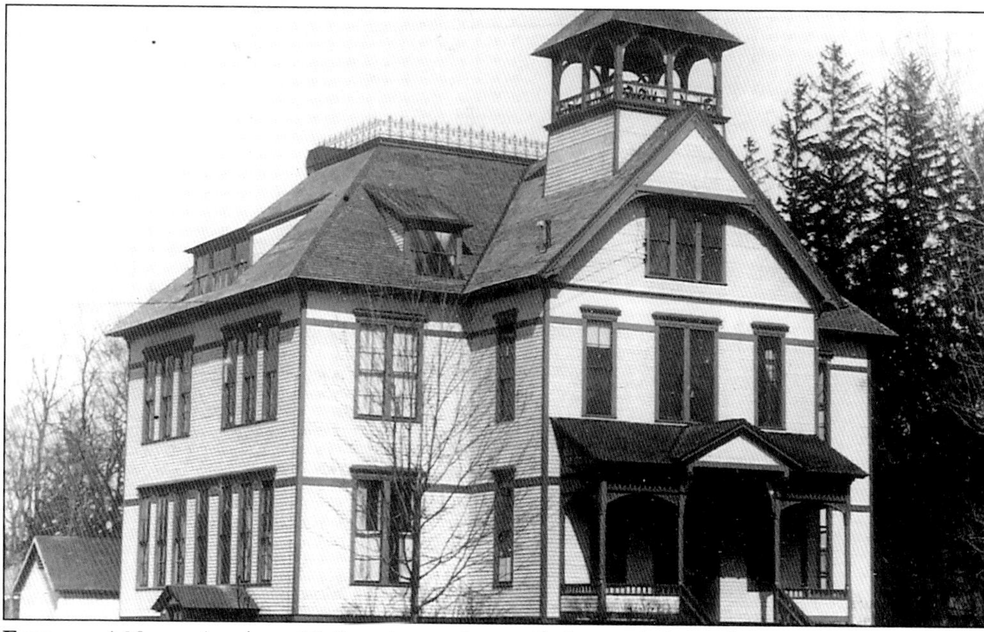

Founders' Hall. Academy Hall, as it was then called, was dedicated on October 17, 1884. It is the oldest Seventh-Day Adventist educational building still existing in the denomination's educational system. Used for classroom instruction, administration, and as a music department, it is currently a religion center and contains Adventist memorabilia in addition to full-length portraits of William Miller and his wife, Lucy Paulina Miller, by American primitive artist Horace Bundy. (AUC.)

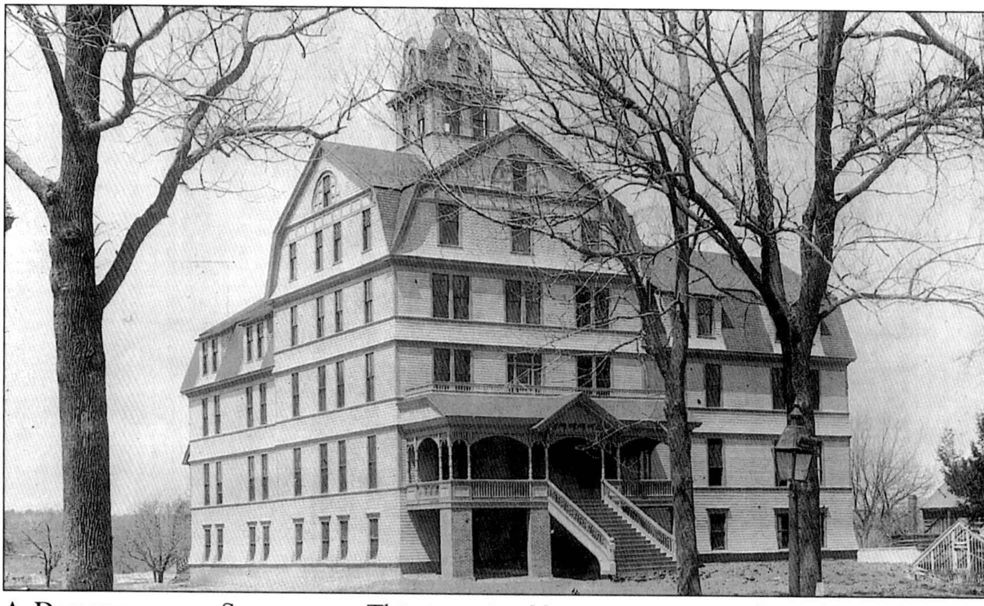

A Dormitory and Sanitarium. This imposing Victorian structure, formerly on the north corner of Flagg and Main Streets in the South Village, was built and used as a dormitory for South Lancaster Academy from 1895 to 1899 and then as a sanitarium from 1899 to 1902. Shortly thereafter, Col. John E. Thayer bought the property, the sanitarium was relocated, and the Thayer Bird Museum was built on the site. (Grout.)

THE SOUTH LANCASTER SANITARIUM

Is a place where chronic invalids of all classes are trained into healt by the aid of systematic regimen, scientific hydrotherapy, massage, Swedis gymnastics, and other rational means.

It is located in one of the most picturesque and beautiful villages of Massachusetts—affording a delightful haven for tired brains and nerves. South Lancaster adjoins Clinton, and is readily accessible from Boston and other principal cities. This well appointed institution is [illegible] in affiliation with the world-renowned Battle Creek (Mich.) Sanitarium. All of the Battle Creek Sanitarium health foods are included on its menus.

Special attention is given to diet and digestive disorders. Baths of every description, includin electric light baths. Electricity in every forn Massage and Swedish movements by trained m nipulators. Aseptic operating room and surgic ward. Accurate diagnosis assisted by laborato investigations, chemical, bacteriological, micr scopical. A large corps of physicians and train nurses of both sexes. Special departments for th treatment of diseases of the Eye, Ear, Nose, an Throat; and diseases peculiar to women.

For circulars and further information, address

C. C. NICOLA, M. D., Supt., or

THE SANITARIUM, South Lancaster, Mass

State-of-the-Art Healthcare. This card advertises the short-lived South Lancaster Sanitarium, which was operated from 1899 to 1902. It was affiliated with the world-renowned Battle Creek Sanitarium in Michigan, which was under the direction of medical superintendent John Harvey Kellogg. The "San" was moved to Stoneham, Massachusetts, where it continued for many years. (Grout.)

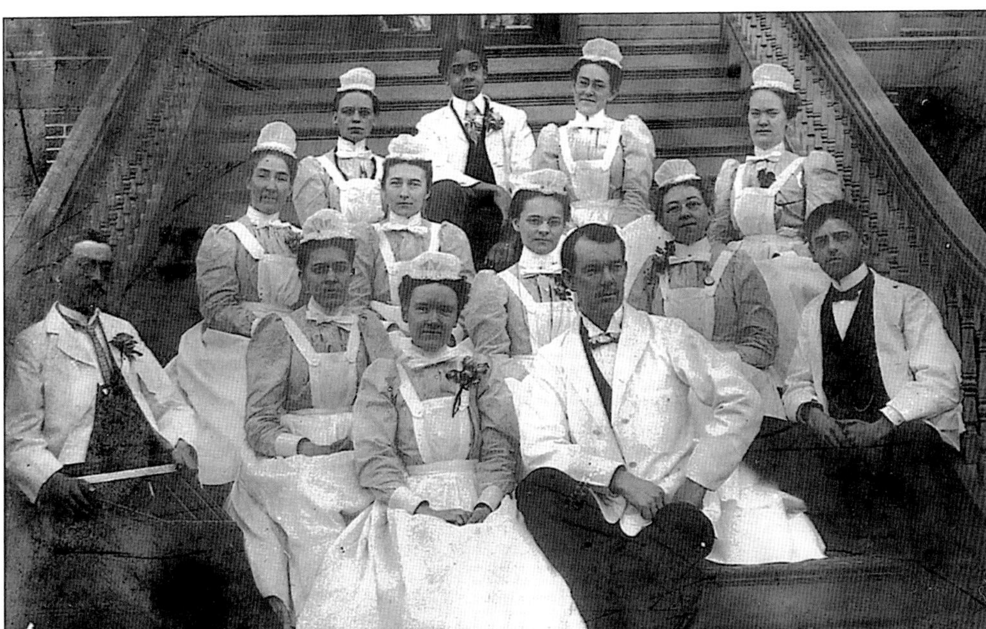

The Medical Staff at San. The medical staff of the South Lancaster Sanitarium take time out to pose for a photograph. (Grout.)

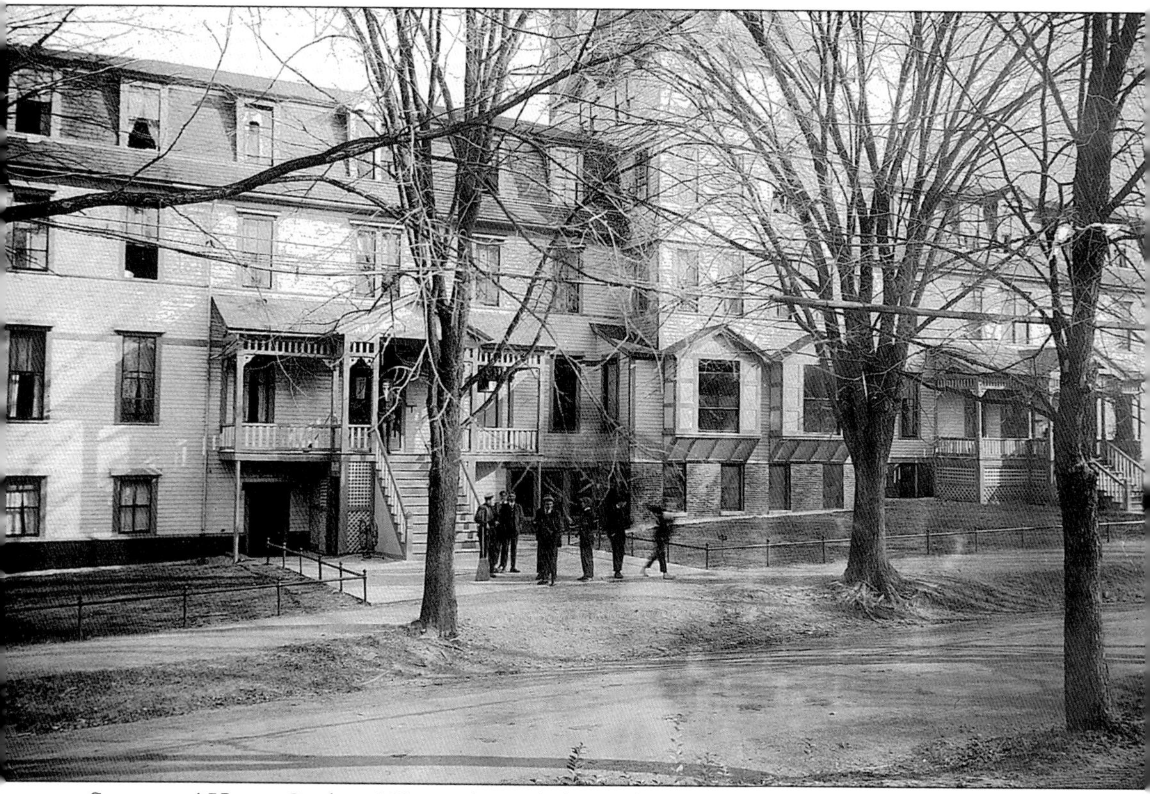

STUDENTS' HOME. Students' Home, formerly located on Prescott Street where the Chan Shun Dining Commons stands today, was built in 1884 to provide much needed housing for students attending South Lancaster Academy. Life was not easy in the early days. On cold mornings, a student's first task would be to coax a fire to start in the little black stove furnished in every bedroom. Also, those living on the second floor had the advantage over those above with the luxury of running water in their bathroom tank. The pumping system lacked sufficient force to reach the third floor. Later, a west wing was added to the rambling building, and it became known as East-West Hall. In its last years, the building was used only as a girls' dormitory and was torn down *c.* 1965–1967, when South Lancaster Academy (which used the AUC campus) ceased to be a boarding school. (AUC.)

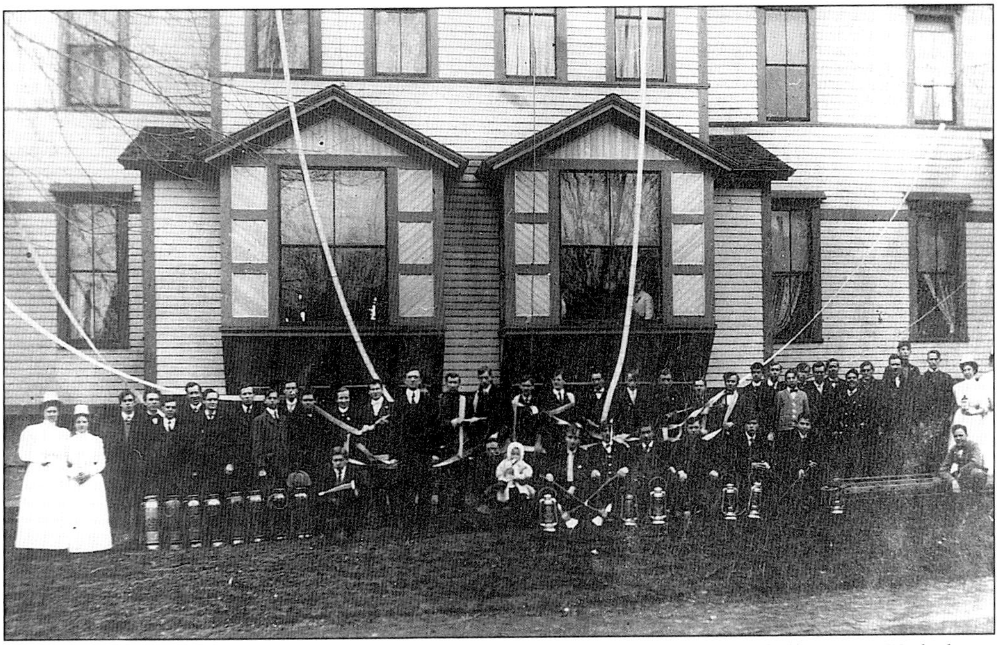

THE FIRE DRILL TEAM. Shown here is an early boys' dormitory fire drill team. With large wooden structures, fire was a very real danger in the early days. The Academy building did, in fact, have a fire on December 4, 1907. It damaged about half a dozen rooms and half of the library's collection. The estimated damage was $2,700. (AUC.)

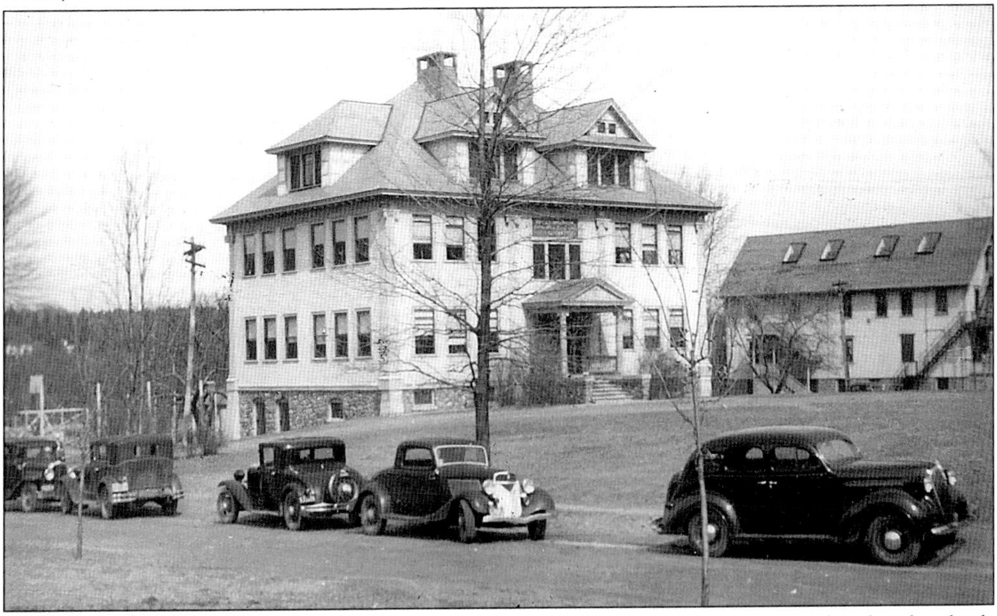

THE BROWNING MEMORIAL SCHOOL. Shown here is the Browning Memorial School, which once stood on the site of Atlantic Union College's Jones Library. Funds to build the school were given by Hansa A. Browning of Darien Center, New York, in memory of her brother, New York banker John T. Browning. The $20,000 "normal building" was a welcome addition to the school's teacher training program. The building's cornerstone, dated October 12, 1912, is still on the campus grounds. (AUC.)

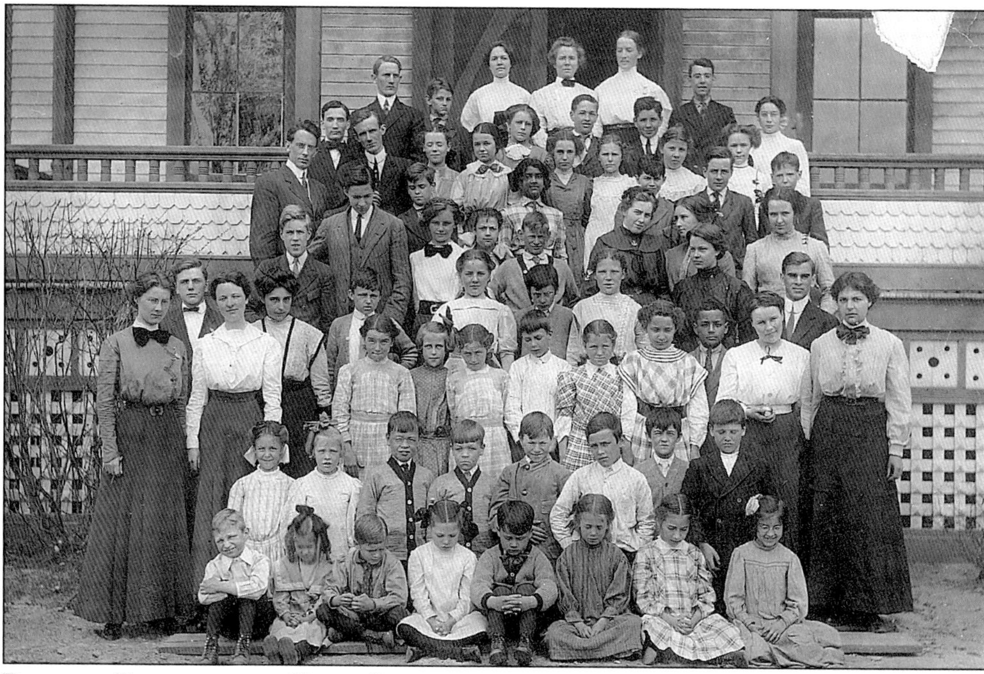

Practice Teachers and Their Students. Posing in front of Academy Hall during the 1913–1914 school year is a group of practice teachers enrolled in the normal course with their young students. (AUC.)

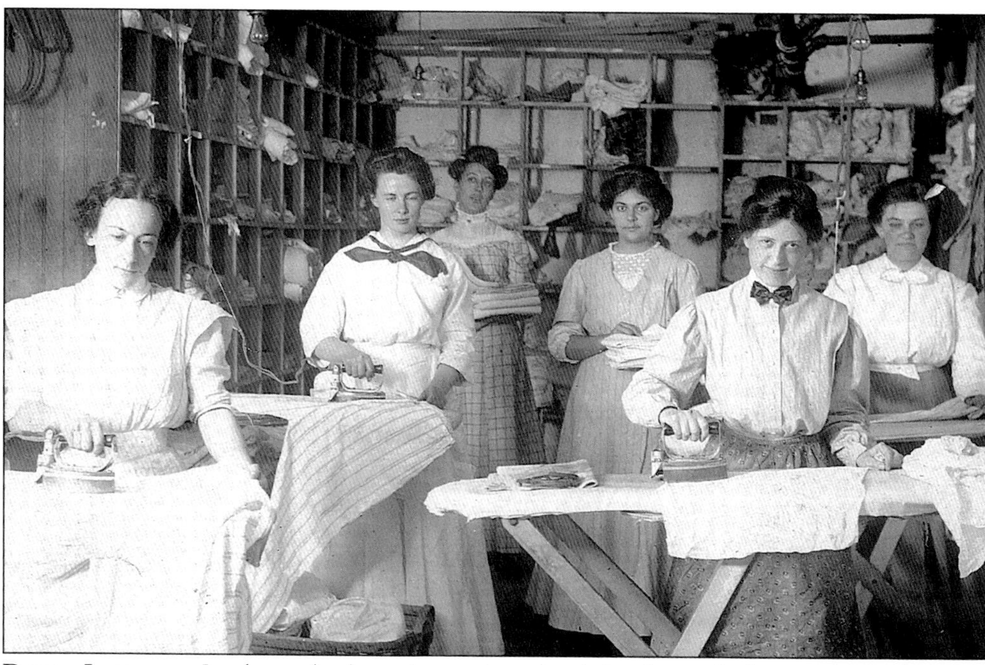

Doing Laundry. In the early days, the entire school family pitched in to keep the place running smoothly. Here, laundry workers diligently tend to their tasks. (AUC.)

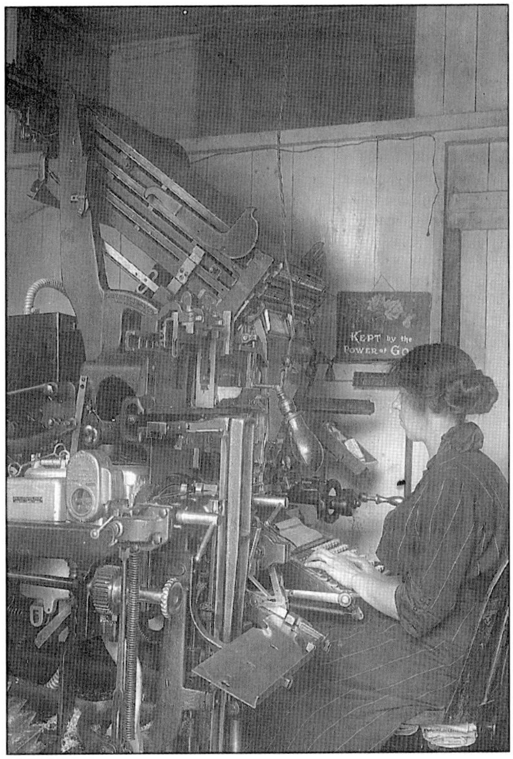

The South Lancaster Printing Company. Reaching people through the printed word was of particular interest to the school's founder, Stephen N. Haskell. Off and on through the years, the school operated printing establishments (in various locations) using student labor. Shown here on her linotype machine is a young woman on the job at the South Lancaster Printing Company. (AUC.)

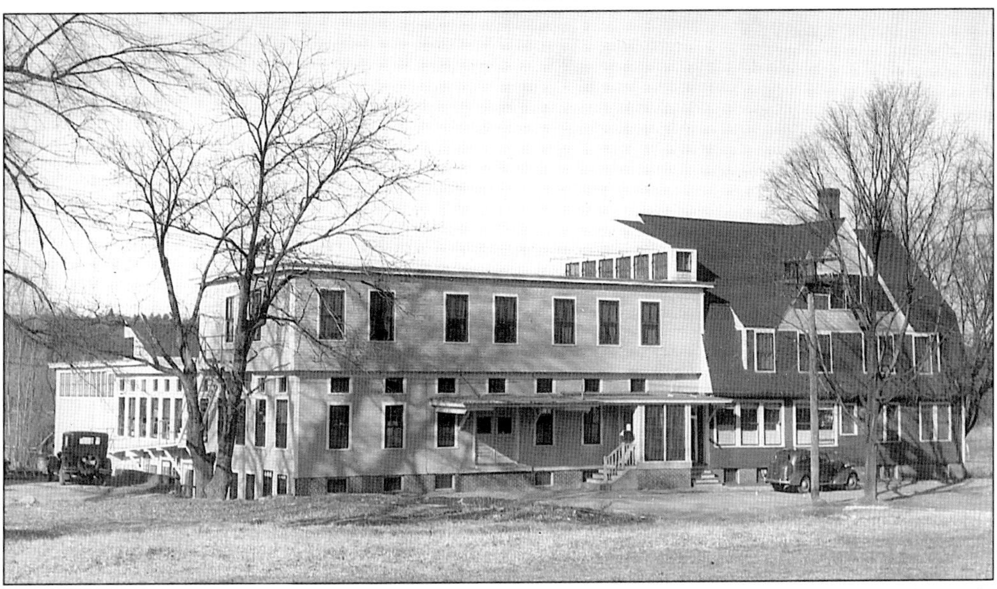

The E.E. Miles Bindery. This photograph shows the E.E. Miles Bindery, which was formerly located on the west corner of Flagg and Orchard Streets. Miles, who originally came to head the Bible department of the Academy in 1886, decided in 1902 to expand his home-based "vest pocket" dictionary sideline by building a bindery to provide students employment to help them work their way through school. To give the plant an architecturally pleasing appearance, he built it to resemble a house. Additions were later made to the south and west. In 1976, the E.E. Miles Bindery Company ceased operations. In 1993, the building was demolished. (AUC.)

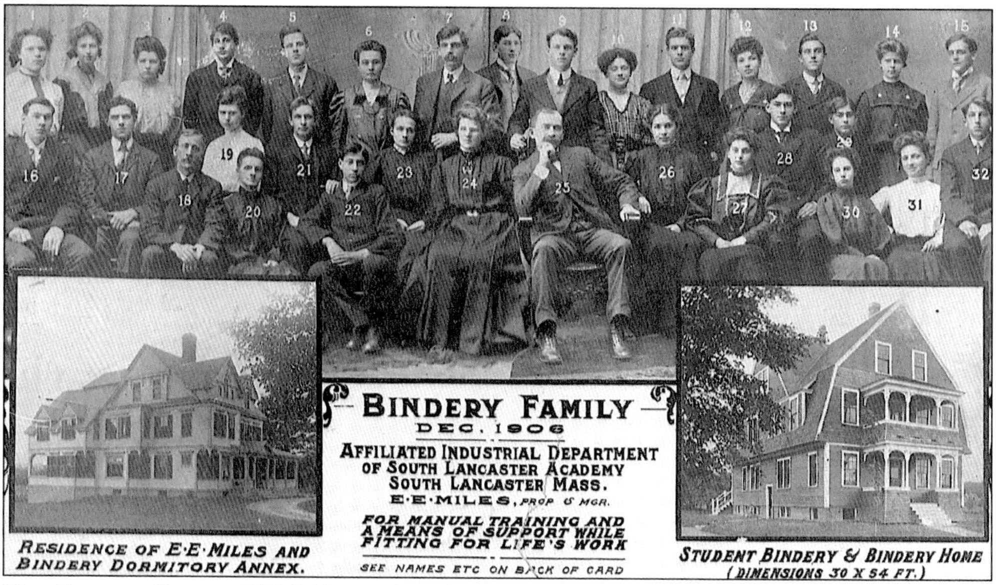

THE BINDERY FAMILY. E.E. Miles took a deep interest in his student employees. Emphasizing character education in addition to learning manual skills, he began each work week with a lecture or sermon to which employees were paid to listen. Once he began, no one was allowed to punch in on the time clock until he was finished. Many former student employees have expressed positive memories of their days in the Miles Bindery "family." (Taylor.)

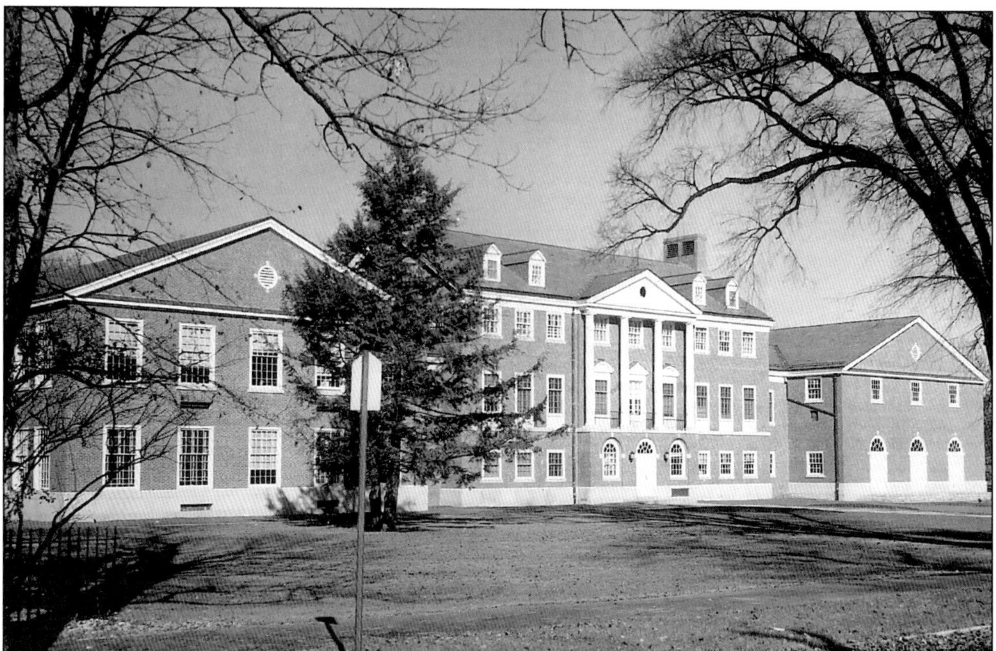

HASKELL HALL. Haskell Hall, on the campus of Atlantic Union College, is the main administration building today. It was begun in 1938. However, due to a shortage of building materials, it was not completed until 1952. It is located near the site of the town's early ministerial lands. (AUC.)

Nine

Points of Interest and Portrait Gallery

"Life has never seemed to me tame or uninteresting anywhere; but this season is glorified in my memory . . . by the objective reality of so many rare individualities congregated together." Educator, writer, and publisher Elizabeth Palmer Peabody was commenting on the years from 1820 to 1822, when she, as a young woman, lived in Lancaster with her family. Through the years, many outstanding and influential personalities have lived in and been associated with Lancaster. Some of the town's special places and people of interest are shown on the pages that follow.

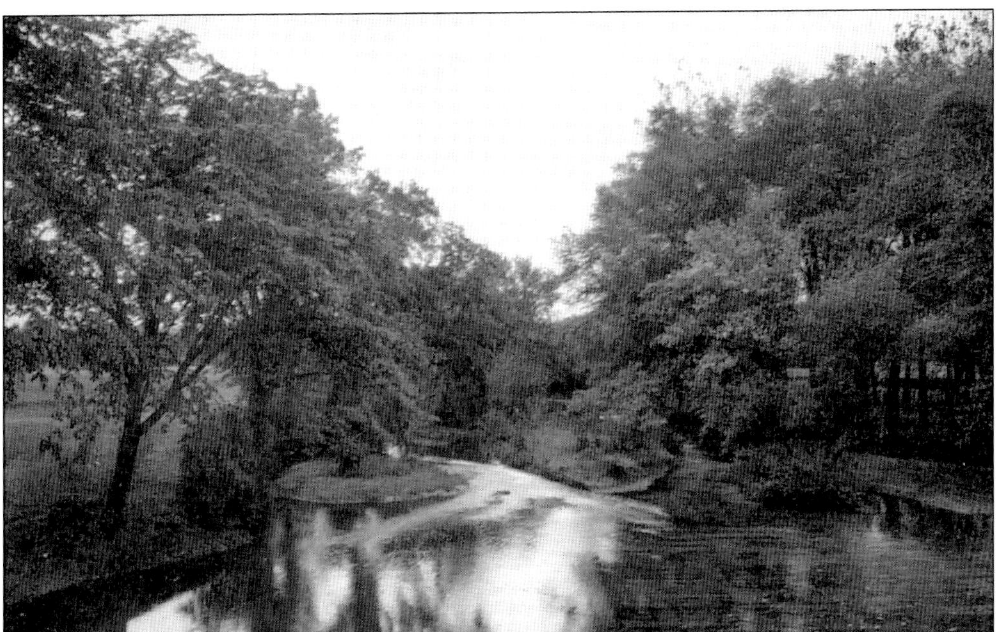

"Meeting of the Waters." Many of Lancaster's earliest families settled in the fertile "neck" area not far from the "Meeting of the Waters," near the bridge on Center Bridge Road. Here, the north and south branches of the Nashua River converge and flow north. Once considered one of the 10 dirtiest rivers in the country, it has made a remarkable recovery over the last 30 years due, in large measure, to the untiring efforts of Marion R. Stoddart of Groton. (Colley.)

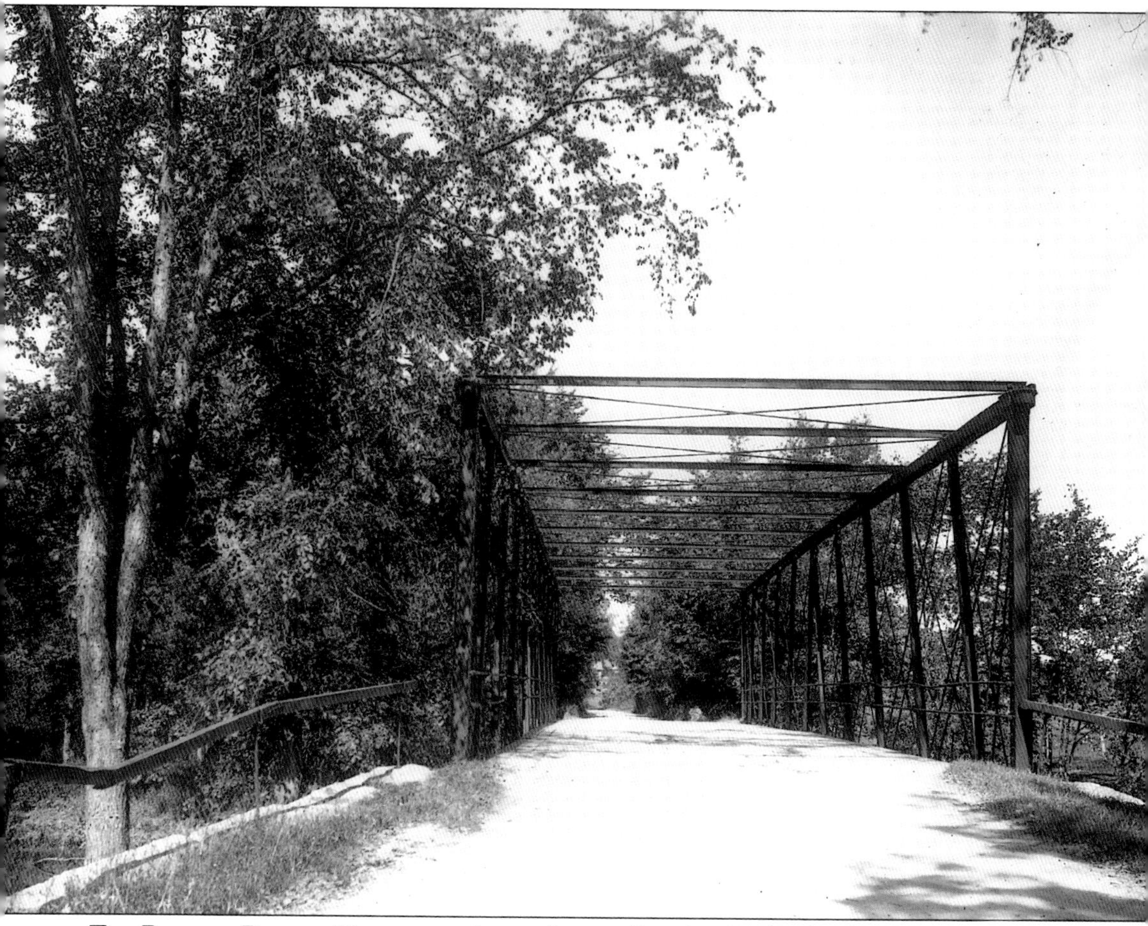

The Ponakin Bridge. The cast- and wrought-iron Ponakin Bridge (no longer in use, but still standing), spanning the north branch of the Nashua River, was built in 1871. Designed by engineer Simeon S. Post, the Post truss bridge marked the transition from bridges made of wood to those constructed of cast iron and metal. The Atherton Bridge, built in 1870, (still standing with a newer bridge nearby) on Bolton Road is also a Post truss bridge. Designed to support the weight of trains, most of this type were replaced by steel bridges as trains became heavier. The two Lancaster bridges, vast improvements over their predecessors, survived because they were used strictly for highway traffic. There are only 69 other structures from the golden age of iron bridges left in the United States.

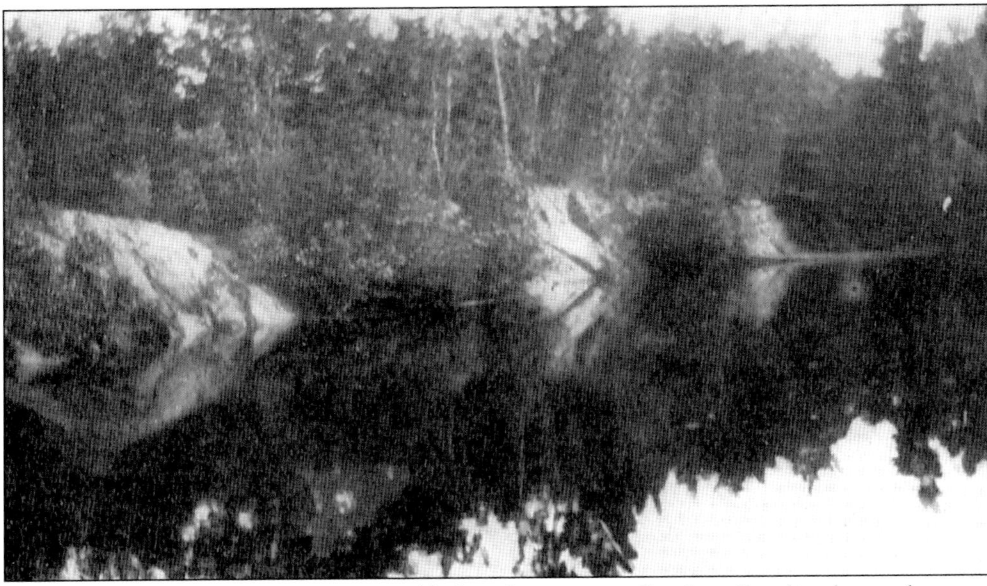

The Old Slate Quarry. Lancaster's Old Slate Quarry, near Cumbury Pond in the northeastern section of town, was discovered by a wealthy Boston architect and contractor Gershom Flagg, who owned a farm in Lancaster. In 1752, he began quarrying slate in what is thought to be the oldest slate quarry in America. The quarry was still used in the first decade of the 19th century but was then given up because transportation was expensive and because water stood deep in the pit. (Kilbourn.)

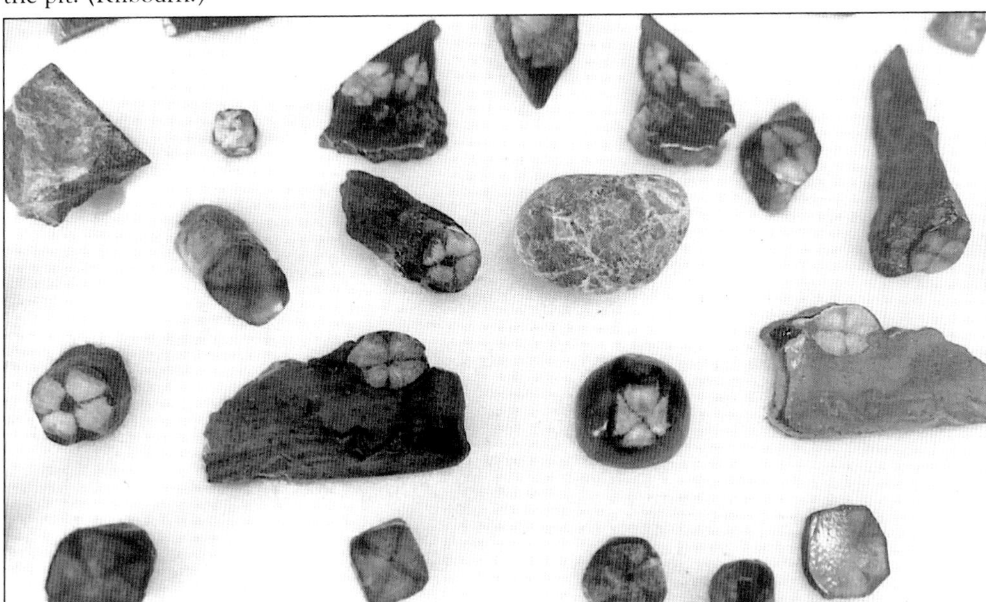

The Lancaster Cross Stones. Cross stones, found in the local hills, have long been prized by many residents. They are a unique form of the mineral andalusite (aluminum silicate) called chiastolite, from the Greek *chiastros* meaning "x-marked." According to local lore, they were worn by Native American braves as charms to give them strength. In the 19th century, it was popular to have them polished and fashioned into jewelry. They are also found in California, Pennsylvania, and Maine. (Christoph, Griffin.)

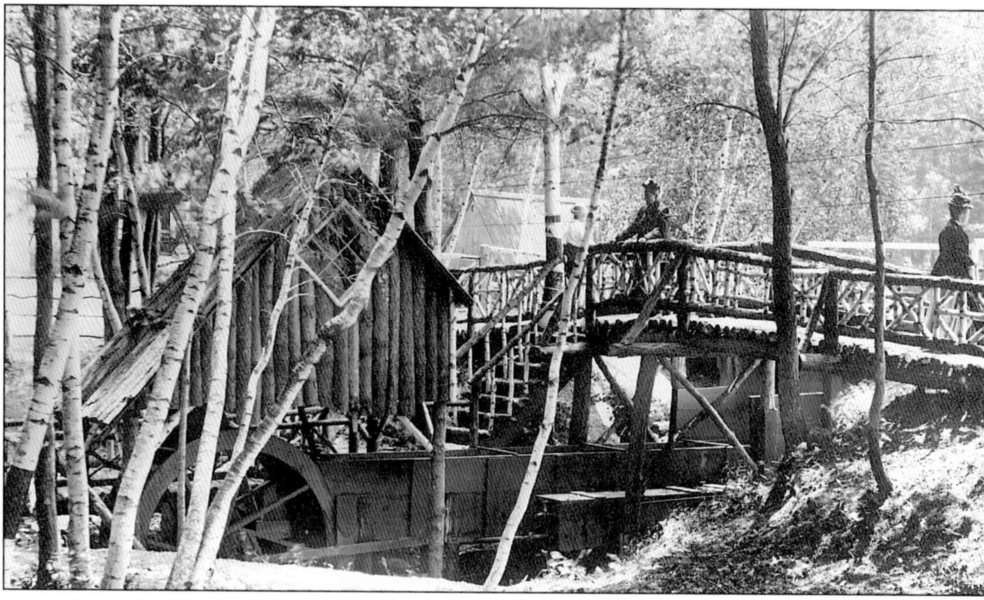

Fort Pond. Numerous private summer camps and cottages dot the shoreline on Fort Pond, near Route 2 in the northern section of town, and the pond has long been the setting for swimming, boating, and general summertime fun. Shown here is a scene from one rustic recreation area that was open to the public for a small fee.

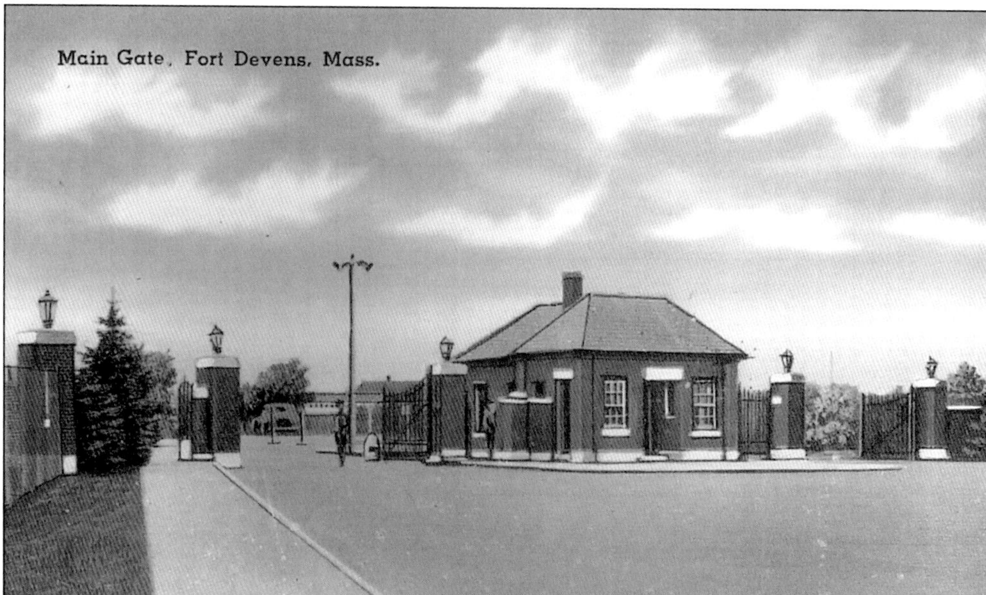

Fort Devens. In 1917, when Camp (Fort) Devens was established, the U.S. government acquired land from residents of Ayer, Harvard, Shirley, and Lancaster. In 1932, when Fort Devens became permanent, the U.S. Army continued to expand the facility. Many fine old homes and choice acres of farm land were lost to Lancaster in 1938. The 4,830 acres became known as the South Post. Although most of Devens was decommissioned in 1996, the South Post remains as a training area for U.S. Army reservists. This view was published by the Post Exchange. (DHM.)

THE GREAT "QUEEN" ELM. This picture showing the Great "Queen" Elm with a visitor beneath, gives a good indication of its mammoth size. Unfortunately, in subsequent years, many of these majestic trees were lost through Dutch elm disease and the Hurricane of 1938.

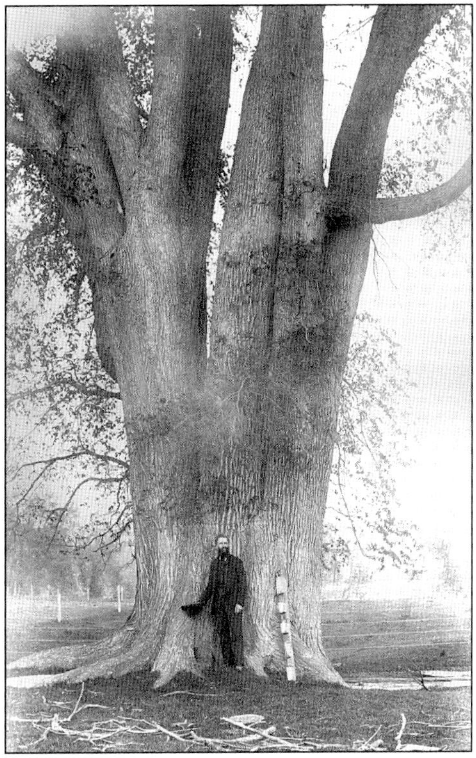

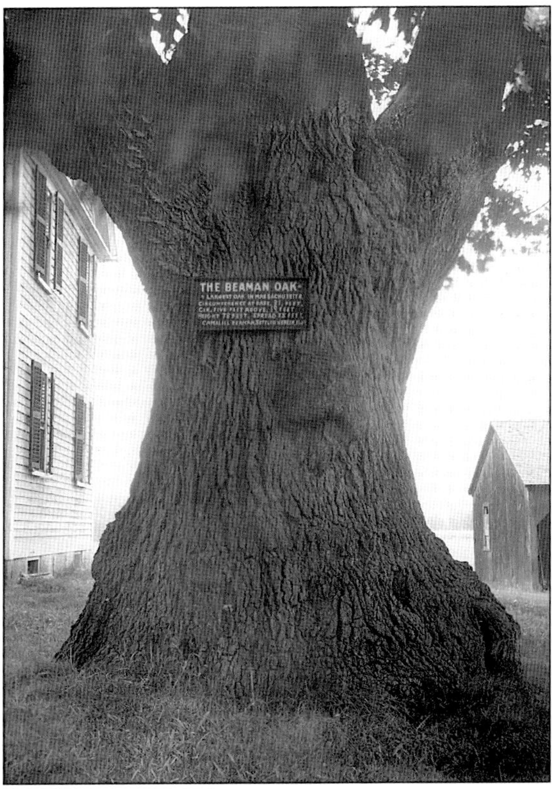

THE BEAMAN OAK. Located on the original grant of Gamaliel Beaman, who settled in Lancaster in 1659, was the Beaman Oak, a large red oak tree (*Quercus rubra*). Once the largest of its kind in Massachusetts, the circumference of the tree at its base was 31 feet and, at 5 feet above the ground, 19 feet. The height was 73 feet and the branch spread was 75 feet. The tree, along present-day Route 117, had to be removed in 1989 because its rotting parts created a danger to those in the surrounding area.

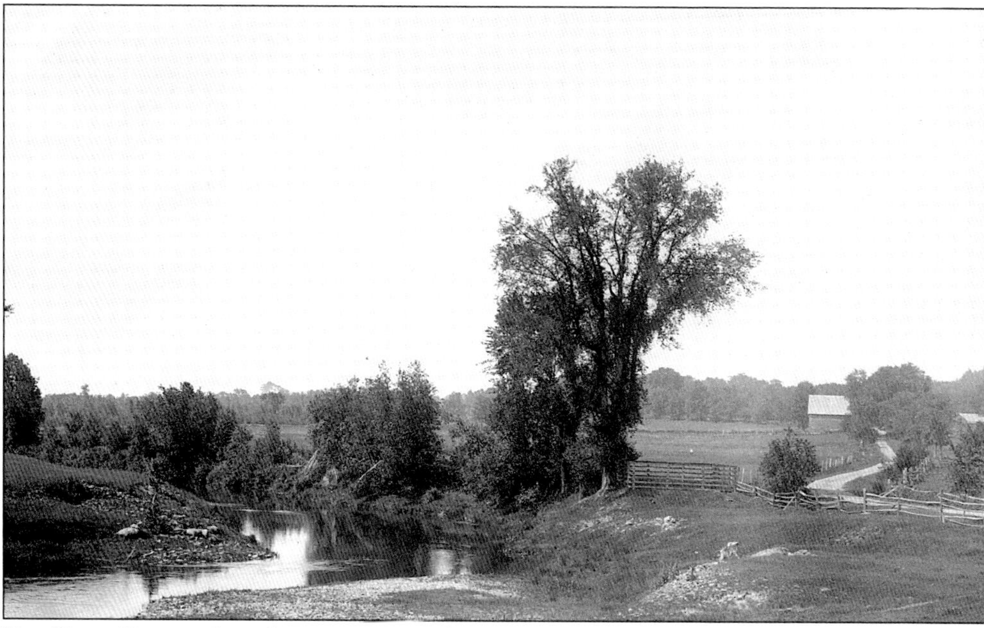

The Town Pound. In early times, wayward animals were kept confined until the owner came to claim them and pay a fee for their release. At one time, the Lancaster Town Pound was located in front of the Middle Cemetery. In 1842, it was relocated to a spot near the intersection of Back Road and Route 117. At the town meeting on March 3, 1964, an appropriation was made to reconstruct the Lancaster Town Pound. It deteriorated and, in 1993–1994, Gregory Philbin and the Lancaster Boy Scouts again refurbished the construction.

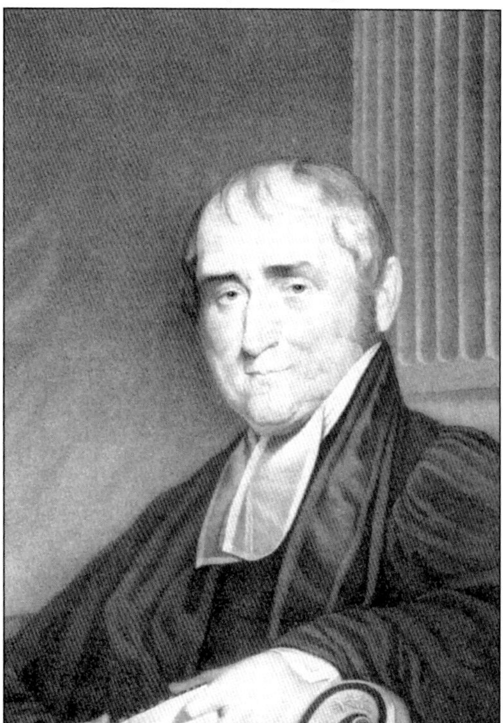

Rev. Dr. Nathaniel Thayer. A lineal descendant of John Cotton, Rev. Dr. Nathaniel Thayer, was the sixth pastor of the First Church of Christ on the Lancaster Town Green. Renowned for his eloquence in the pulpit, Thayer was influential in town affairs and the last minister to serve before the separation of church and state in the mid-1830s. His 47-year pastorate ended when he died suddenly in Rochester, New York, on June 23, 1840, at the age of 71. He is buried in the Middle Cemetery. (FC.)

REV. DR. GEORGE MURILLO BARTOL. During a pastorate that lasted an extraordinary 60 years, Rev. Dr George Murillo Bartol served the congregation of the First Church from 1847 to 1906, through the reign of Queen Victoria to the beginning of the 20th century. (FC.)

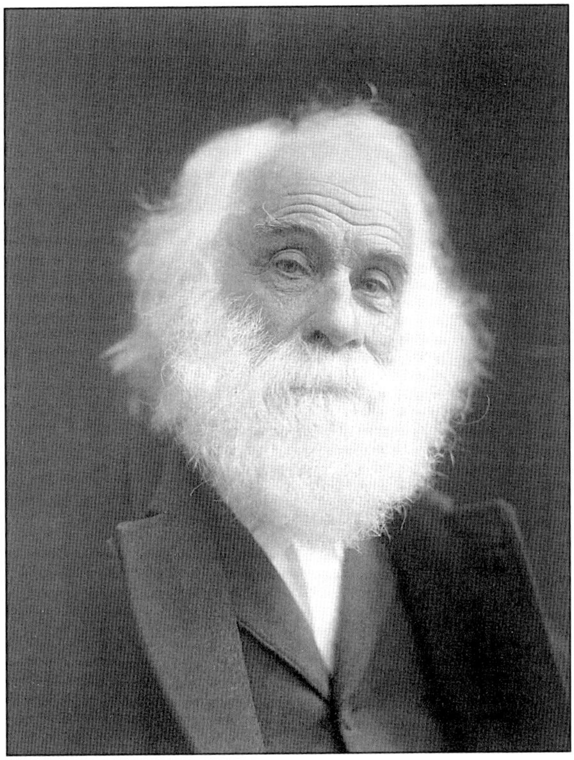

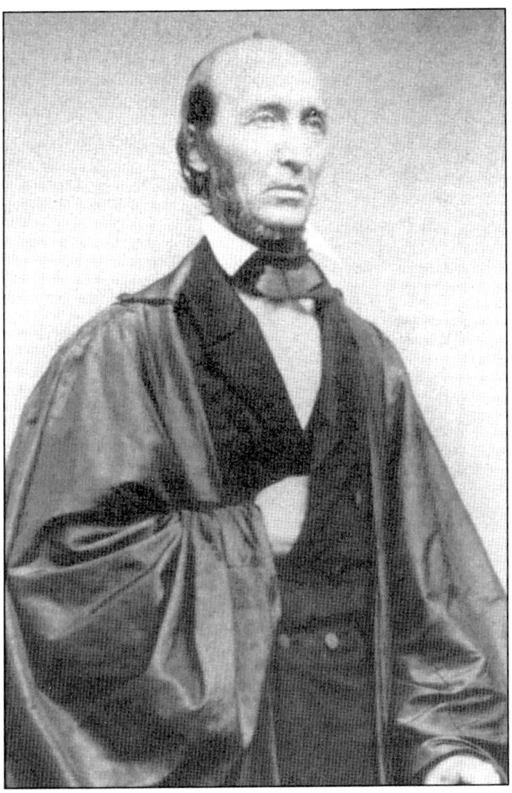

REV. EDMUND HAMILTON SEARS. The Rev. Edmund Hamilton Sears was the seventh minister of the First Church of Christ, serving the congregation from 1840 to 1847. Also a poet, he is perhaps best known for having written the well-known Christmas hymn "It Came upon a Midnight Clear." (FC.)

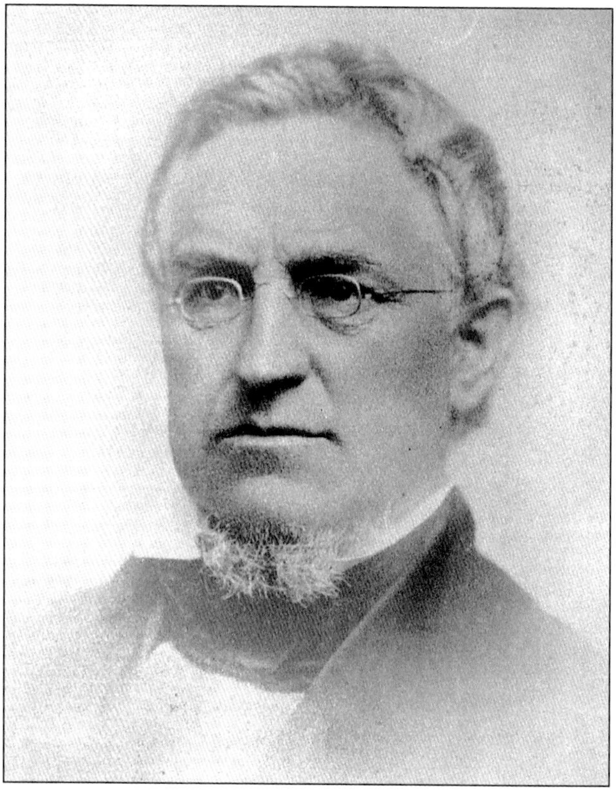

REV. CHARLES PACKARD. This is Rev. Charles Packard, who was the first minister of the Evangelical Congregational Church in Lancaster Center. Also trained as a lawyer, he served the congregation from 1840 to 1854. Considerations regarding his children's education caused him to leave Lancaster. As he was held in high esteem by his congregation, they requested that his remains be returned to Lancaster for burial when he passed away. The family, however, denied the request. (Watson.)

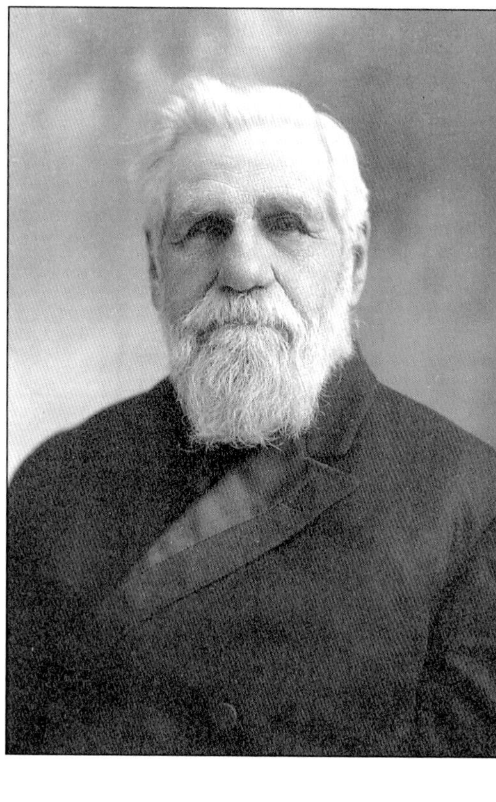

ELDER STEPHEN HASKELL. Born in Oakham, Massachusetts, in 1833, Stephen Haskell, who moved to South Lancaster in 1864, was an ambitious minister, missionary, and organizer within the early Seventh-Day Adventist Church. He is credited with being the founder of "that New England school" in 1882, which later became Atlantic Union College. (AUC.)

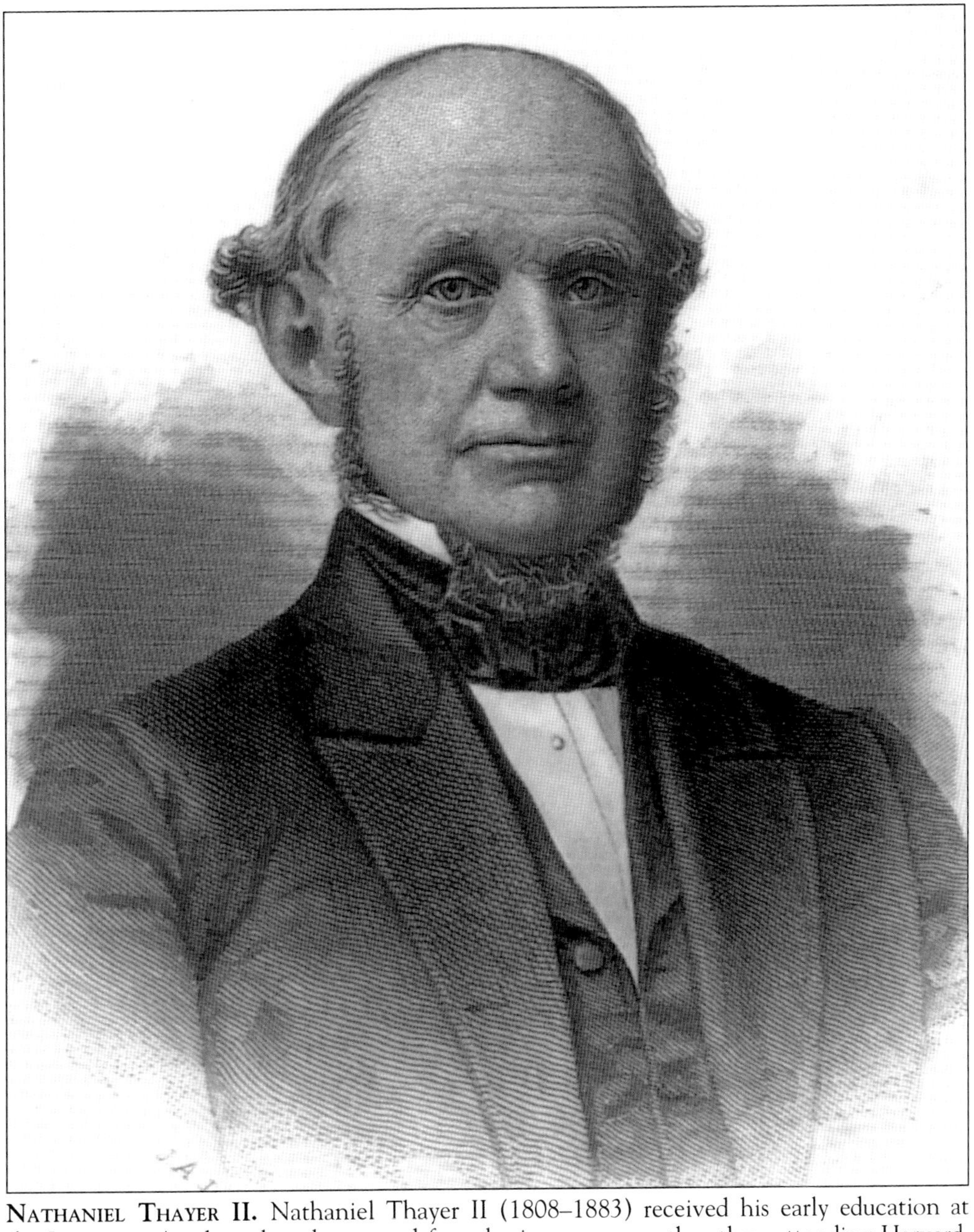

Nathaniel Thayer II. Nathaniel Thayer II (1808–1883) received his early education at the Lancaster Academy but then opted for a business career rather than attending Harvard. According to family legend, he and his elder brother John Eliot "walked to Boston and made a fortune." Both gained valuable experience in Boston's financial district and, in 1839, became partners in the firm of John E. Thayer and Brother, catering to an elite clientele. The banking house they established invested heavily in the expanding railroad industry. After the elder Thayer died in 1857, the firm was reorganized as Kidder, Peabody and Company in 1865. Rather than retire, Nathaniel Thayer II continued to invest his personal fortune not only in railroads but also in land companies, textile firms, and mines. Although he lived in Boston, he and his sons always maintained close ties to Lancaster. His family's legacy to the town is well known.

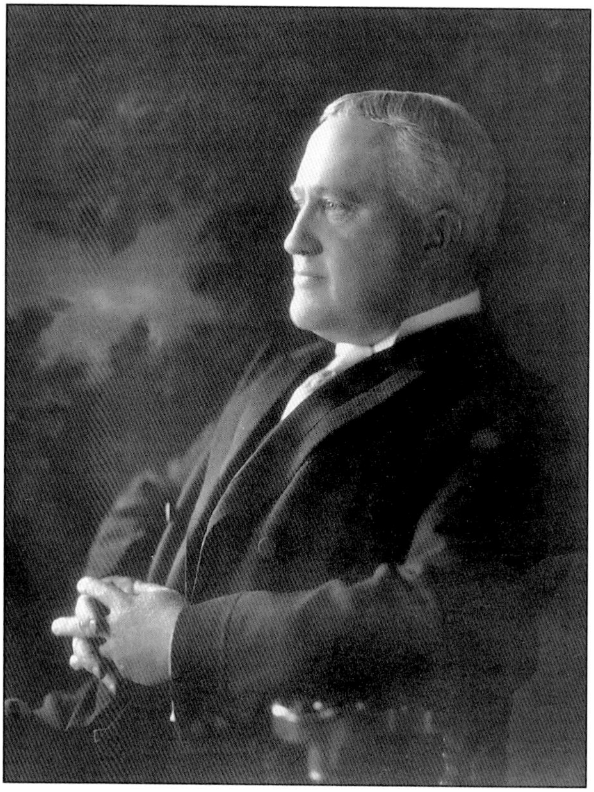

Col. John E. Thayer. Col. John E. Thayer (1861–1933) was one of twin boys born to Nathaniel Thayer II and Cornelia van Rensselaer Thayer. The longest surviving of the four brothers who maintained estates in the town, he is perhaps best known for his vast collection of North American bird specimens. Thayer's interests were broad and, in addition, he raised a variety of dog breeds and harness horses at his Maplehurst Stock Farm. He took an active interest in town affairs, serving as selectman and tree warden for many years.

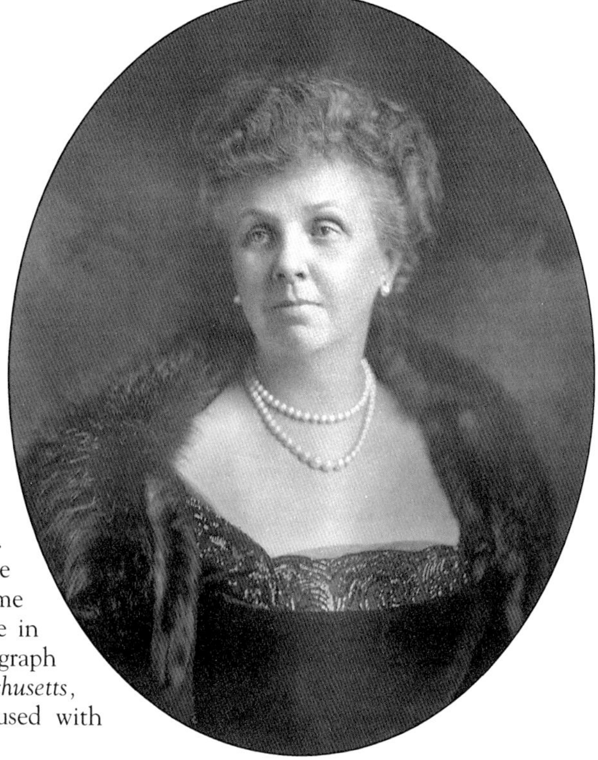

Pauline Revere Thayer. Pauline Revere Thayer (1862–1934) great-granddaughter of Paul Revere and second wife of Nathaniel Thayer III, lived in the Homestead for many years after her husband inherited it. Known for her many philanthropic endeavors, she was the "acknowledged leader of Boston society" in her day. Nathaniel Thayer III and Pauline Revere Thayer also maintained a home called Edgemere on Bellevue Avenue in Newport, Rhode Island. The photograph is from *Famous Families of Massachusetts*, by Mary Caroline Crawford. It is used with permission. (LB.)

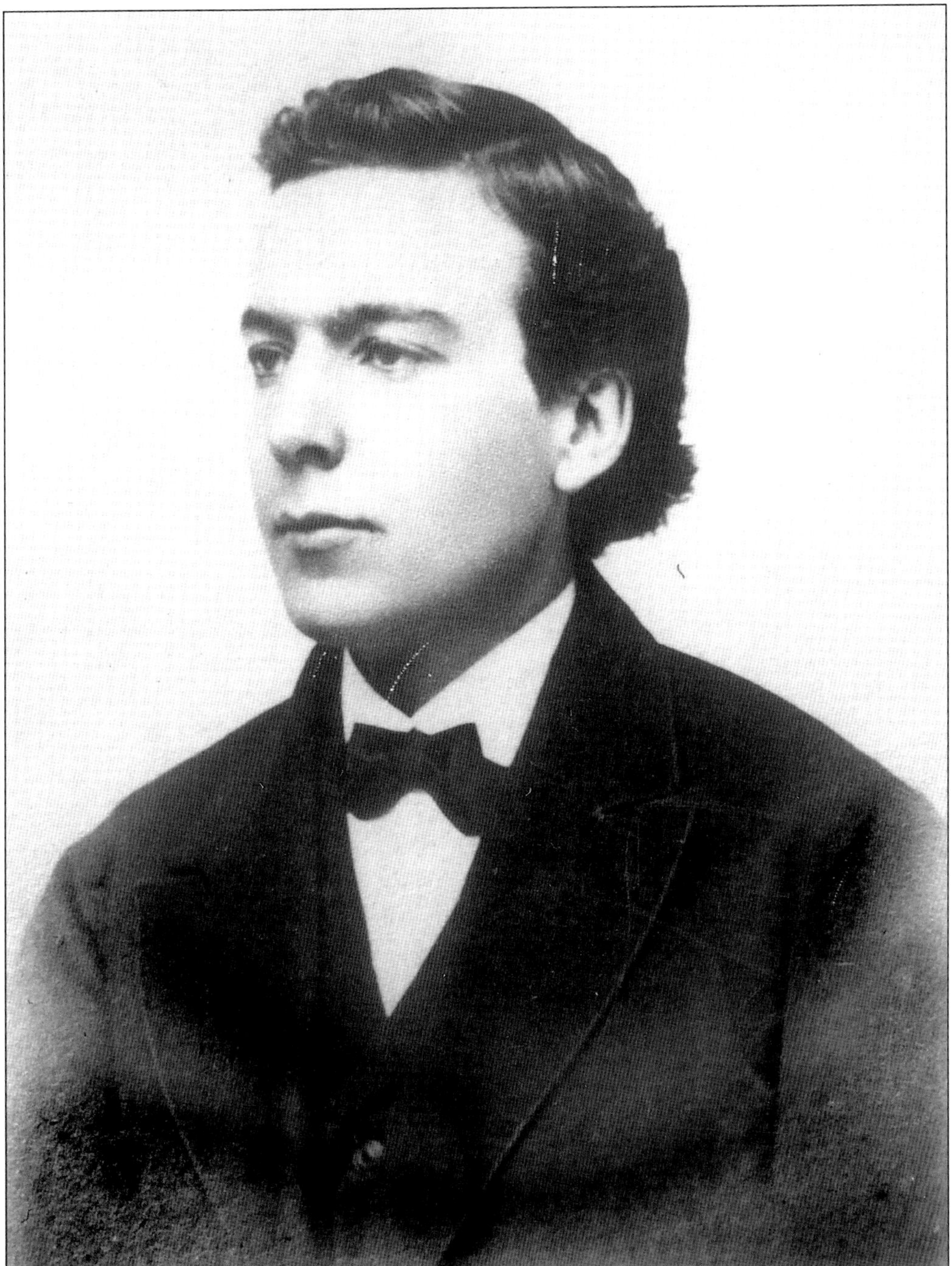

LUTHER BURBANK AT AGE 19. One of Lancaster's most famous sons, Luther Burbank was born on his family's homestead in 1849. As a young man of 21, he purchased a farm in Lunenburg. After developing the famous Burbank potato, he moved to California. During his career, he introduced more than 800 new varieties of plants, including the spineless cactus and the thornless blackberry vine. After his death in 1926, he was buried (according to his wishes) in an unmarked grave on his California property. (LBHG.)

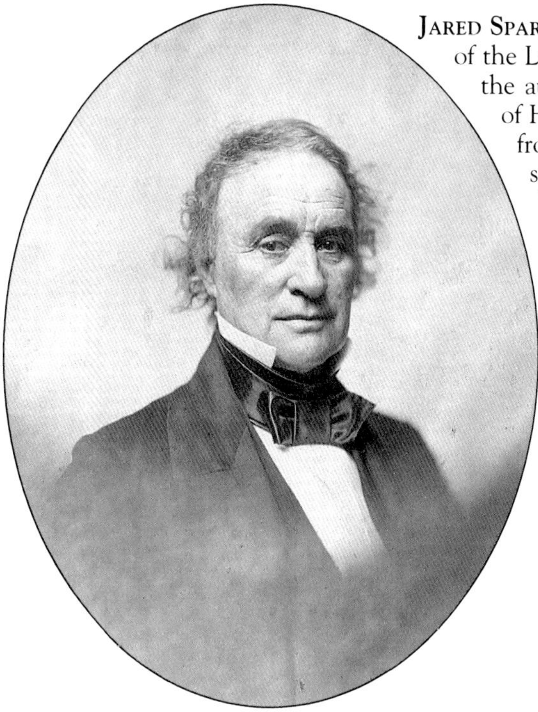

JARED SPARKS. Jared Sparks (1789–1866) was a master of the Lancaster Academy for one term, starting in the autumn of 1818. He later became president of Harvard University, serving in that capacity from 1849 to 1853. Earlier instructors in the school's predecessors included Gen. Joseph Warren (of Bunker Hill fame) and the prominent Unitarian minister William Ellery Channing.

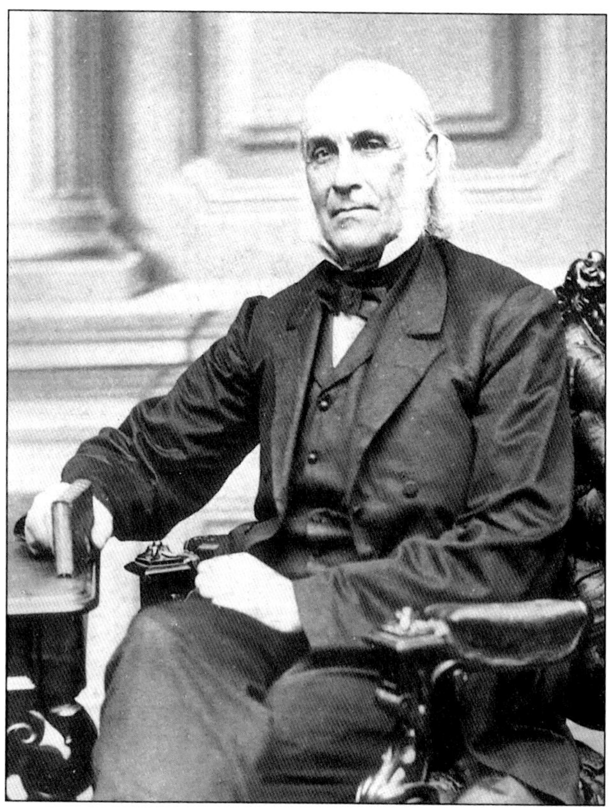

JOSEPH BRECK. Originally from Pepperell, Joseph Breck (1794–1873) came to Lancaster and became the superintendent of the Lancaster Horticultural Gardens, serving from 1833 to 1836. Breck was also a member of the state legislature, an author, and founder of the Breck Seed Company. This picture was taken c. 1871.

MARION FULLER SAFFORD. Pictured in her younger years is Marion Fuller Safford. A lifelong resident of Lancaster and a town historian, she wrote *The Story of Colonial Lancaster*, which was published in 1937.

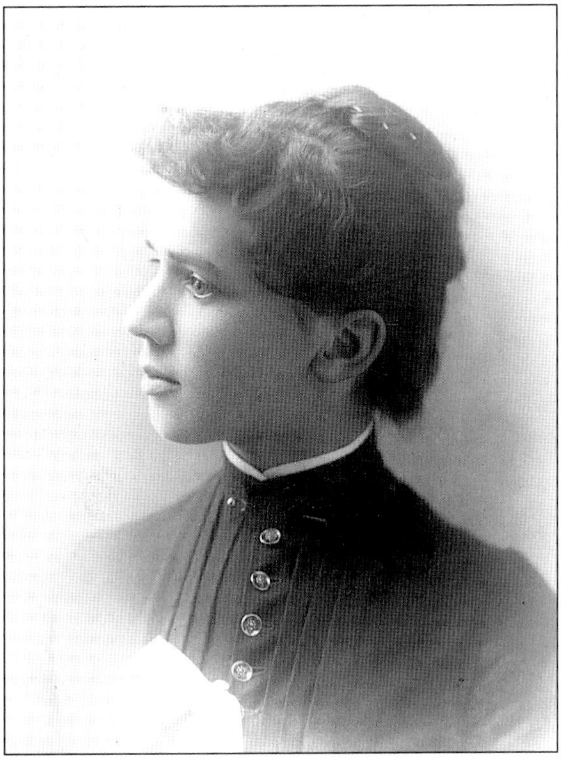

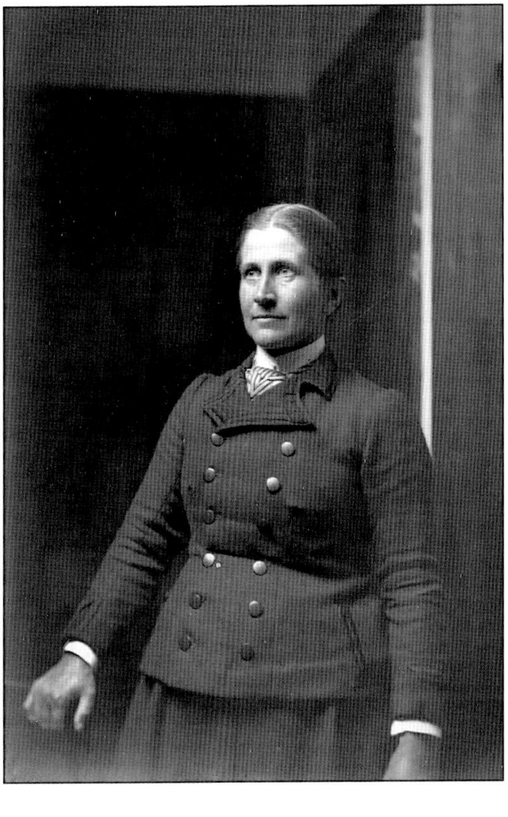

ALICE GREENE CHANDLER. Alice Greene Chandler, who moved from Roxbury to Lancaster in 1867 at the age of 16, was an unusual lady for her times. She served the town for many years as a professional librarian and, in 1891, began making photographs from glass negatives. She took pictures in and around Lancaster until 1900, when she turned her camera over to James McDonald. Many of Chandler's finely done photographs appear in this book.

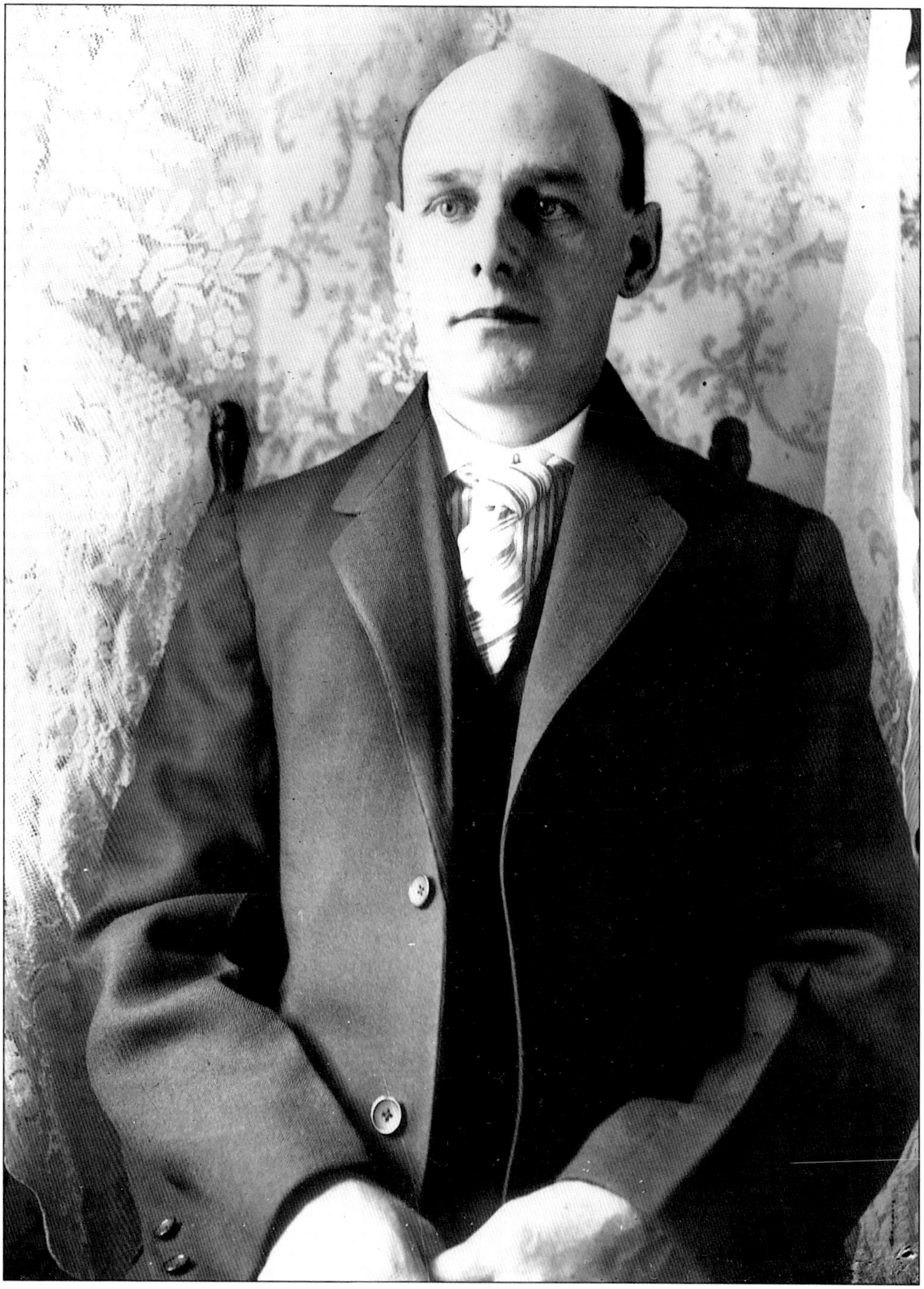

JAMES MACDONALD. James MacDonald moved to Lancaster in 1900 and worked at the Center Railroad Depot as the Lancaster freight agent. From 1900 to 1938, he also took pictures of the town by carrying with him his camera, tripod, and pieces of glass for printing the negatives. He died in 1947. Later, his wife, Esther, and son Duncan gave the entire collection, 2,500 pieces of glass, to the Lancaster Historical Commission. Many of the beautiful images shown in this book are from that collection.